LIVE
BEYOND
your
DREAMS

From fear and doubt to
personal power, purpose, and success

Dearest Kayla —

It is Time you Learn The Mindset
for Success Way of Thinking + Being!
Once you do, Your Life will Never
Be the Same. Enjoy the Journey of
Living on "The Other Side"

In Light + Love,

Rian

See what my Readers say about LIVE Beyond Your Dreams! I hope to hear how this book helped or inspired you too!

Please send your testimonial or reviews to – RianaMilne@gmail.com. Thank you, and I hope you enjoy the book!

In Love & Light, Riana

We live in a world where everyone seems to know better about how to live your own life and what goals to reach and what purposes to have. Everyone starting with your own parents and ending with teachers and lecturers and gurus will tell you what to do, feel and just how not good enough you are to live happily in this world. Well, you know what? That's the biggest lie in the world and all you need to do is just tell yourself 'I can' and then go and do anything you like. It's as easy as that, but to reach that state of freedom and willpower you will first need to get rid of all those old habits and beliefs you were brought up with. It's not anyone's fault, really, people around us want (or think they want) only the best for us, but in the end, they just make us feel sorry for ourselves and our self-esteem goes incredibly low, sometimes beyond repair, or so it may seem.

Right now is the time when you (and I, and anyone reading this comment or this book) need to stop thinking about other people, their beliefs and desires. We don't even need to consider what's possible and what's not (because all those things are relative, you will see) and just find out, maybe for the first time, what is it that we truly deeply want? And is there a way to do that, to go there, to get to that amazing place of happiness and high self-esteem? This is where Riana's book 'Live Beyond Your Dreams: From Fear and Doubt to Personal Power, Purpose and Success' comes in. The author explains in a simple and understandable language her own technique that is called the 'Watch-me' mind-set. It will help you use your own experience to the fullest and get hold of your destiny no matter what your background is.

The book is divided into a few parts each with its own theme. 'Part 1' deals with the secret of 5 D's – Devotion, Desire, Dedication, Determination and Dare to Dream. You will learn how to achieve balance in life, use your experience and learn even from what you consider 'bad' life lessons. There are special tips for teens dealing with parents and parents on how to deal with their kids better. 'Part 2' will reveal the author's story and how she came up with the Watch Me! mind-set. You will learn how to let go of your past and start building your future one step at time.

It's incredible just how much work Riana has put into writing this book. I realized a lot while reading this – things I can change right now to start living a better life. It's much easier than we all think! Definitely recommend this book. You will learn lots of new things about yourself. **An incredible confidence boost. By Ivanka**

Something I've noticed and appreciated while reading Riana's work is that at the beginning of each book she lets readers know their money isn't just going to her, she's giving a portion of it to those in need. That's such a gesture of kindness, but after reading this beautiful author's work it doesn't surprise me.

"It is my goal to help you move beyond your current fear". That line right away had me hooked on this book. In an opening statement, the author pulled me in simply by showing the kindness that made this book. As I continued my read I came across something in chapter 5 that I simply adored. Riana has provided a little structure for her readers, a sheet that you can fill in for your own goals. I love, love, love that. Personally, reading the beautiful writing before me I feel inspired. I feel motivated. I feel like a new opportunity is waiting just around the corner.

If you want to feel that kind of feeling, then I recommend you snag your own copy and set aside time to sit down and really commit to reading. You're not going to want to put any of it down until you finish. **Inspired and motivated! By Asa Henson**

Very inspirational and motivating book. Everyone should read this book, it's a great read for any age group! **It's a great read for any age group. By Amazon Customer**

Having personally worked with Riana as my Coach, I know she is passionate about the 'Watch Me' approach to life. And it has worked for her in many situations. In this book, as well as when speaking with Riana, she is very motivating. She opened my eyes and introduced me to a new way of thinking, of being Mindful, of applying purpose and spiritually to my life. And that helped me through a very difficult time. I have many, many highlighted pages in this book that I continue to re-read and inspire me. I definitely recommend this book...you will not be disappointed! **I definitely recommend this book. By Lisa Domlija**

If you are annoyed by this book it's because you don't truly believe in either God, nature, or Karma. Or maybe you just get annoyed because you have done the same thing to your children. Anyways, I only read 30 pages so far but this is the realest book I have ever just read for my own pleasure. I'm not saying you can compare it to the Bible and maybe some words or phrases can be overbearing but that's the entire point of this book. It's not to make you feel bad it's to help you love yourself and believe in yourself. I'm just saying I truly believe that people should at the very least consider living in this way. A 10/10! **Best Self-help book I have ever read. By Amazon Customer**

Live Beyond Your Dreams is one of those books that could really set you free. You can sit down and read cover to cover, and then revisit for advice on those difficult days. There's a chapter in here for everyone. I, for example, could really do with changing the negative little voices in my head that drag me down, there's a chapter for that. I also enjoyed the chapter on spiritual importance and how useful it is for growth and healing. If you are in the mood to be happier and more successful this is the book for you! **Live Beyond your Dreams. By Kaite**

I've read a lot of self-help books but have had trouble with integration. I really enjoyed this book by Riana Milne and Alexi Panos; because they write about activities and techniques to integrate the self-help knowledge. Of course, we all want to live fuller lives, but how? This book explains it in an easy and straightforward way to understand and actually integrate. I especially enjoyed the Chapter on Secret of the 5 D's. Desire, Determination, Dedication, Devotion, and Dare to Dream. The importance of each is laid out as well as real life examples, how to personally cultivate each, and the importance of supporting other people in cultivating of each. Very empowering read. **Empowering read! By Amazon Customer**

As a teenage boy who has read her book, I am just starting to go through life as an adult. Whether its reaching goals academically, socially, or through athletics this has without a doubt made me change my perspective and is allowing me to live beyond my dreams. **As a teenage boy who has read her book, ... By Sky Glenn**

I Loved this book Live Beyond Your Dreams, It gave me activities which would help anyone fulfill their ultimate business and personal goals. But there was also a higher purpose a spiritual guide in the book that touched my heart. Author Milne reiterated that I needed to find the motivation to change to HEAL from the pain, anxiety and depression that we all feel from time to time. She confirmed we could find our Spiritual connection that gives us the Courage and new way of thinking. That helps find the determination and devotion required to live their DREAMS with sheer happiness and JOY. Being their best selves by living Riana Milne motivational mindset WATCH ME!!!!

Leave Fear and Doubt behind LEARN the Milne WATCH ME positive Strengths and Strategies. By Lisa L.

I highly recommend this book. Riana is a great lady and through meeting with her she helped open my eyes and truly help me change for the better! **Great book by a great lady. By Jeremy Gayle**

I definitely found enough "nuggets" to make this book worth reading. I easily identified with the "Watch me! " mindset, as I have had this attitude myself for a long time; however, Riana certainly takes it to a higher level and provides great personal examples to illustrate her points. I wish I could have had a resource like this a bit earlier in my life, when it became necessary to re-invent myself after divorce. I think a person in that type of situation is the perfect audience for this book. Not being a parent of younger children, this section was basically superfluous for me, but as a whole, it is a great resource, well-written, and thorough. **A great resource. By sjg**

This book is the closest to a "How to" manual on life. I feel like everyone should read this book, and re-read it at different stages of life as a refresher. I am truly blessed to have Riana as a life coach, and for someone who hates to read I was through this book in a few days. Whether you are struggling in a relationship or to find the right partner, or you need to work on yourself, or your family this book a necessary step to a happier, happy life! **The book everyone needs to read!!! By Sarah L.**

Riana Milne along with her daughter Alexie Panos, have written a powerful book on looking at your own personal life and understanding why you have made some of the choices in your life—good or bad.

Reading it and writing the personal growth goals down is like having a personal coach in your life decisions. It's easy reading and a book you can always refer to when you have self-doubt or other life changing

events. Its' a "must read". **Live Beyond Your Dreams. By Margo S.**
Live Beyond Your Dreams is part true story, part self-help book containing a step by step process to guide you along the way to fulfilling your life's goals. I found this book to be very uplifting and inspiring. Milne's approach to setting and achieving goals is pretty well rounded, and includes the concepts of spirituality (though not religion, specifically) and giving back to community as integral parts of gaining success. I particularly enjoyed the chapter on raising successful children and teens, as it was straightforward and encouraging. She also focuses on balance, and ways to invite more of it into your life. Overall, the book was definitely helpful and I would recommend it! **Live Beyond Your Dreams. By jskate**

Live Beyond Your Dreams is an empowering book on the rewards of positive reinforcement within your life and the endless possibilities a person can achieve by keeping the right mindset. I would definitely recommend this book, especially to those who say to themselves or are told by others, "You can't do (fill in the blank) because (fill in the blank)".
It was interesting to read how Riana's "Watch-Me!" mind-set began. This book guides you in the direction needed to achieve the same confidence for success when you reply, "Watch Me" the next time a challenge comes your way. **Live Beyond Your Dreams. By Tom D**

Live Beyond your Dreams was a fast and easy read! I currently had a clean eating life style change and this book gave excellent advice on how to get through peer pressure and negativity from others. As a mother, it also gave me information on great advice to give my own children to get through the hardships of being a teen. This was an eye-opening book that I feel would benefit any and every, one. It really brings insight into the everyday challenges that people face. Don't pass this one up. **Reaching my dreams. By zootzoot**

In this book, Riana shares her Watch Me! mind-set system that can turn around your life, no matter how bleak things look. She gives many personal examples of difficult and what sounds like almost impossible situations that she found herself in and how she used this mindset to change her life for the better and reach unbelievable goals. She emphasizes that this mind set is not about ego or arrogance, but rather it's a faith-based belief that God has given you all you need to reach your dreams and that you have a God-given right to pursue those dreams in a confident way with hard work and determination. She offers tips on how to stop focusing on the negative things in your life and turn them into positives by using Mind work, Body work, and Soul work. As a licensed professional counselor, Riana sees many people wanting to blame others for their bad situations. She wants to empower people to not get caught up in other people's anger and resentments, but to be positive and look for the lesson and change things. She discusses the five "Ds" that she believes can make anything in your life possible: Desire, Determination, Dedication, Devotion, and Dare to Dream. She takes you step by step in helping you set your goals, including having a Plan B, since nothing in life is guaranteed, and then gives you a ten-step ladder to climb to realize your dreams.

There is a part two that was authored by her daughter, Alexi Panos, which was written especially for young people. As a mother of a teenage daughter, it was good to be reminded of the special challenges and difficulties that she is facing and how to help her cope with disappointment, but it is also very encouraging in how to help her become all that she is meant to be. It teaches young people to never stop dreaming and that anything is possible with hard work, dedication, and making the right choices.

If anyone has ever felt like they got a bad hand in life, they only need to read this book to realize that good can come out of every bad situation and that you do have power over your life to change your destiny. This was a highly motivational book that can help anyone improve their life and realize their dreams. **By T Thompson**

I always want to salute anyone who pulls themselves from situations that have tried to beat them down in life, and rise to victory. This is what you will find in this work. It is a motivational self-help read where inward feelings and happenings that could be life shattering are shared with you, but not for sympathy. These are shared to show how you too can be an overcomer in life and come out a winner. I like the slogan, "Watch Me!" and the mindset that it brings. You can achieve and not be held back from living the dream in your heart, if you are willing to forge ahead. Yes, it may take some readjusting, in your mindset, in your speech (not confessing failure), and in your outlook to name a few, but it can be done.

Live Beyond Your Dreams is a great self-help book, upbeat and inspiring. I believe it still all stems down to how much YOU want to change and what YOU are willing to do to achieve that change, but putting positive words, thoughts, and works into action certainly will speed up the process. If you are looking for a nudge in the right direction in life, some encouragement that others have picked up the pieces and found success, this book is for you, a slice of advice for a better life. **An Encouraging Work. By Shirley J.**

Have you ever been told you cannot do something or felt like you can't reach your dreams? Have you ever lost motivation to accomplish your goals and are looking for something to get you back on track? Everyone at some point in their lives has felt this way, including myself. I picked this book up and my life changed forever.

I was completely blown away by Riana's empowering and strong messages throughout her book. This is one of those books that everyone should be required to read just for the fact that it WILL help you. It's not an opinion, it's a fact. It will help you put aside your fears and anger and focus on believing in yourself and achieving what everyone wants, success. If you are finding difficulties in reaching your goals and dreams, then this is the first book I would suggest you to pick up. Riana will guide you through the obstacles in your life to overcome them and Live Beyond Your Dreams. Anyone of any age can profit from this highly informative book, and should be part of regular curriculum in schools growing up. I have heard great things about Riana Milne's public speaking, and I can only hope that at some point I will get the opportunity to see her speak. Overall, I give this book 5/5! **Live Beyond your dreams. By Elizabeth B.**

This is a very easy to read, down to earth book. Everyone could find some inspiration from it. Money well spent! **Live Beyond Your Dreams. By Doreen**

Are you always feeling worse off when a project is ending than when you started it simply because it never goes well? Do your peers keep telling you that you can never succeed in life or that you're no good at one thing or the other? Do you have a dead marriage and simply want out but fear the other side of the divorce wall? Okay. Breathe slowly in and slowly out. Voila! You have definitely made the right book choice today! Author Riana has succeeded in constructing a success guide for the downtrodden! She tells you in this book how to LIVE BEYOND YOUR DREAMS!

There are many people out there today who don't know how to move ahead in life. Yes, they're just stuck there, in a moment they can't get out of (U2), literally! Okay, instead of quoting rock icons, I should be emphasizing on Riana's beautiful book (BTW, her daughter, Alexi, contributed some chapters). LIVE BEYOND YOUR DREAMS is what the doctor ordered for the people I tried to lump together up there. Those who keep repeating the same mistakes all through their lives. Those who keep marrying the same kind and type of human being and keep praying for a divorce after every marriage. Those who feel they are better off than the next man or woman, while deep down, they know they're not. This is the group of humans I am talking about, as well as the set of people I highly implore to read this book. The author and her contributing daughter relate the topic to their personal life experience, drawing out lessons in the process. This book teaches a lot for those of us who need a lot of wind underneath our wings. Yes, I will recommend it! **Book Teaches a Lot... By George S.**

Common sense and honest to goodness self-worth aren't dead after all! These seemingly long-lost concepts are alive and well in Riana Milne's new book, Live Beyond Your Dreams! Hard work and determination are key factors in making a life one can be proud of and in leaving a positive legacy for our children and grandchildren. Get knocked down? Hop on up, dust yourself off and make a Plan. Whether it be a Plan A, Plan B or Plan M, the hardest step is often the first. Learn to be Brave! Learn to Live Beyond Your Dreams! **Live Beyond Your Dreams. By Ronda**

Riana has a very unique style of coaching that encompasses learnings from some of the great spiritual minds in this and previous times. Don't look for someone to hand you tissues, she will get you back on your feet to start living positively again. You really can "Live Beyond your Dreams." **Some Very Special Coaching.... By Tim**

Riana's first book Watch Me inspired me and helped me move forward after a divorce and a very, very difficult year. Watch Me gave me the strength and direction I needed. These authors are REAL people. Their experiences and how they write touched my heart and my soul. I could not wait to read Live Beyond Your Dreams. I downloaded it as soon as it came on Amazon and ordered two paper copies as well (to share!). If you are considering buying this book DO IT!! **Couldn't wait for this book to come out!!! By Lisa**

All of us have been told, at one time or another, that we "cannot." That we're too dumb to succeed, that we just shouldn't try, that we just don't have (and can't acquire) the necessary skills, education, ability, money – whatever it is – to realize our dreams.

For a small number of people, the author included, these negative statements become a dare of sorts, the fuel to press on. "Watch Me!", she said. For others, negative statements become a self-fulfilling prophecy, smothering ambition and initiative, in some cases for entire groups of people, who have learned that "the odds" are against them. This book provides much more than mindless cheerleading and empty encouragement. It's a road map to help young and old alike stare down the naysayers in our lives and move confidently toward our goals. This book will change lives and it should be required reading in every middle and high school. I highly recommend it. **Don't Get Mad, Get Even! By Michele D.**

From the Creator of the Breakthrough *Watch Me!*™ Motivational Mind-set

LIVE
BEYOND
your
DREAMS

From fear and doubt to
personal power, purpose, and success

RIANA MILNE
with ALEXI PANOS

By the Sea Books, LLC
Egg Harbor Township, NJ, 08234

Live Beyond Your Dreams:
From Fear and Doubt to Personal Power, Purpose, and Success

Send all inquiries to:
By the Sea Book Publishing
15300 Jog Rd, unit 109, Delray Beach FL 33446

For Riana's other books, audiobooks, and info products, go to her Web site:
www.RianaMilne.com or app, *My Relationship Coach*
Alexi's Web site: www.AlexiPanos.com and www.epicthemovement.org
See us on Facebook, LinkedIn, YouTube, and Twitter
under Riana Milne and Alexi Panos
For more information, write Riana at RianaMilne@gmail.com,
or BytheSeaBookPublishing@gmail.com

Edited by Caroline Kaiser
Family photo by Michelle Riordan, Photography by Exposure
Cover design by Dunn+Associates, www.dunn-design.com
Cover copy by Graham Van Dixhorn at www.writetoyourmarket.com

ISBN 13: 978-0-9785965-4-5
eBook ISBN: 978-0-9785965-1-4
SAN: 851-0784

Publisher's Cataloging-in-Publication
(Provided by Quality Books, Inc.)

Milne, Riana.
　　Live beyond your dreams : from fear and doubt to
　　personal power, purpose, and success / Riana Milne ;
　　with Alexi Panos. — 1st ed.
　　2017; 2nd edition
　　　　p. cm.
　　Includes bibliographical references.
　　LCCN 2012919068
　　ISBN 978-0-9785965-4-5

　　1. Self-actualization (Psychology) 2. Change
　　(Psychology) 3. Success. 4. Spiritual life.
　　I. Panos, Alexi. II. Title.

BF637.S4M55 2012　　　　　158.1
　　　　　　　　QBI12-600216

Library of Congress Number: 2012919068
Published in the United States of America.

Dedication

Riana:

This book is dedicated to my daughters, coaching and therapy clients, and prior talent who have such determination and dedication to change, grow, and succeed, and who took the risk and dared to dream despite the doubt and disbelief of others. Thank you for sharing with me your journey of self-discovery to reach your dreams and beyond to live your higher purpose.

Alexi:

To my families and children in Africa, who have enlightened my soul and driven the spirit of my higher purpose.

Since Alexi and I are dedicated to helping make our world a better place, partial sales proceeds will be donated to Alexi's nonprofit charity, EPIC (Everyday People Initiating Change), and The Riana Milne Scholarship Fund for the Arts. Thank you for your donation!

Help Yourself by Helping Others

Table of Contents

About the Authors

*R*iana Milne is known as the "Life & Love Transformation Expert." She is a global, Certified Life,
Dating & Relationship Coach for Singles & Couples,
a Certified Clinical Trauma Professional (CCTP), has
a three-part Master's degree in Applied Clinical and
Counseling Psychology; and is a Florida Licensed
Mental Health Counselor (LMHC) and a Certified Ad-
dictions Professional (CAP). Her practice of 18 years,
Therapy by the Sea, LLC is in Delray Beach, Florida,

USA. For 14 years Riana was an LPC, SAC and LCADC in Egg Harbor
Township, NJ.

Riana specializes in helping those of past trauma overcome the
triggers that tend to sabotage their success in Adult Life and Love Relationships. Her Online Group Coaching programs for both Singles and
Couples are held at the www.LifeandLoveTrainingAcademy.com; and
Riana's app, *My Relationship Coach,* offers convenient coaching for her
clients around the world. Riana served as a Student Assistance Counselor (SAC) within schools, counseling students with emotional trauma
or behavioral and relationship issues from grades kindergarten through
college. She is also an interfaith minister and uses spiritual concepts
with her motivational coaching style. Clients are helped to overcome
Childhood Trauma, Unconscious Emotional Triggers, and the frustration,
anxiety, depression, fear, doubt and pain experienced in Dating or their
Love relationship. Clients learn the exact transformational skills needed
for success in both Life and Love. With increased confidence and a positive
mindset, they consciously are able to attract and have the Love they deserve. Riana uses research-based, holistic techniques for personal growth
in mind, body, and spirit for clients to become evolved as their best selves.

The Watch Me! Motivational Mind-set as discussed in this book,
the first of a series, is an instructional., inspirational program for self-
empowerment that Riana has taught for over 40 years to women and
men of all ages. Now she brings this Personal Life Transformation
System to exclusive Love relationships (called Relationship Rescue!) and

for Singles (called Dating to Mating) both virtually and in working 1-on-1 with VIP Coaching Clients. In her #1 Best Selling book, and 2nd in the series, *LOVE Beyond Your Dreams – Break Free of Toxic Relationships to Have the Love You Deserve;* is a key part of her Coaching programs. Riana's goal for those who experienced significant relationship anguish is to create a safe, loving, emotionally healthy, and lifelong evolved love with a like-minded conscious mate.

Riana is a keynote speaker and offers group workshops, is a newspaper Advice Columnist, and wrote numerous articles for eHarmony. com, Digital Romance, YourTango.com, Beliefnet.com and many other top websites. She's had various radio programs and is seen on many TV shows. Recently, she was 1 of 5 Dating Coaches featured on the Docu-series, *Radical Dating; Finding Lasting Love Over 40;* where her client successfully found an exclusive partner. Her Single and Coupled Coaching clients are women and men of all ages; from teens to seniors, and include those from the LGBTQIA Community. Riana's books are in Barnes and Noble, and sold online; and inspire you to change the way you live and love; giving you the confidence not to settle for less! Visit http://rianamilne.com/ for more tips on life, love and relationships.

Alexi Panos, Riana's youngest daughter, is the embodiment of the Watch Me! mindset and inspiration for the LIVE Beyond Your Dreams book. A leader in the Emergent Wisdom movement, Alexi is on a mission to make personal development mainstream through her books, inspirational videos, transformational trainings, online education community and working with her non profit, E.P.I.C. in Africa. She was named as one of INC's magazines Top 10 Entrepreneur's Changing the World; one of Origin Magazines Top 100 Creatives Changing the World; and is a featured expert in the films The Abundance Factor, Riseup and Age of the Entrepreneur. As a bestseller, she's also authored the books *50 WAYS TO YAY!* and *NOW OR NEVER,* both by Simon & Schuster. Follow her on social media @alexipanos. http://www.alexipanos.com

Acknowledgments
from Riana Milne

So MANY PEOPLE have inspired me on my journey, some whose unending love was monumental when the chips were down. This book, however, is first and foremost dedicated to my two incredible daughters, Stephana Nicole and Alexi Danielle. Your unconditional love and friendship has meant the world to me. Just holding you close or looking into your trusting eyes was all I needed to gather more energy and keep going.

You both always believed in me and knew I would take care of you even when I could barely take care of myself. Yes, we had our moments, as every teen and her mother will, but they were rare, and my unconditional love for you was never in doubt. Both of you are my proudest achievements in life, and you continue to bring me such pride.

I really respect the women you have become. Please always shine your inner light with all you meet and continue to share your many gifts with the world. Treasure all the memories we shared as you were growing up—the fun, exciting, and loving memories as well as the difficult and painful ones—as they contained the lessons that have inspired us all to greatness! Continue your journeys with courage, compassion, and the Watch Me! mind-set leading the way.

Thank you so much, Alexi, for wanting to be a part of this book. Your fortitude and ability to live the principles of the Watch Me! mind-set will teach many others how to aspire to greatness. And what a great gift you are sharing! I am very proud that you have developed the EPIC charity (Everyday People Initiating Change).

All that you have accomplished in your young years is now contributing to your higher purpose and helping the world to be a better place. Your inner being touches all you meet, and your sense of spirituality and ability to choose love over fear has enabled you to accomplish a great deal at an early age. This book is a labor of love, and it means so much more to me because you have chosen to be a part of it. Thank you!

Also Alexi, because I have always believed in your dreams and goals, I am dedicating two dollars from the sale of each book to your EPIC charity. Another two dollars from each book will go to The Riana Milne Scholarship Fund for the Arts, so that I can continue to help other young people realize their dreams and reach their goals.

I want to also thank those who have challenged me to the point of almost breaking, as these teachers have taught me how to find the courage, spirituality, drive, and determination to succeed no matter what the sacrifice.

To the men I have loved, you have given me my fondest memories and my greatest challenges. All the trials and tribulations that I have endured brought me to the successes in life I now enjoy. Yes, guys, you have been instrumental in my journey of finding my true self, my inner strength, and the ability to forgive and to love unconditionally. I'm glad we are friends today; forever you will be a part of my life.

Acknowledgments

To my siblings, Jack H. Milne Jr., Scott Milne, Bobbi Milne, and Robin Terral, and many nieces and nephews, I wish you all great health and unending love and happiness.

I wish to thank another relative, mentor, and one of my angels, Uncle Bob Milne, who read my words of poetry and inspiration early in my teen years and told me I had a gift for writing and touching others with my words. He encouraged me to get "the initials behind my name" so that I could publish my works and follow the Milne family tradition of having a published author in each generation. I am proud that the tradition also continues with both my daughters!

To my mom, Beverly Milne-Ryan; now an Angel who continues to watch out for me; you taught me to be tough and not to give up. Thank you for all your support. Thanks for telling me in recent years that you were proud of me, as those are words a child always needs to hear. Also, thanks for listening when I questioned my past; it was an exploration of loneliness and pain that I had to go through to get answers to difficult questions. You were a great mom who held our family together during difficult times, and who was fiercely strong, loving, and intelligent. You dedicated your life to us five children, and I thank you for everything! I love you.

Many thanks to another one of my angels, my father, Jack H. Milne, Sr., who taught me in our many talks together that no matter how hard life seems, if you have the "five Ds"—desire, determination, dedication, devotion, and dare to dream—you can do anything! That special lesson, Dad, I share often with so many. Your soul and memory continues to touch others. It was your lesson that inspired me to write this book, so that I can share the secret you taught me long ago. Thanks for your calm and loving ways, and for teaching me to be strong and independent and challenging me to overcome anything. This is your book too, Dad!

To my professor and mentor, Dr. Z. Benjamin Blanding, now an angel of God, I dedicate this work to you, as for years you inspired me to be the best counselor and coach I could humanly be. You encouraged me to use the style of counselling that felt right to me—always leading with person-centered approaches, and then infusing motivational, inspirational, and educational concepts with cognitive-behavioral and solution-focused techniques for growth and healing. You are sorely missed but greatly remembered, as each day that I am counseling others, your spirit is with me!

I want to thank my two dear friends who are now angels and who inspired me the most when I was young. They taught me to live each day as if it were my last, to appreciate my many blessings, to not dwell on the negatives, and to always remember that life is a gift. They are Michael Marcucci, one of my best friends since we were six years old, who was killed in a car accident by a drunk driver just 10 years later, and Corrine Redinger, who was assumed to be murdered when we were only 24 years old; these two angels of God live forever within my heart. In my prayers, I swore to them that I would take their soul into mine on the day that they passed, and I would live my life with double purpose, with them a part of it. I became a licensed clinical alcohol and drug counselor (LCADC) in Michael's honor and a licensed professional counselor (LPC) specializing in couples, family, and women's issues for Corrine. You both passed through this Earth school way too early, but you live on forever within my heart and soul, and you have never been forgotten.

Thank you to my most loving lifelong friends: Beth Anderson, Jacqui Martin, Robin Barnett, Sybil Jerkins, Michael Logston, and Annamarie Germanio.

You are there for me during both the happy times and the difficult, challenging times.

Thanks to all my support team in creating this book: my fabulous cover designers Hobie Hobart and Kathi Dunn of www.Dunn-associates.com; the dedicated and precise editor Caroline Kaiser; creative cover copywriter Graham Van Dixhorn of Write to Your Market, Inc; book interior designer, Michele DeFilippoand Ronda Rawlins of 1106 Design; and proofreader Aubri Fouts. Special thanks to my wonderful distributor, Amy Collins of New Shelves Publishing Services and Distribution, who's advice and guidance is so appreciated! Online book marketing by Penny Sansevieri and her team at Author Marketing Experts, Inc; and Bethany Brown of theCadenceGroupandoverallpublicityandmarketingexperts, Corinne Liccketto and her team at Smith Publicity, Inc. are instrumental in the marketing and promotion of our book. Thanks to Lorna McLeod my super dedicated Coach at Mission Marketing Mentors. Alexi and I thank you all so very much for your tireless efforts on our behalf and for our charities.

And a final thank you to my test readers, Beth Anderson, Nancy Pagliughi, Dr. Edward Black, and Senora Cristy Oria; I appreciate your honest feedback and input. I'm glad you found my words inspiring and touching; I pray that I may help and inspire others who are transitioning in their life as well.

May God bless you all on this fantastic journey with peace, joy, personal success, and the discovery of your higher purpose!

Thank you with such gratitude, to my Speaking Coach and Mentor, Lisa Sasevich, who is teaching me so much in how to speak from my heart on the big stage to share my light and message with the world; to help those with Childhood Trauma overcometheirEmotionalTriggerstofindSuccessinLife&Love.

Acknowledgments
from Alexi Panos

A NY JOURNEY THAT YOU START takes the help and inspiration of others, and I want to thank and acknowledge the following people for all of their amazing insight and encouragement:

Riana Milne, my mother and my source of inspiration; she is a determined, smart, beautiful woman who has faced many obstacles with vigor and a positive approach, only to emerge a stronger and more successful person.

Gregory Panos, my father, a thinker who dreams big and never settles for the conventional.

June Panos, my grandmother, who taught me the importance of values and character.

Stephana Panos, my sister, who always reminds me to remain true to my beliefs and myself.

Evan Lagace, an amazing person who provokes me to think outside the box and encourages me to always challenge the ordinary.

Tennille De Freitas, a tenacious artist who aims big and never settles for anything less.

Jacqueline Kemp, a nurturer who always gives despite her own trials. Her strength and heart remind me that there is still hope.

My family, who keep me grounded and surround me with love and encouragement.

The pessimistic, who drive me to prove there is still light in the darkness!

Thank you to my husband, Preston, and our amazing family for all the love, encouragement, and inspiration you provide on a daily basis!

Disclaimer

THIS BOOK IS DESIGNED to provide information on different strategies to better your life. It aims to educate you on various motivational and spiritual approaches to a mind-set that helps you reach your goals and overcome your challenges.

It is sold with the understanding that the publisher and authors are not engaged in rendering legal, psychological, counseling, or other professional services in this book. If medical, legal, or other expert assistance is required, the services of a competent professional should be sought. If you are depressed, feel suicidal, or need immediate mental health care, please call 911 or go to your local emergency room.

It is not the purpose of this book to reprint all the information that is otherwise available to authors and/or publishers, but instead to complement, amplify, and supplement other texts. You are urged to read all the available material, learn as much as possible about this topic, and tailor the information to your individual needs. For more information, see the many resources in the back of this book.

Every effort has been made to make this book as accurate as possible. However, there may be mistakes, both typographical and in content. Therefore, this text should be used only as a general educational guide and not as the ultimate source of self-help information. Furthermore, this book contains information that is current only up to the printing date.

The purpose of this book is to educate and entertain. The authors and By the Sea Books, LLC shall have neither liability nor responsibility to any person or entity with respect to any loss or damage caused, or alleged to have been caused, directly or indirectly, by the information contained in this book or other related information and audio products.

If you do not wish to be bound by the above, you may return this book to the publisher for a full refund.

Introduction:

How It All Began

THE WATCH ME! mentality was born within me at age 16, but it exploded from me at the age of 27. At the time, I was living in Erie, PA. I had just opened my own model and talent agency and was the mother of my two wonderful daughters, Stephana Nicole, age five, and Alexi Danielle, age four.

My husband, and their father, had just torn apart my modeling and talent office, throwing files across the room, upturning my desk, ripping the phone out of the wall, and leaving the office looking like a tornado had hit it. This was all in response to my telling him I wanted a divorce.

"Watch how far you'll get in this town without my last name!" he screamed at me.

With a deadpan expression, I looked him in his eyes, pointed my finger at him, and said with the utmost confidence in a stern but calm voice, "Watch me!"

Where did this sense of confidence come from? How was I so motivated to have a new life, and how would I get there when my world was crumbling? Usually, one final act spurs people to

1

become motivated enough to do whatever it takes to create a new life for themselves.

As soon as my divorce was final, I immediately went down to the courthouse and changed my married name to my maiden name. And I took it one step further; never particularly liking my birth name, I changed that too, making the total name change from Terri Ann Milne to Terriana (Riana) Milne. I have gone by Riana ever since 1987; it's a name I associate with rebirth, creativity, confidence, uniqueness, and a dedication to living my goals and dreams.

The Watch Me! motivational mind-set is what I have lived ever since taking on the name of Riana; therefore, that name connects to everything I have overcome and everything I have become. Changing my name was the beginning of my journey to a new life; at the time I had nothing but a new name and dreams for a more peaceful, happier, and more purpose-filled life.

I am just an ordinary woman; my story is one that many women, men, and teenagers can relate to. It's about conquering stress, fear of change, anxiety, depression, doubt, financial struggle, and emotional pain in a time of difficult transition.

It's about overcoming all the negative messages many loved ones have given us over time, making us feel put down and not good enough. It's for those of us who have been doubted, criticized, or told our dreams were a joke, and that they'd never amount to anything extraordinary; it's for the business owners, actors, models, singers, and dancers who were told they'd never make it.

This is also a story for other single mothers and fathers trying to keep sane while attempting to keep their family lives together, and for parents who are frustrated with depressed or angry children. It's for people who are in recovery or questioning if addiction is a problem for them. As well, it's for those who are stuck about whether to move out of or fix a toxic relationship, for couples who want a more successful and loving relationship, and for teens who are looking for answers about their future.

I understand—I've been in all these situations, and I hope I can inspire you to overcome the negativity of your past or current life. It is my goal to help you move beyond your current fear and the pain of transition toward a more positive, happier future in which you can reach your dreams and beyond, achieving your higher purpose.

My name change to Riana initiated a stronger sense of confidence as a woman; when I changed it, I swore I would never again accept any emotional abuse and I would fight for my sense of being no matter the cost. My journey describes the mental and spiritual resources I needed to survive the poorest of times, when there was no help, little hope, no money, and many responsibilities.

At one particularly low point, I lived on tomato soup, eggs, and cereal for weeks, but I always made sure my daughters had a decent meal and a safe place to live. I endured many extremely difficult transitions, and I was even told once that someone had a contract out on my life. A few times I knew I had nothing to hold on to but my dreams for a better life; yet I was motivated to become a strong and successful mother and woman, one my daughters could be proud of.

My story is not about anger or being vindictive. The Watch Me! mind-set is about an inner journey of growth, developing a sense of spirituality to heal and survive, using meditation and positive self-talk for inner strength and self-esteem, and following a goal-setting system to reach your dreams and beyond.

This philosophy will teach you that your own happiness and success are your best revenge, and you will learn not to lash back in anger or retaliation at the people who have hurt you. Instead, you will discover that someone's doubts about you or efforts to hurt or destroy you can now be the driving force for you to succeed. Chapter 1 explains what the Watch Me! mind-set is, and chapter 2, "Gearing Up for Greatness: Finding the Motivation to Change," addresses this underlying inspirational force.

Pain is our biggest teacher; the struggles from our past are simply the lessons we needed to experience to reach our most powerful and best self. Using a combination of spiritual and motivational psychotherapy techniques to get past your pain, learning a different way to perceive your challengers, and practicing the art of forgiveness are all a part of this plan. Spirituality is an important foundation of your success, as I explore in chapter 3, "A Sense of Spirituality is Essential."

My father, Jack H. Milne Sr., who had a huge influence on my life, once told me, "Babe, if you have the five Ds, you can do anything! They are desire, determination, dedication, devotion, and dare to dream!" You will find these secrets in chapter 4, and they are the foundation of the Watch Me! mind-set.

These inspirational lessons that I am now privileged to teach you are ones I have taught to many coaching and counseling clients, business professionals, friends, acquaintances, coworkers, models, actors, singers, dancers, troubled children, rebelling high school students, and their confused parents, all ranging in age from 5 to 85.

Once you know the secrets of the five Ds, then you must move on to goal setting to make progress toward reaching your dreams, as explained in chapter 5, "Just Do It! Goal Setting for Personal Growth and Success." The techniques in this chapter are what I used for many years, as they helped to launch my individual businesses and allowed me to enjoy many successes.

My stories are all true. As you read them, understand that there are always two sides to every story, and this is my rendition.

I have forgiven everyone along the way who has challenged me, and my past "teachers" are my friends.

My forgiveness of their deeds brought the wisdom and courage I needed to be where I am today. This is fully explained in chapter 6, "Learning from Life's Lessons: Finding the Good from the Bad." Not only do I forgive those from my past, but also I thank them, and send them blessings for a happy, peaceful, loving, and fulfilled life.

(Please note: for confidentiality, all names have been changed for stories related to my counseling practice. Some names have been changed to protect a reputation or purposely not mentioned to protect an artist's or entertainer's desire for a private life. Other names have been used unchanged as a thank you for being part of my journey, or for being my friend, teacher, mentor, or part of my support system.)

Back to the Beginning: Background History

I separated from my soon-to-be ex-husband at age 27 with no money but my first month's rent on an apartment with a grimy green shag carpet, stained walls, and a small patio deck that overlooked the concrete patio of the apartment behind me. It was disgusting, and so was my life at the time. I was flat broke, and my husband had just put me through a bankruptcy for over three quarters of a million dollars the year before due to his poor business decisions. I couldn't get a loan or a credit card to save my life.

I was raised a Philadelphia girl from the Huntingdon Valley suburbs, and I found the small-town conservatism of Erie, PA, to be quite a challenge. I had married into a Greek family, where my father-in-law immediately shunned me because I was not Greek. After I was introduced to him, he peered above his newspaper and said to his son, "Look at her—she's not Greek, and she'll

5

never have your children." I was shocked and hurt that I was not accepted, and I was petrified to marry into a family where I did not feel good enough.

Well, I did have two half-Greek beautiful and talented daughters, and as their strong German-English mother, I adopted the Watch Me! mind-set early in their lives. I only named it that after their father exploded in rage in my office.

I understand his upset today, as he explained to me that he felt a total lack of control over his world, which was falling apart at that time. I had married into a culture without knowing what to expect; he was obligated to both his traditional Greek family and to me, his outgoing, new-world, very nontraditional wife.

I'd taught my girls the Watch Me! mind-set and way of thinking since they were young. I was dedicated to making them strong, confident, worldly, and intelligent young women. They have successfully learned the Watch Me! mind-set for themselves; it emerged most prominently in their mid to late teens and early 20s.

Stephana and Alexi graduated with honors, and Alexi's grades were so good that she didn't have to attend the 11th grade. I taught them both to read books by the age of two and to do math problems before kindergarten, but most importantly, I taught them the love of learning. They experienced the creative arts of music, acting, modeling, singing, and dancing from a young age. My girls grew up learning the spiritual message that we are all God's children, and what is important is the love, light, and soul from within the person. We should not be judged by our race, religious preference, culture, or background.

My 29-year-old daughter Alexi, is contributing three chapters (chapters 11 through 13) in Part 2: It Works for Young People Too! I have asked her to include her story of growth, struggle, and success; as well as the techniques she uses to make the Watch Me! mind-set work for her.

I have always respected both of my daughters' input and opinions, as young people are so bright and have so much to offer! I also believe that respecting a young person's thoughts gives us adults insight into better parenting. I have learned this myself by listening to the young people in the schools and in my therapy office. I help them overcome their pain and challenges, and as I teach them to have a better relationship with their parents, they teach me a better way to relate to my own two daughters.

Alexi is living her dreams of being a TV host and producer while traveling the world. She dedicates time to bringing freshwater wells to Tanzania, Africa, through her nonprofit project, Everyday People Initiating Change (EPIC) (www.epicthemovement.org). As of this writing, seven wells are successfully bringing fresh water to villages with 3,000 to 6,000 residents each. Wells number eight and nine are now being built. Alexi cofounded this charity with her best friend, Tenille Amor, in 2005. It has been endorsed by Quiksilver women's clothing and promoted by MTV and JetBlue's, TrueBlue campaign.

Since writing our first book in 2006, Alexi has also had her own TV show on HGTV called *Run My Makeover,* has been a host for *E! Online Entertainment News,* a reporter for the *Bleacher Report NFL Pro Show,* and a host for SNY (Sports New York) sports trivia show called *Beer Money.* She also models for many top designers and has appeared in many print ads and national TV commercials. She has sung on two multi-platinum CDs, handles her own model and talent bookings, and has appeared in over 12 music videos for various artists. Alexi has also appeared in various advertising campaigns in over 30 magazines.

She also follows a very spiritual path, is constantly reading self-help and inspirational books to learn an even keener sense of focus, and is extremely motivated and organized. I never had to encourage her to work; she *loves* her work, and this passion consistently shows! She currently lives in both LA and the NYC area. You can keep up on her news through her own Web site, www.AlexiPanos.com, and her EPIC charity site, www.epicthemovement.org.

I am also exceptionally proud of Stephana, who is fulfilling her creative passion for the photographic arts. She is extremely talented and now specializes in wedding photography with the company she co-owns, Sona Photography, www.sonaphotography.com, in Orlando, Florida. She also works for a major airline company.

At age 19, she managed a large upscale restaurant on Santa Barbara's harbor; then she managed a large nightclub in Universal Studios at age 21. Stephana then moved to NYC, where she worked in the corporate office of Midnight Oil, Inc., a restaurant hospitality company; she managed inventory for 23 of their locations. She has been self-supporting since the age of 19 and has asked me for nothing.

Many girls that age are still fully dependent on their parents, but Stephana lives the Watch Me! principles. She is highly intelligent, confident, and well spoken, and she is a great people person and has a keen business mind. Stephana is a survivor; she works extremely hard and feels she can succeed at anything she desires, and she supports herself fully in her explorations and dreams. She currently lives with her wonderful husband Charles in Orlando, Florida.

My daughters have learned that there are no limits, no boundaries, and no minimum number of talents or professions we are allowed to have in life. The only limits are what we put on ourselves.

I remember the many choices I had at age 17 when I was thinking about college. At the time, I was a promotional model for WFIL, a Philadelphia Top 40 radio station. My job included working with top-of-the-charts singers, dancing on stage during huge concerts with groups on tour, doing half-time shows at various sporting events, attending movie premieres with the film's stars, and driving hot custom cars to their events. It was a great job for a teenager!

Since I came to love the broadcast entertainment field, I entered Penn State University in speech communications and broadcasting. I also wanted to major in psychology, writing, marketing, public relations, and acting. How could I do them all? Since eighth grade, I had published over 200 poems and written inspirational mini-books that all my friends in school asked to read because my writings were real, from the heart, and touching.

As a teenager, I was confused trying to make the one career choice, so I vowed to one day do them all—and I have!

How did I go from being a Penn State graduate to marriage at 21, motherhood at 24, bankruptcy at 26, and divorce at 27, when I had my own talent school and agency? I use the process of my journey as an example of how anyone can use the Watch Me! mind-set to succeed, even if they're starting under the most difficult of circumstances.

I had my talent school, which reached international award-winning status, for nine and a half years, and then I returned to school for my master's degree. I returned to college at age 37 to pursue my master's in applied clinical and counseling psychology so I could have my own psychotherapy practice. I was the first person to graduate from Rowan University, NJ, in the new major, and I did so *summa cum laude* with a GPA of 3.98. I was also inducted into the National Honor Society in Psychology and honored as being an outstanding graduate student.

I soon after acquired my NJ State LPC (licensed professional counselor), which required the three-part master's degree with 92 MA credits. I am also a LCADC (licensed and certified alcohol and drug counselor). I acquired my CCGC certificate (certified compulsive gambling counselor), and have served as a SAC (student assistance counselor) in several schools for students of all ages who are in emotional crises.

In the Atlantic City, NJ area, I created three radio call-in therapy shows, *Night Moods* on KOOL 98.3 FM, *Talk to Me AC (Atlantic City, NJ) on* WJAM FM, and *Talk Therapy with Riana Milne* on WOND AM. I was also asked to do a news appearance on South Jersey's NBC TV 40 station on 9/11 to advise how to help children and teens handle the World Trade Center terrorist attacks.

Like every other American, I was so shook up that I wasn't sure how the report went, but they used it for two days and then asked me to come back on for a news update on processing fear, shock, and terror. I was honored to have been chosen and to use my new counseling skills, along with my broadcasting experience, to help make a difference where I could. In 2000, I had opened a community therapy center in Ventnor called Inner Vision Counseling, a nonprofit organization that offered free counseling for teens. After 9/11, I also offered free counseling for those wanting help in dealing with the attacks.

In 2001, I was working over 80 hours a week in five jobs, trying to financially survive after my second husband suddenly declared bankruptcy and left town in the middle of the night, leaving Alexi and me to fend for ourselves. Our neighbor Mike Ford took us in from the kindness of his heart. Trying to still stay motivated and spiritual was a balancing act all its own. Stephana was living in

California, working very hard to support herself. But I had Alexi and her talent career to support; I was trying to sell my home, and I worked constantly. After the home sold, Alexi and I moved up to Edgewater, NJ, so she could pursue her talent career. I was employed at both Hackensack High School as a school psychologist and at a counseling center.

Other past jobs included counseling for a South Jersey hospital's child and adolescent unit and for a Center City women's inpatient drug and alcohol rehab center (many clients were from the prison system). Today I have my own private practice counseling and coaching center called Therapy by the Sea, LLC, in Egg Harbor Township, NJ. So I certainly have enjoyed the counseling profession, which I always dreamed of being a part of. Also, as a certified coach, I help people of all ages from around the world by phone, Skype, and FaceTime. See information in the back of the book for my individual and group coaching services.

I also work as an interfaith minister. I became very spiritual in nature after my good friend Michael was killed. I realized then that life is so short, so precious, and such a gift. At age 19 and while at Penn State, I was nominated to be the chaplain for my sorority, Alpha Xi Delta, a job that I took very seriously. I tried to teach love, hope, and spiritual inspiration to my sorority sisters, as I was learning it for myself.

Living a life with spiritual purpose became even more profoundly important to me after my good friend Corrine's death. In 1992, I became more focused on how spirituality was positively affecting my life when I started attending a group and doing self-study in *The Course in Miracles*. I chose to become an ordained minister with the Universal Life Church in 1997.

Being a minister is another career from which I currently derive so much pleasure and joy. My ministry services (Ceremonies by the

Sea, LLC) include performing wedding and civil union ceremonies and vow renewals, offering premarital counseling, and using spiritual concepts for healing for my coaching and counseling clients.

I found that studying the faith-based concepts daily and following them to the best of my ability was the missing ingredient I needed to reach my ultimate personal purpose and destiny. When I first wrote this book in 2006 with Alexi, we wanted to highlight the importance of a spiritual path for success. This book brought together my passion for my daughters, counseling, coaching, the ministry, and writing, so this is truly a labor of love.

In 2010 I acquired my certification as a relationship coach for both singles and couples from The Relationship Coaching Institute. And recently, I completed my app for smartphones and iPads called *My Relationship Coach*. This app provides me with the opportunity to coach clients from around the world, all of whom are accessible through the app!

In today's hard economic times, many adults are holding down several jobs to help make ends meet. Relationships and family life can suffer severely without personal balance. The various techniques explained in chapter 7, "Achieving Balance in Life" were critical to me during all my transitions, moves, and job changes. These techniques kept me stable, sane, and focused on personal and business success during emotional and exhausting times.

Chapter 8, "For Couples: The Evolved Relationship—Being Your Best Self for Your Partner and Accepting Nothing Less," offers advice to single people as to the most important qualities to look for in a partner. It is also for individuals who are not happy in their current relationship, or who are experiencing toxic partners. This chapter helps you to define when enough is enough, as well as how to find the courage to get help individually or as a couple.

Even though my second husband felt overwhelmed and ashamed of his business failure to the point of moving out of town without notifying me, we have thoroughly discussed both our torments at that time, and all is forgiven. He is now a supportive friend. We all make mistakes, and it is important to admit them, ask for forgiveness, and do whatever it takes to make amends to the damaged party.

A few years prior to 2001, Alexi was going through her own challenges. A very successful Grammy Award-winning producer from the Atlantic City area auditioned Alexi at age 15. He and his brother told us that they auditioned over 350 girls on both the East and West Coast, and Alexi was one of two they chose for a callback. They were ready to sign her, but this was in September after Alexi had returned to Erie, PA, to continue the 10th grade. Alexi was thrilled and honored to receive the invitation, and was ready to move to New Jersey full-time with me. But then, her world crashed; her father said she was not allowed to quit McDowell High School in Erie and move to the Atlantic City area to sing.

"You think you can become a singer and a model in Philadelphia or Atlantic City? That's a f–ing joke!" Another relative from Erie said, "Well, why should *you* become famous? What have you done to deserve that?" Even though both my girls had been involved in my model and talent school since the ages of five and six, leading them to become successful child models and actors in our area, people still wanted to put them down and tell them they weren't good enough to succeed in the arts.

This is the kind of poison that can destroy our kids. This is the kind of parental negativity that drives teens to use drugs, drink alcohol, and give up on themselves and their dreams. People they love and respect—parents, teachers, mentors, peers, siblings—or anyone else telling them that they can't do it or they aren't good enough to go for their dreams kill their spirit. I refused to let them believe any of the negative comments and did everything to encourage them to go for their dreams!

The Watch Me! mind-set addresses this question: How do you still realize your own dreams when those who supposedly love you tell you that it is impossible, that you can never do it? These relatives and friends who doubted Alexi had forgotten that she had years of modeling, dancing, and acting classes at my modeling school and at other training centers. She had singing lessons for a few years with a coach in Erie and an outstanding Seth Riggs Coach, Badiene Magaziner, in both New York and Cherry Hill, NJ. She had always loved performing and creating new acts; it had been a part of Alexi's life since she was three. She was perfectly in tune with her childhood dreams and desires; it was everyone else who didn't understand her passion to do it professionally.

I could not take Alexi across state lines myself and bring her to New Jersey full-time even though she wanted to (it's called kidnapping!), and I had a joint custody arrangement. An attorney advised her that if she wanted to move, she should leave on her own volition once she got her driver's license at age 16.

Alexi finished 10th grade with all As, and drove herself— along with all her belongings—to my home in Ventnor, NJ. It was the day she told her father, "Watch me succeed—I am going to do this no matter what, even without your blessing!" It was the start of Alexi's greatness, and the moment she adopted the Watch Me! mind-set completely for herself. The rest of the story is in her section of the book in Part 2: It Works for Young People Too!

Holding a child back from their desires, goals, and dreams out of parental selfishness, insecurity, and fears during the most exploratory and courageous time in a child's life is a huge mistake.

Chapters 9 and 10 are for parents and young people who are encountering difficult challenges within their families and describe what they can do about it. It is difficult being a good parent; our children don't come with an instruction book! Chapter 9, "For Parents: Raising Successful Children and Teens by Teaching the Watch Me! Mind-set," addresses some important issues on positive parenting and gives parents tips on raising assertive, emotionally intelligent, responsible, and street-smart children. These children will reach success early in life and throughout their life span. Although there are many challenges between parents and their children, by learning these various techniques and a positive communication approach, you can break through the wall of silence. And if you still can't break down the wall, you will have the courage to jump over it!

Chapter 10, "For Teens: Advice from 'Mom,'" offers words of encouragement and inspiration to the young people I think so highly of. I remember all too well the suffering I endured during my young teenage years, how not feeling good enough caused a huge sense of depression. This chapter reaches out to you—in celebration of your quest for independence, your creative magic, your unique individuality, and your fierce fight to hold on to your dreams.

Alexi was strong and independent and soon able to handle her own career without me. In spring 2004, she was 21 and confident enough to move to NYC on her own. In less than just one year, she learned to navigate the city like the back of her hand, and was part of the "in" crowd who knew where to go in the city.

I began to envision my life now that I was in my mid-40s and alone, missing my kids terribly. I needed a new plan to reinvent myself and to set fresh goals for the final years of my life, without my children as my primary focus. This was a huge change for me, as it is for any woman and mother.

I moved back to my mother's house in Ocean City, NJ, temporarily while I was looking for a home to purchase and a place to reopen a therapy center. I felt like I was starting from ground zero all over again. I decided to take a trip by myself to Cabo San Lucas, Mexico, to reflect on my life's struggles, accomplishments, and purpose. I had taught the Watch Me! mind-set and attitude for years and had always wanted to write a book to inspire many others to risk change and grow to become their personal best. It was finally my turn to focus on this goal, so I wrote the first edition of this book in 2006.

It is my sincere hope that the stories, examples, and lessons shared within *Live Beyond Your Dreams: From Fear and Doubt to Personal Power, Purpose, and Success* get you inspired and motivated to become your highest, best self as you reach your goals and dreams.

It is your God-given purpose and destiny, after all. We pray you enjoy the book and then give it to someone else in their time of emotional need and challenging transition.

Part 1

~ ~

The Watch Me! Mind-set:
How to Make It Work for You

by Riana Milne

Chapter 1

What Is the Watch Me! Mind-set?

⌒ ⌒

Y OU BOUGHT THIS BOOK FOR A REASON. Maybe you have this burning desire to accomplish a certain goal, but your fears paralyze you, preventing you from getting started. Or you have been working toward your dream, but friends and family laugh at your endeavors and make you feel as if you're not good enough to succeed.

Perhaps you have this nagging, negative, critical inner voice that constantly puts you down, ruining your confidence, self-esteem, and chance of reaching your goals. Just maybe, something in your life may not be working quite right or you are experiencing a horrific, unexpected transition, making you feel overwhelmed, stressed out, anxious, and depressed.

Possibly, you have dared to dream of achieving exactly what you want in life, and you wonder how to go from dreaming to living the reality of that dream. It is one thing to think, ponder, and imagine the vision of the ideal life; it's another to absorb the vision, have it be your driving force and purpose, and live each day on the path to actually achieving those dreams.

The Watch Me! mind-set will inspire you to reach and live your inner vision, enabling you to keep an intense focus to create the exact life you want. By living totally in the now, you will realize that each day is truly a gift. Each day is an opportunity to take one more step toward a well-balanced life full of purpose, peace, inner light, a sense of spirituality, and the contentment of a life fully lived. Meditating on these concepts is how you prepare daily for personal lifelong happiness and success.

Would you believe it if I said that *you*, no matter what your current age, can reach that degree of personal happiness, joy, peace, and success if you learn the techniques of the Watch Me! mind-set and the secrets to balance in life?

The Watch Me! mentality is simply an inner motivational program that helps you to reach your goals, dreams, desires, and purpose. It is a motivational self-talk system that helps you to ease your stress, anxiety, and overwhelming depression during a difficult challenge or transition in life. Humans are normally quick to jump to fear-based thinking when faced with an unexpected traumatic situation. They can also be quick to go into the "pity-me" attitude and feel sorry for themselves, retelling the stories to all their friends of the injustices that were forced upon them. This negativity comes from overwhelming emotional pain and a faulty coping system.

There is a better way to handle unplanned painful challenging transitions. I discovered this for myself when I was only 26 years old and had two small daughters. My husband's business failure had left us $750,000.00 in debt. I was afraid, stressed out, depressed, and anxious, and knew I had to do something to change my life.

20

When I told my husband I wanted a divorce because I couldn't take the stress of his poor financial and business decisions any longer, he tore apart my model and talent office. Everything I had built with just pure energy and my first month's rent was destroyed. Looking at the mess of his tantrum, he screamed, "Watch how far you'll get in this town without my last name!"

"Watch Me!" I said boldly. I didn't know where the strength had come from, but it signified my newfound confidence that I could do anything if I set my mind to it and become the woman I knew I could be. I knew my life couldn't get any worse. It was time for a change, and to reinvent myself for a better life for my daughters and me. I didn't know exactly how to do it in that moment, but I knew I was ready! It was the birth of the Watch Me! attitude and a new mind-set that would change the rest of my life.

The Watch Me! mind-set is *not* walking around with a sense of entitlement, an arrogant, selfish, self-centered personality, or a defiant attitude! It is just the opposite; the program consists of constant mental positive self-talk, daily reflection or meditation, and following the core lessons and spiritual principles with every choice you make. It involves knowing what you want—defining your goals and using the five Ds (desire, determination, dedication, devotion, and dare to dream) to reach them.

The Watch Me! mind-set also includes clarifying what you want and need in a healthy relationship. It is important to know the traits that a healthy, evolved person has, and to know what a toxic person is and have the strength not to settle for an unhealthy relationship.

A toxic person is someone who is negative, controlling, angry, addicted, demanding, or demeaning, someone who lacks integrity, constantly lies, or who tries to hold you back from your higher purpose because of his own lack of self-esteem.

When you are an evolved, spiritual human being, you will find you cannot possibly endure a toxic relationship that is full of anger, deceit, and abuse. Having the inner strength to move forward, release this person in love, and get out of the toxic relationship is often very difficult, especially for a woman with children to support. I know, as I have had to do this myself. Even though it is not easy, you will develop the inner strength to do whatever it takes to have peace in your life for you and your children.

Men with children also hesitate to leave a toxic relationship because they hate the thought of breaking up the family and becoming a part-time dad. I have counseled these fathers who have given their toxic partners chance after chance, but eventually they leave due to the heavy emotional toll it takes to stay. I encourage them to get even more involved with their children once they are separated by becoming a coach, doing hobbies together, traveling together, and making sure their time together is quality time.

No matter your situation, or whether you are male or female, through prayer, study, meditation, and living with this philosophy, these motivational techniques will carry you through these tough times. This program will help you acquire the inner wisdom to make wise choices based on your personal purpose in life, and will give you the strength to pursue your passion without letting anyone else bring you down in the process.

Even though we hear negative comments from those we admire and love that we'll amount to nothing, and that we're not good enough, pretty enough, talented enough, strong enough, smart enough, or privileged enough to succeed (this list can go on forever), we can develop the strength and inner fortitude to move on with our goals and dreams despite what others think or say. Unfortunately, we are often told at a young age that we won't succeed by those we trust: parents, siblings, teachers, and coaches who feel that we just aren't as good as someone else. We then become programmed to think negative thoughts that defeat us before we even try.

Many people who were emotionally or physically abused or abandoned when young often turn inward as adults, with self-doubt and low self-esteem. This could eventually develop into various mental health disorders that may include depression, anxiety, adjustment disorders, bipolar disorders, borderline personality disorder, and antisocial personality disorder (dissocial personality traits), and could lead to a variety of addictions. The ACOA (adult child of an alcoholic or other childhood traumas) personality type may also have many of these disorders emerge after entering into a long-term love relationship.

Individuals who may be suffering with a mental health disorder could be toxic to your soul and your life, and it is best to try to identify these people early on. You can save yourself a lot of heartache if you see the red flags, the warning signs of one or several disorders. These toxic partners can drain your spirit, causing turmoil in your life as well as mentally or emotionally depleting you.

As children we were born with a perfect innocence, able to do whatever we dreamed to do. But along our journey in life, we become jaded because our mentors/parents/teachers tell us in many ways that "we can't."

Once you know the methods in this book, you will be able to say silently and in a strong and assertive, yet calm and confident way, "Watch Me!"

Watch Me! is where the journey begins. These two words could become a living and loving motto in your mind, almost like a chant that you repeat over and over again. This is the starting point or point A. This can happen at any stage or at any age in life. Each person has at least one gift or talent. We are all God's children, whoever you see your God to be. Therefore, we are all perfect in our own way and born with a purpose to contribute to the world in the best manner possible. Only when you find your purpose or talent in life and use it to serve others will you feel truly content with yourself.

Your talent is something you do extremely well and derive incredible joy, satisfaction, and pride from. Your talent could be a variety and multitude of things: writing, singing, dancing, speaking, teaching, painting, building cars, cooking, decorating, fashion or hairstyling, working well with numbers, creating scientific experiments, being a great people-person, working with children, animals, or the elderly, being organized, being a entrepreneur, being a homemaker, or working with details. Your talent can literally be anything, as long as you feel confident about your abilities and love exercising them. While engaging in your talent, you feel your passion: you have increased blood flow, and you often feel "in the zone." This state of being is commonly described as the best high ever!

The zone or flow is almost a trance-like state, a spiritual, unconscious flow of energy, like a peaceful yet energetic high. The gift of the writer or painter, for example, is having the ability to touch our emotions through words or create an image on canvas effortlessly, almost without thinking; it just comes.

Sometimes this state is called channeling. Channeling the energy from God into your work gives it a higher purpose—a way to please or help others in our society. Isn't that what really brings true happiness, the ability to touch another human emotionally?

Knowing you have inspired others in some deep and meaningful way, your creation or work brings you incredible joy. Through the fruits of your labor—an income, a product created, words that inspire, art that is appreciated, or acts that inspire peace by giving back, you will have true purpose, success, and joy by living a loving, spiritual life and receiving gratitude from someone who was hurting or needed you in some way. Without an inner motivation to reach your higher purpose or to give back to others, your talent or success will not bring the personal happiness you thought it would.

Think of all the movie stars or singers who have reached "great success" according to most standards, but have committed suicide, self-medicated with drugs or alcohol, or engaged in high-risk behaviors to numb their pain and feelings of unhappiness. You may think, "What could they possibly be unhappy about? They have all the fame, fortune, toys, hot cars, fashionable clothes, jewelry, art, and mansions a person could dream of! How could they not be happy?"

It is not until you contribute to others or give back that you feel a deep sense of satisfaction and personal success because only then are you living for a higher purpose. Fortunately, many of today's actors, singers, and models appear to have found the secret of how to strike the balance in life that brings both happiness and a sense of accomplishment. Many have found an incredible sense of calm by studying the lessons of the enlightened leaders of our past and present. Ask any of the accomplished, effective, and contented leaders we have today, and they will tell you they continue to study, live, and breathe the techniques of a spiritual, faith-based, balanced life.

The people who dream of being successful singers, actors, dancers, models, politicians, or business leaders all wonder how the people who made it actually did so. What were the differences, the approaches, the knowledge, the strategies, the education, and the privileges they were given that got them where they are?

How did these individuals go from being normal kids to incredible leaders in their field, examples and mentors to others? How do people go from A to Z, especially when they grow up without privileges, lack good parental role models, come from broken families, have negative peers trying to influence them, and live in an uncertain world filled with terrorism, uncertainty and a crumbling economy?

The good news is, the lessons are the same for everyone. I have taught the Watch Me! mind-set to people of all ages, from children as young as 5 to a senior citizen, Hildi, who was 83.

Hildi was a wonderful woman who wanted to model, and her husband laughed at her desire. She joined my talent school anyway, had a blast, and became a huge inspiration to her fellow models! She told me that she confidently said to her husband, "Modeling is something I always dreamed of doing, and if I don't do it now, then when? I'm 83 years old. I don't care what the training costs—I'll pay for it. I don't care what you think because I think it's about time!"

Hildi learned the Watch Me! mind-set and became one of my busiest booked models. I was so proud of her. I gave her a knowing smile the day her husband came in to apologize to me for giving his wife and me a hard time during her training. He was amazed at all the money she was earning as a "real people senior model," and he wanted to thank me personally!

Always remember, your personal success is the best revenge; you'll have no anger or defiance, just pride in succeeding. There is never a wrong time to live, breathe, and work the Watch Me! mind-set; and once you start living it, you will never want to turn back. It is something you develop internally, deep in your heart, mind, and soul that becomes a part of your conscious existence.

When people hurt or doubt us, it is only human to often respond in anger and defiance, and to want to seek revenge against those who belittle us. When you have adopted the Watch Me! mind-set, you will find this is not necessary; you will not respond with anger at all. Instead of being angry, you may say, "I'm sorry you feel that way, but I do not. Watch me succeed in this business, pass the test, make the team, find a better relationship," or whatever you dream to accomplish. You now know that your doubters have given you the gift of becoming driven to succeed.

You will see that your enemies have become part of the journey, and in reality, they are the teachers who help you reach the God-given greatness you were supposed to achieve all along. You will no longer harbor any anger or have any enemies. Your life will become peaceful, and your personal success will come from knowing you are living your life with passion and a higher purpose.

This mental mind-shift in how you perceive people and what they have attempted to do to you will make you very strong. There will be a time to stand up in a firm and assertive way, but you'll make your point and move forward. You won't waste time in wondering how you will get back at them, for you know that the only purpose this serves is to keep you stuck in negative thoughts.

What is most important is removing the perception that others can bring you down to make you look small. Your sense of strength and confidence will be so evident that you will leave them in the dust as they try to figure out why they can't upset you any longer.

At this time, you will start using the secrets of the five Ds—desire, determination, dedication, devotion, and dare to dream—to become motivated and to reach your goals one step at a time.

Also, becoming a spiritual, loving person is an extremely important part of this program. Being an interfaith minister, I found value in many religious books, but I share in this book just a few highlights of the studies that have been very important in my journey thus far.

When I mention the word "God" within this book, I want you to relate that word to how you see *your* God, the Divine, or higher power. If you do not have a sense of a higher power or have God in your life, I sincerely hope I can inspire you to connect with and live in a spiritual way that works for you. It is that important.

Without it, the Watch Me! mind-set could become about defiance and inner anger; if that happens, *it will not work for you.* This book is not about winning with your ego or selfish pride, but instead, living with spiritual grounding and inner strength so that you can confidently move forward in your toughest times by taking your God-given talents and reaching out to the world to serve others.

The rewards are many! Once you begin on your path to greatness by living your sense of higher purpose, the happy, evolved human being that you are becoming will emerge. It is that high, that exhilaration, that incredible feeling of living a peaceful life full of purpose that will keep you in the zone and help you reach your highest degree of contentment, joy, and personal success.

Welcome to *Live Beyond Your Dreams: From Fear and Doubt to Personal Power, Purpose, and Success.*

Chapter 2

Gearing Up for Greatness: Finding the Motivation to Change

~

YOU MUST DEVELOP your talent or passion in a variety of ways to reach your dreams. If this talent becomes your work, then you will always love your job and have a life full of purpose, pleasure, and abundance.

Also, when you love what you do, then your work becomes a daily passion and enjoyment, and you will never begrudge going to work each day. You will find that your joy, energy, and excitement for what you do is contagious, and others will want to share it by being part of your talent or product. People will desire to be around you, like and trust you, and feel comfortable with your product, service, or company.

Did you ever hear the quote from Marsha Sinetar, "Do what you love and the money will follow"? It is so true, even in a spiritual sense. When I taught a sales course at Gannon University in

Erie, PA, I told the students, "You *must* believe in and love your product, or you will not be able to sell it well, no matter what sales techniques you learn. You must find a product you believe in and respect. Only then can you sell it with passion and conviction."

With the Watch Me! mind-set, the product you are selling always begins with *you*. If you believe in yourself, know you are prepared, work hard, study, practice, learn, seek help from mentors in your field, and have a spiritual purpose as to *why* you want to succeed, then you will. If you don't believe in yourself, why would others believe in you? If you are not confident and proud of yourself, you must do everything in your power to become so before selling anything.

That could mean going to the gym to become physically stronger, healthier, and in better shape, or eating properly by staying away from junk foods and eating primarily vegetarian and protein foods. Ladies, look your best by doing your hair and makeup each day and choosing clothes that make you feel wonderful and accomplished. Men, good grooming includes being clean-shaven and wearing clothes that are neat and professional. If you desire a higher position within your organization, dress the part that you wish to become. It is better to be overdressed than underdressed in most situations.

Do take the specialized training or educational courses you need to help you grow, to stay informed regarding new developments, and to become more accomplished within your chosen field. Go to networking events to promote yourself and your business, and look for ways to help others do the same. Giving business referrals to someone else usually comes back to you tenfold. Always carry your business cards with you, and hand them out on a regular basis. Leave them in places that allow you to display your card, especially in businesses you frequent or that are related to your type of business. My business cards are displayed at my health spa, my gym, and my hair salon. I have sent these businesses many referrals, and they are happy to refer me also while displaying my card.

Find the time to engage in inspirational and motivational daily reading for your mental health and well-being. Go to the self-help, psychology, and spiritual (new age religion) sections at your local library, bookstore, www.amazon.com, or www.barnesandnoble .com to find many of the books I recommend in the References and Recommended Reading section of this book. Choose books that are motivational and inspirational. Reading an uplifting book keeps your thoughts positive and helps you to become strong and focused. Remember, you are retraining your mind to think in a better and different way. What you think about comes about! Reading something optimistic each night helps eliminate dark and depressing thoughts. Most shows on TV are depressing; watch TV less and read more. Stay away from any shows that involve murder, fighting, negativity, anger, or cheap drama.

Keep in touch primarily with healthy and positive friends, and avoid those who constantly complain or belittle others. It is good to be supportive to friends, but those who are constantly negative are wearing emotionally and take up too much of your positive time. Limit the time you spend on the phone, texting, and e-mailing. When a friend's conversation turns negative or destructive, tell him you must go and will talk later.

Organize your finances to become debt-free, and have at least six to nine months' worth of living expenses in savings. Read Suze Ormon's books, watch her TV show, and get help from your accountant to eliminate overspending and debt in all areas. Start by eliminating credit card debt. Call the companies and ask them to reduce your interest rate. If possible, get a 0% card and transfer high balances to it to buy you some time. If you are not able to get another card, try to get a part-time job that will help pay down these debts. If you are over $25,000 in debt, seek a bankruptcy attorney's advice to see if this option is best for you. Refinancing your home is another option to pay off large debts, but today's banks require a healthy credit score of at least 740 to get a mortgage. Get your credit reports from TransUnion, Equifax, and Experian free once a year at www.AnnualCreditReport.com. Be careful; this is the *only free* government-supported site for credit reports, but you will still have to buy your credit scores. It is a good idea to get these reports once a year. Be sure to correct anything wrong on it and then ask that a new report be sent to you. Review it carefully. You may also get a free report anytime you are turned down for credit, so do get one to review and correct.

Eliminate all unhealthy habits or addictions. If you need help, seek a specialized addictions counselor. There are many free, 12-step self-help groups in your area. Just google AA (Alcoholics Anonymous), NA (Narcotics Anonymous), SA (Sexaholics Anonymous), GA (Gamblers Anonymous) or OA (Overeaters Anonymous). Try a few of the groups in your area to see which one feels right for you. You don't have to speak right away; just listen. Once you go a few times, ask for a sponsor to help you in your sobriety.

Tell your friends you are trying to stop an addictive behavior and ask for their support. You need to drop anyone who encourages you to engage in the destructive habit (like drinking alcohol). Avoid all people, places, and things that trigger your addictive behavior. Read books on how to help stop your particular addiction. A great spiritual-based counselor, self-help group, positive reading for change, and avoidance of the triggers that lead you to use are all great places to start. You may need a rehabilitation center for treatment in your specific addiction. Ask your certified counselor for her recommendation. If you need to withdraw from a toxic substance like opiates or alcohol, a rehab center is usually best. Take the first step to get help and don't get discouraged. There are many sources of help, but the most important component is your desire and determination to have a better life, addiction-free.

Be someone whose company is desirable. Do not vent or be negative when you talk to others. Do the spiritual work (reading and meditation or prayer) you need to remain positive. If you need help in becoming a happier person, seek counseling or coaching and stay with it until your thoughts are more positive and optimistic. Do not be judgmental, jealous, envious, racist, close-minded, rude, or demanding. Smile often and keep the conversation light when you are out. Be forgiving and a good friend, but maintain boundaries to avoid negative friends or family members. Protect your peace of mind.

These are but a few suggestions to help you become more confident. When you like who you are, it shows, and other people will want to be around you. Having a high sense of self-worth is essential in selling any product or service. If people like and trust you, they are most likely willing to buy from you.

Steven Tyler once said, "Fake it till you make it." This means you should act as if you are already a success in your chosen endeavor. In other words, how would you act, what would you wear, how would you treat others, how would you treat yourself? With love and compassion? Would you walk proudly and with confidence?

When you think about it, do you enjoy spending time with someone who whines, complains, and moans about everything? People who are generally unhappy often blame others for their misfortune and are usually angry and depressed. These people do not attract joy or positive energy into their lives, nor do they feel this energy from others.

The vicious cycle of loneliness, discontentment, spiritual emptiness or disbelief, feelings of failure, and a lack of positive relationships all add up to a life not fully lived or appreciated. If you find yourself in this type of rut, get counseling help immediately with a therapist who uses a motivational, solution-focused, and spiritual/holistic approach, one who addresses mind, body, and soul for healing.

I often advise my psychotherapy clients to use a different frame of reference when they are in a self-pitying mode. After they complain about how bad their lives are, I ask them to compare it to the people who lost a partner or loved one in the 9/11 tragedy. All of a sudden, they stop complaining—their lives don't look that bad after all. They are alive! Now they must learn to appreciate what blessings they *do* have and learn to cultivate or repair the rest. There are many versions of this quote, but Joan Rivers said it best: "Yesterday is history, tomorrow is a mystery, today is God's gift, that's why we call it the present." Learn to appreciate that with each new day, you have a new opportunity to work toward your goals and dreams.

If you are stuck in a negative pattern of feeling stressed, angry, lonely, and depressed, or if you feel as if you are years away from realizing your dreams, then get ready! Living and working the Watch Me! mind-set system can begin to turn your life around. It is a new lifestyle, a new paradigm shift in thinking, being, behaving, believing, and living. It is about reaching your full potential *now*, not thinking you will reach it sometime in the future. Live consciously and presently, aware of today and each day from now on. Focus on your blessings with happiness, joy, peace, purpose, and goals.

You *must* believe in your product, yourself, your talents, and your convictions, and you must be real in wanting to serve and succeed for a higher purpose. You will succeed in your work if somehow, and in some way, you are doing God's work—work that helps others and the human condition.

Why get motivated to change and live with a Watch Me! mindset? Because you deserve to be happy. Children are born with such greatness and the full potential to become whatever they choose to be. But as children grow, unfortunately, their beautiful sense of creativity is often put down, ridiculed, and criticized.

Consider your own child within, your creative child who may have been forgotten years ago, whose talent was locked inside and never allowed to express itself. Now is the time to release this child for yourself! Think back to what you absolutely loved to do—what you may have spent hours doing while you were young. Or, what did you dream to do? What skill did you see yourself performing in your mind's eye, even though you never actually trained for or tried it for real? Brainstorm on a piece of paper exactly what it would take to perform this skill professionally. Don't worry right now about *exactly how* you will be able to take all the necessary steps to reach your dream, as you will learn that in chapter 5. For now, just freely write down *what* you think you may need to do to reach your desired dream. Visualize yourself performing this skill or job every morning and night when you pray or meditate. After all, what you think about will come about!

Why does a parent forget how important it is for a child to have the chance to express himself? Why is this parent trying to make his child a "mini-me?" Is he the perfect individual his child must become? Why can't a parent celebrate the similarities each child has inherited from both of his parents, and at the same time, celebrate the uniqueness his child develops on his own?

An overcautious mother stifles her child's sense of risk or adventure. A wild, independent flair for fashion is belittled by a parent who is too conservative or confining. Yet this parent was the '60s hippie who wore love beads, had long hair, and smoked pot!

I get so frustrated when parents put down their child's choice of fashion, music, or hairstyle. How can they forget their own desire for individuality so long ago? Don't they remember how their own parents hated the Beatles and their wild hair in the '60s, thought Elvis Presley's dance moves were obscene in the '50s, and were shocked when Donna Summer mimicked a fabulous orgasm in her '70s hit, *Love to Love You Baby!*

My generation was making love to the sexy words of Marvin Gaye and Barry White. Who am I, or any parent in his 40s, 50s, 60s, or 70s, to criticize the love music of today? Whether it's the feisty music of rap, R & B, jazz, country, pop, or rock, music is usually about feeling wonderfully in love, feeling sexy, or stating your need for individuality and independence. Whatever the words may be, music is a universal language that bonds young generations in a multitude of ways.

In the way that music connects people from different cultures, so too can a spiritual connection bond people of different ages and backgrounds. When two people are spiritual, they will find each other in a crowded room. It is as if our inner beams of light extend outward and meet another person's inner beam of light.

Two people instantly know when the other one lives in a spiritual way. Spiritual people have a sense of calm or peace about themselves. Those who are enlightened also know that there are no mistakes in life; everything happens for a reason. This is one of the highest beliefs in the spiritual world, that the pain from our past is supposed to teach us lessons and make us stronger, wiser, and more empathic. We meet new people at a certain time or place because they are part of our journey. Everyone and everything is important and interconnected.

I met a dear friend of mine when he was presenting a speech to the staff of an elementary school. My own school was doing testing procedures for our in-service, a topic that I, as a student assistant counselor, didn't need to know about. I asked the principal if the school social worker and I could go to see the motivational speaker, and she said yes.

The speaker and I made a spiritual connection right in the middle of his speech. Everyone in the audience remarked on it and remembered it—the way he looked at me, stood still, stopped what he was saying, and then spoke to me directly about something totally off topic. I knew right then that I must personally get to know this man. There was a spiritual lightning bolt between us!

The social worker asked me two months later, "Riana, did you ever get a chance to get back in touch with the motivational speaker from North Jersey?" I said that we had been in touch and asked her why she'd asked. She said that we had such a strong connection that we seemed as if we would be good for each other, as we had very similar personalities. We did become good friends and still are today.

Watching him speak that morning had inspired me to get my own goals for public speaking back in motion. Whether it was being in that South Jersey school when he spoke, my good friend telling me that he would be speaking at the other school, my principal allowing me to go, or the vibe between the speaker and me because of our spiritual natures, there was a reason for us to meet that day. We continue to inspire each other in our work and daily lives.

My journey back into public speaking began after completing the original Watch Me! book and forming my professional singles networking group, an idea I had started a few years earlier that would combine doing business with the pleasure of meeting other available singles. This group began in May 2006, and each meeting gives me the opportunity to speak on a topic that pertains to single people, and to provide a forum to help others find love and friendship, a higher purpose goal of mine.

I encourage the group to be "real" with each other by bringing truth, honor, integrity, and social graces back into the dating scene. I encourage them to build friendships first based on these higher character traits and principles; this in turn will help them in both their personal lives and business endeavors.

We may not know why or understand it at the time, but everything happens just as it is supposed to in the spiritual world. Take the night I was in Florida, when I met the top-of-the-charts recording artist who ultimately did two songs on his multi-platinum CDs with Alexi; it was just meant to be that we were both at the same club, on the same night, without Alexi being there.

A wonderful friend of Alexi's and mine, Joe Gray, who is also very spiritual, actually spotted the singer, took me by the hand, and said, "Come on, Mom; we're going to have to make the connection for Alexi!" We went together to go say hello to the superstar, and that is when I approached him about Alexi's singing. He was very open to me, listened politely, and he remarked on the spiritual connection we both immediately felt.

Within a few weeks, he ended up recording with Alexi, and then she went on a world tour, which brought her through Tanzania. It was during that tour that she discovered her higher purpose in life was to help the people of Africa who were dying from waterborne illnesses. She decided not to sign the record contract offered to her, but instead returned to Africa to start building freshwater wells. But without the singing and world tour, that realization of her higher purpose may not have come to her. It all happened the way it was supposed to, and she was consciously aware of everything that came across her path.

Realizing there are no mistakes or coincidences in the spiritual world makes life an exciting and amazing adventure! Incredible miracles come your way when you believe, are open to receive them, and live in the present; but more about this in the next chapter.

Alexi has met a lot of wonderful people in the music and entertainment industries, but she certainly has had her challenges. Although many people say the music industry is full of sharks, I don't believe most people have bad intentions. It's just a fast-paced, big-money industry full of competition. In any business where there is fierce competition, you must be careful and investigate carefully any promises made. A team of professionals you can trust—your agent, lawyer, manager, accountant, PR rep, and so forth—is essential in the music and talent industries. Your team must be the family you stay close to and can count on for advice.

Timing is everything. Alexi appreciated all that she learned and experienced, the good and the bad, because it helped her to become stronger, wiser, and more sympathetic and appreciative. She remains friendly with all the people she has worked with in her past because of their shared experience.

Alexi and I have learned the spiritual concept that it never does any good to harbor any anger for another person. Instead, we ask ourselves, what lessons did we learn from the difficult or painful experience? We then bless that individual with thanks and move on, becoming more deeply soulful from those lessons learned.

Although she was disappointed her first invitation for a record deal didn't work out because her father delayed her move from Erie, I explained to Alexi that for some reason, that deal just wasn't meant to be at that time. I advised her to keep positive, stay spiritual, practice her talent, and work hard. The opportunities would keep presenting themselves and she needed to remain positive to receive them. When that one door closed, many other doors opened for her to explore and enjoy. Within the year, Alexi ended up performing her first duet with that superstar on his multi-platinum CD!

As an adult, you have choices! Focusing on the negative will blind you to the positive because you will be so swept up in damaging energy that you will miss the fabulous opportunity looking right at you. Pray daily for healing from any pain and for a quick recovery, and learn the lessons from the disappointment. With the new lessons learned, you will be wiser and gentler to yourself, yet more determined to reach your goals. Know that these difficult lessons and the steps to overcome them make you more appreciative when the real opportunities come along, and they always do.

Being prepared is essential when it is your time to shine. Even though Alexi missed her first recording break, she had even more time to train for her auditions with the producers and recording artists who wanted to work with her soon after. She was older and more confident, and she had paid her dues by working hard throughout the years. This was extremely evident, not just in her ability to sing, but also in her television hosting and modeling work. It was obvious in her positive outlook, mind-set, and confidence in living the Watch Me! principles. This way of living was an essential component of her success thus far and continues to be in her other endeavors.

The motivation to want to change your life comes from the spiritual fire and unending passion within you. If you suffer from depression, your fire and energy are low. You must start the sparks of emotional passion one small step at a time. Approach depression holistically, addressing the needs of your mind, body, and soul. For your mind, read inspirational books and eliminate your negative thoughts through prayer and positive self-talk. Every time you have a negative thought come up, cover it with a positive thought. For example, you might think, "I don't want to go to work today. I hate it there." Top this thought with a positive one like, "I'm so happy and thankful I have this job, which enables me to pay my bills and live in my pretty home. I'm so grateful I get paid this week. I think I'll treat myself to something special because I deserve it!" Continue to speak positive statements in your mind about the blessings you have. Start each day with acknowledging your blessings and being grateful. Listen to motivational CDs in your car on your way to work. Don't talk on the phone; instead, be inspired during your commute to work. You will see an amazing difference when you start each day in this way.

You need this passion, along with mental preparation that keeps you positive throughout the challenges, tests, and hardships. Without the mental preparation and spiritual grounding, many people quit when things become too difficult.

If you expect it to be hard, and you are prepared to work hard, then there should be no surprises. The Watch Me! mind-set and successes will not come if you are not prepared to work hard. Daily, weekly, monthly, 6-month, and yearly goal setting and doing your mind, body, and soul work is all a part of this holistic approach that will lead to reaching your goals and living beyond your dreams. Let me explain this further:

Mind work is the mental preparation of reading books and listening to tapes about spiritual lessons from the masters every day. It involves thinking before each choice you make and trying to make the "higher" or spiritual choice. It is about mentally letting go of anger and fear, and praying for the strength to forgive and to have peace. It is about thinking of the lessons learned and thanking silently the person who taught those lessons to you. Mental work also includes using positive self-talk and refusing to endure emotional abuse from others or yourself through negative put-downs. Always cover every negative thought that comes to you with a positive one. It takes about 30 days to break a bad habit. Negative thinking is a habit created from your past experiences and messages given to you as a child. You can learn to think differently, and when you practice daily thinking in a more positive and spiritual way, your depression lessens over time.

Body work is the physical fitness, nutrition, and daily care of your body, both on the inside and the outside. If you want to be a singer or model, you had better look like one! If you want to be a professional manager within a corporation, you have to present yourself as one. Dress and act the part. Getting enough rest is required to have the energy you need to live a full, productive, and positive day. Don't pollute your body with too much alcohol or other toxins like cigarettes or drugs. Outer radiant beauty begins with the care you're giving your body internally.

Soul work is "the knowing" that God helps those who help themselves. It is practicing meditation, living the secrets of the five Ds, doing the daily goal setting, working on your plan, and revisiting your purpose for living every day. It includes making choices that your spirit knows are the correct ones to launch you toward your intended higher purpose.

Each day, awake with a prayer to bring you one step closer to your life's purpose. Take at least 15 minutes to meditate on the end result: seeing yourself helping others by the fruits of your labor. On the way to work, listen to a motivational or spiritual tape from one of the masters.

There are many I personally consider masters, but my list may differ from yours. I enjoy listening to the wisdom of the Dalai Lama, Wayne Dyer, Stephen Covey, Gary Zukav, Marianne Williamson, Anthony Robbins, Barbara DeAngelis, John Gray, Thomas Moore, Eckhart Tolle, Joel Osteen, M. Scott Peck, Dr. Phil, and Oprah, to name a few. Many of their books and tapes are listed in the References and Recommended Reading section of this book.

Some of my mentors are everyday household names, others specialize in relationships, most are spiritual leaders, and some are experts in psychology. They all motivated me, and each one has a lot of valuable information to share. Using books and audio recordings full of positive messages is part of this daily success plan, as well as doing everything in your power to avoid negative messages and conversations.

Throughout the day, do at least one thing that will bring you closer to your goal. I usually strive for three goals to complete each day, but it depends on how focused you have become on your end result. At the end of your workday, relax to some classical music or jazz to unwind. Eat a healthy dinner high in protein before 5:00 p.m.; do not eat too late at night.

Each week, arrange to do at least three 45-minute workouts at the gym. Try to walk in the country or at the beach at least once a week, or any quiet and serene place where you can enjoy the blessings of nature and your higher power.

At night, read a book that inspires you or helps you to develop the skills needed for your intended goal, new business venture, or mission. Try not to watch mindless TV; instead, pick up to three shows a week that emphasize learning or spiritual messages. Joel Osteen is a great TV minister, and his show airs at least three times a week., Watch some comedy and avoid negative shows about murder and distressing world news.

As you progress toward your goals, reward yourself by buying or doing something special. For years, I have celebrated my growth by treating myself to an exotic trip once a year around my birthday in September. I take this vacation with my daughters, a friend, or by myself for personal reflection. But I always go to escape, rejuvenate, explore, laugh, enjoy romance, and have lots of fun. On weekends, I choose either Saturday or Sunday to make special plans to go out and enjoy myself too.

The Watch Me! plan doesn't mean you can't have any fun! Believe me, I love fun and need it in my life. I work hard and play hard! I put in such a great, productive workweek that my fun always feels well deserved, and I engage in it freely and without guilt.

People who know me say they always see me smiling and laughing, and they feel it's a genuine response to inner happiness. This simple, spiritual, psychological, and motivational system, done daily, weekly, and monthly, will bring you to your desired dreams and goals year after year. Try it and see! What do you have to lose?

And I ask you seriously, one more time, what *do* you have to lose? Then ask yourself what you have to gain. When you can honestly answer this question, your motivation to live beyond your dreams has truly begun!

Chapter 3

A Sense of Spirituality Is Essential

~~~

I STARTED WRITING the first Watch Me! book in Cabo San Lucas when I took a one-week vacation alone to write without interruption. What happened there really ties in with this chapter on spirituality.

Hurricane Marty hit. The winds and rain possessed me as I stood on the sixth-floor balcony of my hotel resort on the beach. What an absolutely incredible rush! The sheer power of nature is magnificent and a wonderful reminder that *we* are not in charge. God (however you see Him, Her, or It), Mother Nature, The Divine, or some other higher power calls the shots!

When Hurricane Marty hit us, I was quickly typing my book on battery power, as the resort had no electricity; once that ran out, I was back to a notepad and pen! The electricity was off for four days, there was no running water for two days, the streets were all torn up, and the main city was flooded. Oh joy! Finding the good from the bad, I laughed and said to myself, "Well, God certainly gave me writing weather." That hurricane was the start of a new phase in my life.

Similarly, in late October 2012, just as I was completing this book, Hurricane Sandy struck the Eastern Seaboard. It was the most devastating storm ever to hit Atlantic City, NJ, the eastern NJ shore resorts, and many areas of New York City. While it may be simply a coincidence that I just happen to be writing books when major hurricanes strike, I have the feeling that once again a cosmic event is signaling the beginning of a new, very spiritual chapter in mine and other people's lives. It offers a time of reflection to feel the blessings of the most simple things: food, water, safety, shelter, and the love of family and friends. It offers a time to simplify our lives and to look at what is truly important to be happy.

We humans are so small in the scheme of things. In relation to the ocean, rainforests, animal kingdom, and the highest mountains, we are just mere specks in the cosmic creation of nature and life. Experiencing the storms that Mother Nature has unleased caused me to reflect on the lack of control we humans have, and the importance of the spiritual saying, "Let Go and let God" and being open to what the world presents to us.

All books of faith talk about a higher power and the importance it should have in your life for peace, happiness, serenity, and success. Spiritual guidance helps provide the balance you need in life to move on to your higher purpose goals and ultimate self-actualization.

For example, the yin and yang symbol represents the Taoist faith's understanding of how opposites such as masculine-feminine and light-dark exist in our world and within ourselves. Spiritual reflection on this symbol reaffirms the following:

1. Each dark event has within it some light of hope.

2. Each positive event or person has a negative element within it.

3. People have both a light and a dark side to them, and the two often intertwine.

4. Even the darkest soul contains some light within it. An example of this is Ted Bundy; despite his horrible killings, his neighbors use to say what a nice man he was. It was a small spot of light within a dark, confused man.

When you are spiritual and have faith, a feeling of inner peace and outer confidence emerges. It is a sense of knowing and a quiet sense of trust. A spiritual person radiates light and a sense of calm. One can sense a person with these qualities. Did you ever notice people who walk into a room with an aura of light around them? They exude energy.

None of us live a perfect life, and we all have the ability to live on the dark side and have a dark day or a dark mood. But we are here on this earth to learn how to be and live in a spiritual way. This takes time, study, and practice.

We are all human; we all make mistakes. It is important, however, to quickly admit your mistakes and make sincere apologies. It is really egotistical not to apologize for a harm done to another. It tells someone he is not worthy of your apology, even though you really *do* know you committed a wrong against that person. To apologize is a spiritual practice, not a sign of weakness. It is a sign of strength, character, and inner light.

Although I am Christian-based and an ordained minister with the Universal Life Church, two of my favorite spiritual teachings are from Buddhism and *A Course in Miracles* (ACIM). The Course has taught me that we are all God's children and angels of God. We all can minister to and help our fellow man. Helping others through your work is one way to serve a higher purpose.

I am so happy that I became a minister, relationship coach, and a psychotherapist who uses motivational approaches along with spiritual concepts in my client's sessions to teach them a happier way of living. By showing them a different perspective, I can guide clients toward their spiritual inner light, toward a sense of calm and away from the darkness of fear, anxiety, depression, and anger. Helping one or more people each day is a beautiful reward from my work. It is my passion, my talent, and my gift to and from God as one of his angels.

So, the Watch Me! mind-set for personal power is not about ego, arrogance, or bullying another. It is a faith-based belief that God has given you all you need to reach your dreams, and you are merely defending your right and ability to pursue those dreams in a confident way. Once on the path to realizing your dreams, you must appreciate and enjoy the journey. You can't go from A to Z overnight; it is a goal-oriented system, and it takes time to reach optimum success. This is a learning and growth process; you must be motivated yet patient.

When you begin the journey, if you have pure intentions and thoughts that enable you to give back by serving others, your spiritual purpose will guarantee your success. Once you become personally successful, you must continue to give back, otherwise reaching your goals will seem empty and unfulfilling.

You often hear stories of people who reach their top goals yet still have a sense of emptiness. They might think or say, "Is this all there is? All that hard work, and I feel nothing." They feel this way because they lack a higher purpose goal or spiritual fulfillment in their work.

Many years ago, I wrote a quote I have used in all of my business endeavors: "Help yourself by helping others." It means that when you reach out toward others to help, you in turn become your best and happiest self.

The Gift of Spiritual Presence

Many of my clients come to counseling after the death of a loved one. Often, people fear death and get stuck living a life of depression after a loved one passes. Sylvia Brown and John Edwards have done a beautiful job explaining what happens on the other side when someone passes. They bring great comfort to many when they tell members of their audience that their family member or friend is just fine on the other side. It also helps to believe that when people pass, they are never truly gone. They become one of your angels who are always with you in your heart, mind, and soul.

I feel the spiritual presence of those who have passed. This presence is often referred to by others as "seeing ghosts." I have had many experiences with spirits, although I have never seen one. One experience I define as a "great experiment" occurred at the old mansion of a gentleman friend. He had just bought it in

Erie, PA, and was renovating the house for his magazine's office. We went out for dinner that evening, and later, he wanted me to see the remodeled office.

As we toured the bottom level of the three-story house, I felt very uneasy, especially when climbing the steps to the second floor. I said, "The house seems a bit spooky to me. Did you ever do a history search on it?" He said no. When I started climbing to the third level, my heart was pounding in my chest, and I broke into a sweat.

When I reached the top floor where the steps came into a kitchen area, I said, "Something is wrong in this house; I feel it!" He laughed and negated my feelings and then directed me into a small living room/study area. My negative feelings subsided a bit but then escalated again when I left the study that led into a small bedroom and a bathroom. When I was touring the bathroom I said, "I'm going downstairs—I have to get out of here. You don't understand!"

My friend knew what a strong lady I was, as we had been dating for over a year. He said, "Riana, I've never seen you like this."

I said, "Let's go. And do me a favor—do a history on the house because something bad happened in here on the third level."

About 10 days later, he came over for a date and told me to sit down. He said, "Riana, I have to tell you . . . what you felt in that house . . . well, you have a special gift. There was a murder in that house, back in the 1800s, where the father hung his son from the rafters in between the third floor kitchen and bathroom. You felt the negative spirit!" It was confirmed; I can feel spirits of those who passed, and I feel fortunate to have the gift.

A month later we wanted to show my daughters his new office, as they both had modeled for his magazine. I told him not to tell them about the murder, as it might have scared them, since they were only 10 and 11 years old at this time. Nothing was said; however, when they were both climbing the steps to the third floor, Alexi said, "Mom, something is creepy in this house!"

I looked at my friend, wide-eyed, and I said to Alexi, "What do you mean?"

She kept going up, but by the time she entered the kitchen, she said, "Mom, this is really creepy up here. I'm going downstairs!" Stephana kept looking around the third level with us, but later told me she also felt very uneasy in the house.

I later told the girls about the incident in the house and that they must not be afraid of spirits, that it is a gift to be able to experience them. When Alexi was six and my dad had just died, the next day she told me that Granddaddy had come to visit her. I asked her what he said or did. She struck a pose against the dresser and crossed her arms, as my dad would have done. She said he told her, "Hon, I'm sorry I had to go, but Granddaddy is safe and up with God now. I need you to help me take care of your mother—she's a real special lady."

I asked Alexi if she was scared, and she replied, "No, I was glad he came to say goodbye." Alexi was so sure, so matter-of-fact that it happened, that I thought she may have the gift. But what occurred in the old mansion in Erie years later confirmed it.

Since then, both Alexi and I experienced spirits again in our home on South Dorset Avenue in Ventnor, NJ. Soon after moving in, the doorbells at both the front and back door ceased to work. My husband was very handy, so he replaced both bells. They worked for only two days before they stopped working. However, a loud single bell, like a gong, would go off in the house at random times. I would run to the door, but no one was ever there.

Soon after the bell incidents began, I started to smell cherry pipe tobacco in the house, especially in the master bedroom. None of us smoked, so this smell was inexplicable. I wondered if a spirit was in the home, because they often present themselves through certain odors or electrical occurrences.

Also, after moving in, I was tending a dead rosebush that surrounded the concrete archway of an exterior stucco wall. I remember my husband laughing at me as I tried to get roses to grow. He said, "Ri, just tear it out—that bush will never grow!" Within days, beautiful red and yellow roses started to bloom; it was a miracle! The first season, they lasted and grew into December, which was extremely rare for roses.

I asked a friend of mine about the history of the house. He'd grown up in Ventnor, NJ, and as a police officer, knew the history of our well-known home, which dated back to the late 1800s.

"Raucci was the last name of the man who lived here for many years," he explained with dramatic flair. "He was a South Philadelphia mobster who was shot in the house. The doorbell rang, and he opened the large front door and was blown away right there." (This explained the doorbell situation!)

"He used to stand on the large front stoop on summer nights and smoke his pipe." (This explained the pipe tobacco I smelled). "People from all around the Shore used to go by the house and look at his fabulous rose garden. Once he died, the roses died, and never grew again on the stucco wall until you moved in." Ah! Italians always loved me! And Raucci was watching over us as we lived in his beautiful home.

They say the more spiritual you are, the more you are able to tap into the magic of feeling the spirits of those who have passed. I am not sure if this is true, or if the ability is inherited, or both. Having this small gift makes me believe that there is a life beyond this Earth school.

One of my therapy clients, Bob, presented an example of the process of passing on. He was pronounced dead from a heart attack, his third. He and his loving wife told me the story. "I *did* die—I heard the doctor pronounce me dead at an exact time. I went toward the light, and it was very peaceful; I was not afraid. My relatives were there to greet me, and I felt happy to see them. But then I saw and heard my wife Marsha in the hospital hallway, sobbing as she said, 'How can I tell my niece he's gone? She will be devastated, and we need him!'" They did not have children, but their young niece was like their own child. Bob quoted Marsha's exact words and where she was when she said them, information he never could have known because he was in the operating room.

I have read many stories like this and seen them reported on the TV show, *I Survived . . . Beyond and Back,* but this one was from a couple I knew well and trusted.

Of course, most religious books mention the afterlife as "a given fact." Experiencing the presence of spirits is an awareness that you should never be afraid of, as they are just reaching out to connect with you, another spiritual soul.

What Is Karma, and How Does It Affect Me?

A chapter on spirituality would be incomplete without mentioning the laws of karma, which can help you to grow and learn from your current or past painful experiences.

Karma is the result of a particular deed and the chain of cause and effect that connects various deeds to each other, affecting your life or, as it is often referred to, "fate." Therefore, karma is the accumulation of your actions in life that is carried forward, affecting your fate. Each deed, whether positive, negative, or neutral, has a part in defining or altering your karma. Each event is unique and is a part of the whole experience of your life.

Humans are attracted to many illusions about what is valuable in this world and within themselves. These illusions can separate us from our best selves and our spiritual destiny. Attachments to false hopes or illusions bring about adverse events that can ultimately affect your karma negatively. Not living your higher purpose in life can bring about despair, depression, anxiety, and an internal disconnect.

When you have a disconnect between knowing what your intuition tells you to do and procrastinating because you're afraid of repeating the past as you try to correct it, you will stay stuck in pain and dysfunction. Going to therapy can help you understand how the past affects your present and future decisions. Even though at first this may be uncomfortable, this is extremely important for you to do to get beyond your emotional pain and destructive, repetitive patterns.

The Laws of Karma

The laws of karma teach us to confront the dysfunctional attachments that we are tempted to latch on to. They teach us to free ourselves from the painful illusions that delay us from reaching our spiritual greatness. The laws tell us we have the power to attach or remain unattached to a thing or a person, explaining that the state of "unattachment" brings peace.

The Karmic Law of Cause and Effect states, "For every action, there is an equal and opposite reaction." The laws and lessons of karma help us to remove the obstructions that life often presents. There are four axioms that will always exist and explain the nature of the universe. They are:

- things are cyclical

- there is a universal oneness

- balance is the goal for peace

- all things change and must change. The "winds of change" will forcibly change things not ready for change.

I often speak of the winds of change with reference to those going through a difficult transition. We don't often understand at the time why we were forced into a change we didn't want, like losing a job unexpectedly, discovering a cheating spouse, being diagnosed with a sudden illness, or going through an unexpected breakup. These forced changes should make us stop and reflect on why they happened and what we are supposed to learn from them.

Mediation and prayer during these difficult times helps us deal with the "Why me?" question that so many humans resort to. Although we don't understand a change when it first takes place, faith-based trust must then take over so our thoughts turn to "Everything happens for a reason. I don't understand why this happened to me, but I trust that there are no mistakes in the spiritual world, and I must now refocus on how to handle this change for myself."

God redirected your path for a reason. Here are some examples of how to get through a forced change:

- You have just been laid off at the job you didn't like much. You are distressed because you need the money, but you will have unemployment insurance for a while to help get you through. Job loss has now given you the time and incentive you needed to start the business you've always dreamed of. Instead of feeling sorry for yourself, get busy with goal-setting strategies for your new business and go for it!

- You knew deep down that your dysfunctional and toxic boyfriend wasn't a good partner, but you loved him and hung in there to try to make things work. Your shock over his suddenly leaving you was the catalyst for personal change. The winds of change are forcing you to move on to reinvent yourself and take the time you need to meet someone more healthy and loving toward you. Keep in mind the world is abundant, and you will meet someone even better once you are emotionally and spiritually centered.

- You have received notice that your home is being foreclosed on. You have been working three jobs, but the bank won't refinance you or help you get a new loan. You love your big home, but you have felt a slave to it. This is the forced change you needed to simplify your life, to downsize to a more modest home, giving you the financial freedom to enjoy your life and relationships more.

You can see how these everyday examples fit into understanding the laws of cause and effect, and they demonstrate how to handle the winds of change in a proactive and positive way. This is a new way of thinking for most people that gets away from the pity-me attitude by using basic spiritual teachings along with the Watch Me! mind-set.

Here are some of the highlights of the 13 Laws of Karma as I have interpreted them from my studies:

1. *As you sow, so shall you reap.* Known as *the great law of karma,* it asks, "Are you creating negatives in your life by focusing on negativity in others?" Start with where you are; do

something positive about you. If you are helpless and fearful, do you cause that by the illusions or negatives to which you are attached? Learn to let go of your need to control others.

2. *You attract what you are, not what you want.* If you want a healthy, evolved mate, develop within yourself the qualities you envision in a potential mate, and life will bring that person. Living in a healthy and successful way requires your participation; if you want to attract loving people, then be loving. This is the *law of creation,* which states that you can create your own situation, starting in your mind with what you think about and in your soul with what you feel about yourself and others.

3. *What you resist persists for you.* What you object to reflects who you are on the inside. Do you deny the truth about yourself, and in turn, create your own pain? This *law of humility* states that you choose your own enemies and give them strength. Is your false or heightened ego so lost in dysfunction and illusion that you deny the greatness of who you really are—a wonderful spiritual being?

4. *Wherever you go, there you are.* This *law of growth* states that if you don't change, nothing is changed. Wherever you go, your problems come with you. Changes learned slowly will last. You can physically move from one place to another, but until you are ready to live in the now, your past will come with you. Do you seek the growth and forgiveness it will take to stop recreating those same negatives all over again? When you have the courage and focus to accept and cultivate change, life and karma sees to it that negative environments go away all by themselves.

The Laws for Personal Action

5. *Whenever there is something wrong, there is something wrong in you.* You reflect your surroundings; therefore, this is the *law of mirrors* regarding personal responsibility. If you are with negative people, then there is negativity within you. If you become healthy and loving, then you will attract others with these characteristics. Whenever you get angry, you allow it. This means you have a choice either to get consumed with anger and resentment or to perceive it in a different way. No one "makes you get angry"; you allow the other person to make you mad. Choose to not let another affect you in this way. Do you blame others and say it was their fault? Or do you accept your own contribution to the problem, and then seek to make a positive change after examining the lessons you have learned from the experience?

6. *Whatever you do may be very insignificant, but it is very important that you do it.* This is the *law of synchronicity*, which is about the chain of connection from the lowest to the highest. Do you respect people for their work, no matter what their work is? Do you accept only what the ego craves from your work, seeking only the rewards, or can you also accept the daily grind? This lesson says that you must have discipline and humility and demonstrate these qualities in your character and the work that you do.

7. *You can't think of two things at the same time.* This *law of direction and motives* speaks of higher spiritual values versus lower human natures. If you focus on higher values, then there is no room for thoughts of anger, selfishness, and greed. What do you focus on? You cannot be consumed

with self-centered, egotistical thoughts or crave material things and still grow spirituality. Each morning, you must connect with your higher power and pray for spiritual growth and the ability to live faith-based principles; then give your family and the world the love and attention they need. Knowing your priorities helps you to be mentally free at work to concentrate on your job. The compulsion toward greed only feeds your lower nature and material-ism. In the end, when you are facing death, you cannot take anything with you except your memories, spirit, and peace of mind, so nurture those things.

8. *If you believe something to be true, then sometime in life you must demonstrate that truth.* This law is about what you have learned in life and your willingness to show it. If you don't demonstrate what you know to be right, there will be consequences for you. Are you afraid to grow because it is hard? Do you procrastinate about doing what your intuition tells you is the right thing to do? This *law of willingness* questions whether you are willing to learn and grow from your lessons of pain from the past, and if you are ready to make the changes needed to become your higher spiritual self.

The Laws of History and Results

9. *You can't go home again, but you must try.* "Home" refers to the psychological and emotional home of your past. Are you trying to recreate the past to fix something in old relationships? Are you trying to get it right this time, or to find the emotional value that you thought you missed? You cannot rewrite your past, no matter how hard you

try. There is nothing more that you need to go back to. Do you feed old dreams that keep you from being in the present here and now? According to this *law of be here now,* you must try to live in the present or the past will continue to haunt you. Instead of living in the past, understand what lessons you have learned from it, and bring that insight into the present in a positive way so you will not repeat the painful emotional mistakes you have already endured.

10. *The more things change, the more they stay the same.* History will repeat itself until you learn the lessons that change your path, according to this *law of change.* Are you doing the same things, making the same choices, and yet expecting different outcomes? Do you keep recreating past events and problems in new relationships? What are the lessons you must learn to move forward and not feel stuck in a cycle of despair?

11. *When you focus on your life, good things happen.* This *law of reward and patience* refers to doing a job that highlights your inner talents and spiritual being. Joy and peace comes from a sense of doing work that you are supposed to do—work that benefits family and community. Are you instead focusing on what you don't have? Do you seek flashy, materialistic things or people who are shallow and who draw you away from your God-given purpose and values? Do you start your day with thanks and an attitude of gratitude for all the blessings you do have?

12. *What you put in, you get out.* This law of *values and upliftment* refers to the idea that whatever you contribute will either

increase (uplift) or decrease the whole. The rule asks you to consider what you are putting your energy into, as there is value in that energy. Are you choosing the right things to devote your time and energy to? If you direct your energy to the good of the world, the universal whole, and your higher purpose, then you will receive the rewards of your time and work.

13. *The law of letting go: you truly don't have something unless you can give it away.* When you can let go of your ego and allow others to be right and have their say, you have even a truer, greater ego because you don't have to prove anything. When you give away money, you prove that you have the power to get more and open the space to receive more. The true test is to let things go, for only then do you know that you have them. You have heard of Richard Bach's saying, "If you love something, set it free; if it comes back, it's yours, if it doesn't, it never was." Only when you let it go can your love be mutually shared and enjoyed.

The Law of Unconditional Love

When you give away love, you prove you also have the power to get more of it in return. This law is one of the most difficult tasks to master. When someone hurts you, usually your first reaction is to get angry, defensive, and find a way to get back at him.

However, those in toxic relationships often turn their anger and their fear of their partner inward. The abused partners become submissive, withdrawn, and depressed as they try to change themselves to please their partner. In doing this, they slowly give away their own power and personality, losing their God-given greatness.

Fear takes them over, and they become stuck and their self-esteem plummets as they try harder to hold onto the angry partner. Until the "victim" becomes strong enough to let go of their dysfunctional lover, they will remain in emotional pain and cannot move forward in life.

Only from strength can they let go, thank the partner for the love they once had, learn the lessons from this suffering, and forgive the partner. Then space will be created for God to present a new, healthier love in their lives.

The universe and your higher power have given you the gift of free will. You have the peace, drive, and choice to create greatness in your life, without your toxic partner telling you that you can't do it. Letting them go with forgiveness and unconditional love gives you the power to do the right thing as you release yourself from the toxic anger that held you in depression and anxiety.

Each one of these very deep and heavy lessons is actually quite simple; they apply to the past, present, and future. I present these important laws and lessons of karma to encourage you to overcome your fears and to live fully present in the here and now. If you feel fully alive in the now, then you can live your future with purpose and clarity—one moment, one hour, and one day at a time.

A Course in Miracles (ACIM)

The lessons from *A Course in Miracles* are also important in understanding growth, change, and healing. I first heard a lesson from Marianne Williamson on the tape called *On Intimacy*, in which she talked about what elements a quality relationship had. It was the first explanation of what I was seeking in a love connection that I felt was completely accurate. After hearing this tape years ago, I wanted to know more about *A Course of Miracles* as a spiritual study.

That was the beginning of my intense journey into the spiritual world and its lessons. I actually found an ACIM study group in Erie, PA, that I attended every Thursday night. I really looked forward to going, as it grew into quite a large gathering of spiritual souls. The group was very diverse. Everyone was invited, but most importantly, everyone was accepted. Each week we would read a new lesson together and then talk about how we could relate this lesson to our lives.

The Course is based in Christianity, and it combines psychology, spirituality, and philosophy in its teachings. I would describe it as a book on spiritual faith in God that is written with a modern, down-to-earth, easy-to-understand approach.

The goal of ACIM is to achieve atonement or a reuniting with God. It could be considered a course in positive and personal mind control. Here is a summary of the most important concepts that may help you through your challenges and growth:

1. Your self-esteem flows from your beliefs. You cannot believe you are a loving child of God and still have low self-esteem. To change your self-esteem, you need to have a high motivation to live in a spiritual way. Self-esteem improves as you release your anger and eliminate fear of change.

2. You have two choices in every decision you make: to deal with your situation with love or fear. If fear rules you, then you have a faulty belief system, usually arising from painful childhood messages. Fear impedes your ability to receive any spiritual gifts, but this can disappear when

your belief system changes. How to accomplish that change is the process of learning ACIM. Remember, you always have a *choice* for every decision: to approach it with either love or fear.

3. Fear gives rise to anger in how you see yourself and how you choose to see others. When your ego controls your life and you don't trust in your higher power, your ego becomes superior, and you will live a fear-based life. You hurt yourself if you feed the ego, and how you experience the world mirrors your beliefs and feelings. What you see or believe is what you get (this is also one of the karmic laws). Evil, pain, problems, arguments, anger, revenge, or jealousy are all experiences you create in your mind with a controlling and ego-based belief system.

The ego (our dark side) is in a constant tug-of-war with our inner light. The Holy Spirit is a message within us, given to us by God. When you can tap into this light, this spirit along with "the answers" and miracles will constantly come to you. The separation from God was caused by choosing fear (ego) instead of love (God's light, trust, and spirit).

Replacing pain with joy requires replacing your ego-based beliefs with messages from your inner spirit. The power struggle between fear and love choices keeps you in turmoil known as hell on earth. Anger means you are choosing fear, which makes you project your own insecurities onto others. Your perception creates your reality. If you choose love, you will live in love and peace (heaven on earth); if you choose fear, you will live in your ego world full of fear, anger, power struggles, resentment, and chaos (hell on earth).

4. ACIM presents three core beliefs for you to consider, and says with these concepts, your entire life will change for the better. These are the following:

   a. Your God is loving, not vengeful, angry, or punishing. You must trust in the path He presents to you. Do not fear change; instead, trust in change as you trust in God.

   b. You are a holy, loving child of that loving God, or you are one of God's angels. You are here on earth to discover your wonderful gifts that you can give to others in service.

   c. All other humans are also children of God; you should treat them accordingly, with love, kindness, and respect.

5. When you have these core beliefs, three things will happen:

   a. Your enemies will disappear, as you will have a new way to intellectually and spiritually interpret negative deeds done against you.

   b. You will learn to distinguish between what ACIM calls love versus a call to love. A call to love is any action other then love, and instead of looking negatively at what a person did, look at the gift or reason for his doing it.

      Did it come from his sense of fear? Can you help him through this fear with love and understanding? If he won't accept help, can you forgive him? Forgiving releases any anger or negativity you may hold inside, and is very important for you to do for your own healing and peace of mind.

65

    c. Once you can distinguish between love and a call to love, you will know how to react in a way that will always work for you, creating a positive result.

6. Your feelings are the windows to your beliefs. If you work on your feelings and thoughts, you can change your faulty beliefs. Look for the "gifts" in that difficult person, and the opportunity to learn to be a better, more understanding, and loving person yourself.

7. There are no mistakes in life. Everything happens for a reason. You cannot force change. Be open to the messages of God, and you will be given the answers. Learn to trust your spiritual intuition. This does not mean you should sit aside and wait for change, because God helps those who help themselves. Instead, trust in the change process; do not fear it. Any mistake made along the way is merely a lesson to be learned, one that will make you a stronger and more spiritual, emotionally aware, and intelligent individual.

8. An important ACIM theme is that the world and your fellow man are but a mirror of your perceptions that you create. These perceptions determine how you act, and then how you act creates your reality. Act with love, not fear.

9. Motivation, spiritual faith, and personal positive mind control are the three most critical beliefs in successfully carrying out the messages of ACIM. It is lifelong learning, as you were put on the earth to learn your lessons. Because you are human, you can be weak, and when you are, you must call on your higher power and the teachings of ACIM to create a healthier perception of your obstacles, lessons, and the difficult people you encounter. When you choose to

look at these obstacles with love instead of fear, you learn to live life in peace and trust in a loving God. He knows what is best for you, and you must trust this process.

10. This new ability to trust in your higher power will bring more peace, love, and a joyful contentment in life. This is the feeling of living in heaven on earth. Spiritual people instantly bond. The more spiritual you become, the more you will meet the knowing—other spiritual people on the path to a better, more contented life. You know each meeting with another person has some purpose, as there are no mistakes in life!

Two of the prominent summary lessons from *A Course in Miracles* are:

1. ACIM shows you the path of growth from pain to joy. You become aware of those faulty parts of your belief system that may block you from living with joy. Your intellectual choices will now involve an emotional, spiritual belief system based in love.

2. Your way of solving problems will become so much easier when you trust that the answers will come. Meditate or pray for the answers. You will approach each problem in a calm, peaceful, and loving way, versus an angry, revengeful, and fear-based way.

A quote from the ACIM text reads, "I am responsible for what I see. I choose the feelings I experience and I decide upon the goal I will achieve. From my perception flows my reality." This is about living a conscious life in the present here and now. It is about being proactive, versus reactive, in your choices. It is about consciously choosing a love-based reaction over a fear-based, negative reaction.

An example of this occurred when my second husband left town in the middle of the night when he knew he had to declare his business bankrupt. He was too afraid and ashamed to tell me about it. I discovered at that time we were eight months behind on our mortgage, and our home was about to be padlocked. I immediately put the house up for sale, and Alexi and I needed a place to live, and fast. Our neighbor took us in. I could have been reactive and angry at my husband, but I focused instead on being proactive and planned Alexi's and my next move. It was right after I met the singer in Miami, who wanted her near NYC to start recording. I told her it was time to make that move. The reason had presented itself, and it couldn't have been more clear that it was time to make a change—for her future.

I prayed to find the forgiveness I needed to relieve the emotional pain of my husband's leaving us due to his fear and shame. I didn't focus on anger or resentment; I prayed to forgive him and bless us with a positive change and meaningful transition. I looked at this forced change as the winds of change making me do whatever I could to help Alexi and to reinvent myself yet again.

Years later, I met my husband for lunch, and tears streamed down his face when he told me how bad he felt that he'd left us while we were sleeping and that he had let us down. I knew he had a good heart and really did love Alexi, Stephana, and me. I understood his childhood turmoil and ACOA personality type, and his tendency to run when he was afraid. I told him I had forgiven him a long time ago. We became friends again; he helped me move into my new home and assisted me with several issues throughout the years. I chose a love-based reaction over a fear-based one.

These were only some of the general lessons of ACIM that were presented. Please understand that I am not looking to push a certain religion or any particular faith on you. But you must find a spiritual path and study that *does* work for you. There are so many wonderful religious books with such magnificent messages for growth and healing. Take the time to learn your chosen faith, and do your best to practice it daily.

There are many paths to God, the Divine and your inner light. There are no mistakes, only lessons, and everything happens for a reason. Trust in the path; when you choose love instead of fear, a type of self-assurance in doing things God's way—not your way—will prevail.

Soon your inner light will shine to the world, and people will feel the power of its energy. As one of God's angels, it is up to you to spread the light in any way you can. The more light and love you share, the more you will have and receive.

When you live focused on your inner light, you will be amazed at all the miracles that happen for you in life. You will have peace as you intuitively know the answers to all of your questions.

I think one of the most impressive examples of *receiving miracles* happened to my best friend, Beth. She was going through a very painful divorce, and I was encouraging her to get some books based on ACIM. I told her to listen to *On Intimacy* and to try to change her faulty, negative belief system about her relationship.

She read and listened to what I suggested, and after two weeks exclaimed, "I don't get what these miracles are; I haven't gotten any miracles! Everything negative keeps happening to me. Where are these supposed miracles?" I laughed and then told her to keep studying, to trust, and to be willing to change how she perceives things that happen to her.

Within a few days, I got a distressing call from Beth. She said in a weak voice, "I will never question again what a miracle is!" Beth was calling me from the hospital. Earlier that morning, her car had gone over a 150-foot cliff. There was only one tree at the base of that cliff, and the nose of her car hit it perfectly, breaking the fall of the car, half a foot from the ground. The front page story in the Lancaster, PA, newspaper confirmed what really happened: "It's a Miracle She's Alive—Lancaster Woman Survives Fall!" Beth only broke one foot and got some facial bruises. Now that's a miracle!

God saved her that day, and she knew it. God wasn't ready to take Beth yet, as she had more to learn in this Earth school, and more of her purpose to discover before she went. Miracles happen when you least expect it; you must trust, study, meditate, or pray and work the program each day!

There is a lot to learn in our spiritual growth, as we are forever learning lessons in this Earth school. We are all a work in progress, and none of us has all the answers. Life is exciting, and having an open mind to keep learning, growing, and practicing the spiritual lessons is essential in reaching personal fulfillment and success.

Spirituality is at the core of the Watch Me! mind-set; it is the essential ingredient to trusting that God knows what is of the utmost importance for you and will deliver it when it is best for you to receive it.

"Let go and let God" is a motto of many drug and alcohol rehab programs for the addicted. In essence, this means that you must trust in God, not your ego. It also means that you should let go of trying to be in control of others and their choices. Pray for guidance and the answers. Pray for the strength to do what you need to do to reach your God-given potential. Trust and rejoice in the challenges that are the prelude to change, for they propel you to move forward to the next level of greatness.

Share your inner light with all you meet! Wake up with a prayer thanking God for all the blessings you have, and then ask God to lead you as you strive to reach each goal and dream that ultimately will fulfill your life's higher purpose. This is the way He meant it to be.

Chapter 4

The Secret of the Five Ds— Desire, Determination, Dedication, Devotion, and Dare to Dream!

⌒ ⌒

M Y FATHER, JACK HOWIE MILNE SR., taught me the importance of the lessons of the five Ds. He said, "Hon, if you know the secret of the five Ds, you can do anything in life!" I remembered his words, share them often in the speeches I give, and have tried to live them since being a teenager. Many people are amazed at how many careers I have enjoyed and my wealth of experience in many different areas. I can attribute much of my growth and various successes to this valuable lesson.

I admit, I can get easily bored. I am a risk-taker and considered gutsy, and I always look for the next challenge or goal I want to meet. I have always been extremely focused and yet I have still dared to dream. Perhaps that is why I felt there were no limits in life.

Usually, I find that the children and teens who come to my therapy center who have been diagnosed with attention deficit hyperactivity disorder (ADHD) tend to be creative and risk-taking personality types. If the parent or I as their therapist can help find the child's or adolescent's passion and talent, then we can channel the traits of the person with ADHD—risk-taking, impulsivity, and being easily bored—into something very positive for them, and they can truly enjoy their chosen career.

I often hear about the ADHD child who can't focus in school but can sit and play video games for hours. So they *can* focus on something they feel they can do well and are passionate about—the goal is finding that talent within the child.

When speaking to a group of high school kids, I have found they are often concerned about choosing the one career they will work at for the rest of their lives. This is the tradition that most parents instill in their children because it is what they have known and done. Many adults who are now 70 to 80 years old worked at one company for 50 years and retired with a bonus and a gold watch.

Today, there is no security that your job will exist next year or even next week! I advise young people to go for their current passion and dream. My daughter Alexi wanted to be a singer, and even her own father said it was impossible! She proved him wrong, and in going for her passion and dream and getting it, she has felt satisfied enough to move on to the next dream. This is the idea of living beyond your dreams. Once you meet one challenge, plan a new goal, meet that goal and move on to another one. Today, seven large villages in Tanzania have freshwater wells due to Alexi's dream to help change the world, which occurred after she satisfied her dream to sing.

In creating your own goals and multiple dreams, you create your destiny and your future. Your own dreams come true every time you achieve another goal in your path in life. Many people have decided not to settle for just one career or goal. As soon as you meet your first goal, start working on your second one. You will then find you are living a life with total purpose, fun, excitement, a sense of achievement, and a great deal of personal esteem and gratification.

It is important that you realize there are no limits in life. If you choose to work at one career at a time, you may eventually feel you have fully experienced it, and boredom or exhaustion may set in. That is the time to consider going for career number two or three on your list.

As a 17-year-old girl, I wanted to be a counselor, a writer, a model, a radio and TV talent, and an executive in marketing and promotions. I ended up going to Penn State University for broadcast communications, and my first job after college was as a DJ at WLVU radio in Erie, PA. Soon after, I was hired at a CBS TV Station, WSEE TV 35, as continuity director and head of public relations. My job involved writing and creating most of the local TV spots, as well as creating the newspaper and *TV Guide* ads. I also did voice-overs for many of the commercials. It was an excellent creative job, but the money was just above minimum wage. After a couple of years, I was looking for a job with better pay.

To make a long story short, I held a lot of jobs, and many of them were unusual ones. At the age of 24, I owned a chocolate company and factory called 24 Karat Candies, and Maron's Chocolates, which had four locations in Philadelphia. I was responsible for the total marketing of the product and packaging, as well as remodeling each store location. I also went into custom chocolates and created a chocolate museum. I did so well that I was given the Philadelphia Chamber of Commerce's Business Person of the Year award, and I was the youngest recipient ever! I developed corporate logos in chocolate for the Philadelphia Flyers, Ciba-Geigy Pharmaceuticals, The Golden Nugget Casino, Meritor Financial Group, and Boeing, to name a few.

After the chocolate business, I opened my own model and talent agency and school in Erie, PA, in 1987. Over nine years, the school won three International Modeling & Talent Association (IMTA) awards for Model and Talent School of the Year, and many successful models, actors, and singers were trained there. After nine years of 80-hour weeks, I was growing exhausted and bored again, and really longed to get that degree in psychology. I found I was doing a lot of counseling and advising to those who sought my opinion on various things within my modeling school. I really enjoyed helping people in that capacity and found I could assist them on some important issues.

I was able to help several girls stop their eating disorders, aid women in regaining their self-esteem after horrendous divorces, help teens stop using drugs, and assist a few young gay men in coming out to their families. Most importantly, I helped many people reach their dreams.

I felt a nagging urge to make counseling a legitimate career for myself. After winning my third Model and Talent School of the Year award in NYC, I decided to close my school and agency by posting a thank-you ad in the newspaper to all my models and actors.

I informed them that I was going to move on to get my degree in spiritual psychotherapy. When I discovered later that this wasn't an official degree, I felt that becoming an interfaith minister as well as a licensed professional counselor (LPC) would fill that double desire within me.

I got a three-part master's degree in applied clinical and counseling psychology in 2000, and opened my own psychotherapy practice. It was exciting to combine psychotherapy and broadcasting. I created three different radio call-in therapy shows, like the one on the TV show *Frasier,* on three different radio stations in South Jersey. Also, I was the therapist chosen to address the 9/11 crisis on the NBC News Channel 40 in the Atlantic City area. This is my fourth book, and I am writing my fifth to be released Spring 2013. So through the years, I did combine my love for acting, modeling, counseling, writing, marketing, promotion, and radio and TV performance. And I'm still not done! Today I am focused on doing Life and Relationship coaching for people around the world. I am so excited to provide both individual and group coaching services through my app, by phone, Skype and FaceTime! Information is provided at the back of the book regarding these services.

In summary, it is important that today's teens know that change is okay and not to fear it. If they choose college, they should pursue the career that excites them the most at that age. Their career interests may not include college, as was the case with Alexi. She wanted to sing, model, and act, and those choices did not require college. Once she was chosen to host the HGTV home design show, *Run My Makeover,* she got a certificate in interior design.

Each career choice did require hard work and living the secret lessons of the five Ds and the Watch Me! mind-set. With growing up and learning these approaches, Alexi has succeeded in these careers; and at the age of 22, she moved on to live beyond her dreams with EPIC. Engaging in all her desired dreams and talents has given her the opportunity to create her own business that helps those in need. Everyday People Initiating Change (EPIC) was a fitting title for Alexi and her cofounder Tennille Amor, two young women making a difference in the world. Once EPIC was established, Alexi then began to focus on her TV career, and at age 25 she reached her dream to be a TV host on several top networks.

College is not the only path to success for teenagers. Some may do better in a technological or a specialty school, like one for computer/graphic design or fashion design. Don't try to convince your children that you know what they want to do; instead, *listen* to what they want and consider their passions and desires.

Please don't laugh at them or criticize what they want to do, for you will kill their spirit and their motivation to succeed. Encourage them; tell them you are sure they will succeed because they seem dedicated to their own cause. Reassure them that you will help them reach their dreams however you can. Remember that what you tell them, they will believe. Tell them to set goals, and once they reach them, to move on to live beyond their dreams. Teach them at an early age the secret and importance of the five Ds. Start by teaching *desire.*

Desire

This is a longing, wish, craving, yearning, need, or aspiration. Our desires act as the fire that burns within us to propel us toward our goals. Without desire, we have nothing to strive for, which then causes stagnation and uncertainty.

Goal setting begins with desire, as goals are the dreams we are willing to work hard to achieve. When we set goals, we take responsibility for our lives and choose to devote ourselves to doing whatever it takes to reach these goals and dreams. Taking small steps toward them is all it takes to begin living a life of purpose. Achievement of these goals takes time and dedication, but with a strong initial desire, living the lessons of the five Ds and the Watch Me! mind-set, these goals will become our reality.

It is so important not to mock your children's desire to do something. You take away their passion by mocking it, and you attack their self-esteem by not giving them credit for having the intelligence to choose what they wish to do.

During the teenage years, kids often choose to escape the critical voices and put-downs of their parents by turning to drugs and alcohol to self-medicate. When teens start self-punishing by cutting their bodies, becoming bulimic or anorexic, or engaging in risky sex, they are acting out in pain and seeking to control something, even if their behaviors are destructive.

If their self-esteem is extremely low, it is very difficult for them to climb out of this abyss alone. Get them help immediately. And parents, know that you are both part of this problem and part of the solution, because teenagers don't become this way all by themselves. Family therapy is required to change the family system and make it a more positive and supportive environment for everyone.

Determination

No matter what hurdles we have to jump over to reach our goals, we need determination to get there. No matter how much we doubt ourselves, determination wins out, and we are willing to take the risk despite feeling the fear. We do it anyway. It is human to fear change and the unknown. There are no guarantees in life, and we might fail. So what!

With the Watch Me! mentality, we would rather try and fail than live with the knowledge we didn't have the guts to try at all. That is harder to accept than realizing we gave our goal the best shot we could, and it just didn't work out at the time.

Perhaps from your attempt to reach a goal another dream emerged that became a new passion, stronger then the first. Remember the spiritual message that there are no mistakes in life?

79

And that everything happens just as it should? These messages are part of having faith in the notion that it is important to live in the now, to just *be,* and to trust the process of life as it unfolds and the answers come to you.

So perhaps you had to struggle in your attempts to achieve the first goal so you could get to the second one, which took you ultimately to your higher purpose. So in this respect, you did not fail at all, did you? Perception is everything. From this perspective, perhaps you were not supposed to complete your first goal because your second goal was more important to your ultimate final purpose.

Change is always scary, but usually good. You must be willing to take risks to reach your goals. Otherwise, you remain stuck in fear without change, and depression can develop. The Watch Me! motivational mind-set is what gives you the guts to go for it and to make the changes necessary to grow and reach our best self.

Determination takes risk, personal push, and the ability to work beyond the fatigue when you are in the zone. Determination means trying again after a series of failures.

Many well-known entrepreneurs had several business failures and often bankruptcies before finding their successes. Walt Disney is a great example. Our most respected scientists had numerous failures before discovering their greatest inventions and breakthroughs. These people have all had an unending sense of dedication, determination, and of course, they all possessed the secrets of the five Ds.

Positive Self-talk

Having drive is part of being determined enough to succeed. Drive includes having the energy, motivation, initiative, hustle, and inner incentive to make every effort to succeed. What we say to ourselves can either drive us toward success and happiness, or toward failure and depression.

Knowing how to use motivational positive self-talk is essential in keeping your drive and determination alive. What you think and feel has a critical effect on how well you perform and directly affects the final outcome of your goals.

I taught my models and actors to use positive self-talk when going to an audition. If they were scared and thought negative thoughts, they would not get the part. Handling rejection and failure to get a part is a large piece of the talent game.

It is the same in a business interview. I remember when I went to apply for the student assistance counselor (SAC) position at a southern New Jersey school district, and there was a lady next to me with eight years' experience, and a gentleman being interviewed who had 15 years' worth of experience. I had done my six-month SAC internship at Atlantic City High School, but the superintendent at the time never filed my paperwork with the New Jersey board of education, so I never received my final SAC certificate.

I had done SAC work within several schools after the internship, but all without final certification. At the interview, I could have thought, "I'll never be able to compete with these two—I'm not even certified yet!" But instead, I went into the interview and sold myself (my product) and the talents I did have and could bring to their school.

For example, the fact that I worked with kids as a licensed therapist in my own practice and with a hospital-based child/adolescent counseling center showed that I had worked professionally with troubled children. I also had experience with the juvenile justice systems and multicultural settings, using the creative arts to instill self-esteem in kids, and I had served one year as a school psychologist. All this was experience that most standard SACs don't have. I focused on *what I did have to offer,* not what I didn't.

As I was leaving the interview, the school principal came running after me and asked me to return to the conference room. The committee offered me the job on the spot! Always believe in your product, and you will be able to sell it, even when the product is you. Don't focus on the obvious negatives; instead, use constant positive self-talk and the Watch Me! mind-set before entering the room.

It is essential to remain optimistic and to use positive motivational self-talk to succeed in the long-term. By cultivating this habit, you'll feel more self-control and confidence while achieving your goals. Being positive doesn't mean hardship won't come or that you should ignore limitations or difficulties. But it will help you to approach challenges with a clear, open mind leading to outside-the-box thinking and creative solutions.

Evaluate your degree of talent honestly, and then do whatever is necessary to work on areas that need improvement. Your levels of success will greatly improve with positive thinking. Instead of dwelling on any challenges or problems, be confident enough to relax and look at solutions to overcoming your obstacles. You are more likely to find positive solutions and strategies when you stop focusing on the inevitable negative roadblocks.

In the spiritual world, the teachings advise you to imagine yourself as already successful, happy, and accomplishing your desired goals. By meditating on being successful, you will succeed. In the incredible Rhonda Byrne book and DVD *The Secret,* there is the quote, "What you believe, you will achieve." Be sure to watch the DVD several times to learn the many valuable concepts taught there.

Positive self-talk sounds easy, but you must overcome years of negative conditioning to do it. Most people hear a critical, scolding voice in their heads. Many say that the voice is their mom or dad—whoever was the harsher, angrier parent who enforced discipline. To change this harmful conditioning, you must immediately correct any negative thought that comes into your mind, exchanging it for a positive one. With repeated practice, you can condition your mind to dismiss self-defeating, angry, or fearful thoughts. It takes 30 days to instill a good habit or to break an undesirable one. ~~75~~

For example, if you are going to an audition and a thought comes up like, "I'll never get this TV commercial—there are so many here to audition!" you must replace it with, "I have a great chance of getting this commercial. Who cares if there are a lot who are auditioning? I'm just as good, if not better than any of them. I have prepared and done the work. I studied my lines, I fit the physical description, I know and like the product, and I think I would be a huge asset to this company if I were the spokesperson they chose! Someone has to be selected, and I think it should be me!"

With that attitude and mind-set (watch me get this commercial), you have a huge chance of getting hired. Actors and models have to accept that they are not supposed to get every role. If you don't get the spot, you can rationalize it this way: "Well, I had a great audition, so maybe they will use me next time. There must be something else I am supposed to do instead of this particular commercial, because now I am free to receive that offer!" You must feel as if you are worthy to receive glory, and you will.

It is within your power to be successful if you do the preparation work necessary to learn the product and the mental work necessary to successfully sell it (even when the product is you). Staying positive affects your moods and the quality of your life experiences.

Once positive self-talk is a part of your constant, everyday way of thinking, you'll feel and believe that everything you desire is within your reach. Just put the plan into action and do it one day at a time. You must be open to trying all these suggestions in this book to initiate the change toward personal power, goal fulfillment, and ultimate success.

I do advise my clients that if they are not willing to be open-minded enough to try various suggestions on their own, then we can brainstorm together. However, they must willing to take some risks for the sake of change, or it will be very difficult to grow out of their present pain.

One client, Miriam, a 38-year-old woman, is an example of someone who refused to take the risk to change. She had never dated or been married, had never moved from her family home, and had never left her 10-year receptionist job that she hated. She felt that the psychotropic drugs she had taken over many years for her depression "never helped."

That's because the answer isn't in the pills—*it's in you!* Although medication is imperative for some clients, this client was more determined to blame her mother than to help herself. Within two sessions, I did get Miriam to understand that her mom did her best to raise the four kids she had without help from anyone. I explained that it was hurting her as a woman to harbor this childhood anger, and it was time to forgive her mother to move forward in life.

When her mom was in town for a visit, Miriam said she took the risk of being nicer to her and put herself in her shoes "to bring about the ability to forgive." Miriam said she did feel a lot better after this visit.

I would not "hand-hold" Miriam like her other therapists did. I was motivating her to change by teaching her a mental mind shift in how she looked at things.

So many people want to blame another person to rationalize their current pain or bad situation. Yes, we all get burned, but after that happens, instead of being stuck in anger and resentment, we must instead make a concrete plan to turn our lives around. What good will anger or staying stuck in blame do us?

After the third session, I had Miriam leaving her house to engage in some hobbies. She went to a bookstore and sat in the coffee shop to read and perhaps meet some people. She was scared to death to do this, but promised to try it four times. The first two times, she kept her nose in the book, but the third time, she actually met someone she became friends with. By now, she was also talking to her coworkers and making friends at work, something she had never risked before.

I had adamantly encouraged Miriam to take risks for change. She was very resistant, but trusted me and went with it. I feel it is my responsibility to help someone become strong enough to get out of therapy. My motivational and coaching approach to counseling does encourage some risk and change, which ultimately leads to growth and a happier, more dynamic life filled with purpose.

Miriam admitted that her therapists over the years were her only "friends" and her only social outlet, once a week. Miriam became dependent on her once-a-week sessions and didn't want to have to leave them.

This is often the pattern of the resistant client. She wants and feels she needs the therapist's support to just get by in life. She is resistant to change because she unconsciously doesn't want to get better.

Miriam tested her comfort levels and found the drive to change. I got her out of the house and her self-imposed isolation and taught her to make some new friends. She now likes her job, and she has made incredible progress with her mom. This all happened within a few weeks of working with the motivational therapy techniques behind the Watch Me! mind-set. Just think of the potential you may reach when you decide to risk growing!

Dedication

To be dedicated to a purpose, project, or person is to live it, breathe it, and be consumed by it from conception to finality. This is a pretty tall order, and tough for most humans to do. In dedicating yourself to clear and definable goals, your choices and actions take on a new significance.

Make a plan to reach your goals, which includes a time frame with step-by-step procedures. Make each step realistic, and one that can be achieved with hard work and dedication. Make sure your goals reflect your inner core of purpose and emotional satisfaction. Announce your goals to friends and on Facebook; write them down if necessary to hold you accountable to them. When you announce your goals, you are more likely to keep them. However, do not tell your family if you suspect they will not be supportive.

Some people paste goal cards all over their home so their goals are always in sight. Give yourself small rewards along the path as you reach each step and get closer to your goal. Celebrate your progress and share it with others. If you find yourself slipping from your dedication to your ultimate dream, talk with others who believe in you and your ability to reach that dream. They could help inspire you to finish.

Do whatever it takes to stay on your path until you reach that final goal. One thing I have found helpful is saying a prayer each day when I wake up to help me focus on what I have to do that day to help fulfill my goals and life's purpose. I then think of three specific things to do and list another one or two things I can do if I have extra time. This daily reflection has helped me reach my goals throughout my life.

Think of how dedicated Mother Teresa was each day to those less fortunate, or how dedicated the Dalai Lama has been in leading people of the Buddhist faith. Consider Jesus and his lofty goal of healing the sins of the world. Just how many disbelieved he was the Messiah? How many doubters did he meet along his journey to greatness? And yet, his story and many followers still exist today! The daily dedication of Jesus must have been incredibly strong and unstoppable given that his doubters were so destructive. He might have said to himself, "Watch me heal the sins of the world!" and "Watch me make a difference to those in pain!" Who knows what could happen for you if your convictions were this strong! Read the Bible, one of the greatest books ever written, to learn more about this incredible journey to greatness through dedicating yourself to helping others.

To be dedicated means that your belief that you will reach your goals is always a part of you. You may be the only one who believes in yourself; and when you have a lot of doubters, you must be even more dedicated to this conviction.

I remember when I wanted to start a model and talent agency in the small, blue-collar town of Erie, PA. People laughed! No modeling school would work there, people told me! Then a John Robert Powers School of modeling opened. I went down to apply as a teacher, and the director, who had a major ego, wouldn't hire me. I had been a teacher at their school in Philadelphia and had 15 years of big-city modeling experience, so I thought I was a great candidate.

I walked away saying to myself, "Fine, you won't hire me? I'll open my own school and be an owner, not just a teacher! Watch me!" But I needed to consider the needs of the market, and I didn't see Erie as a fashion town; it was commercial. So I prepared to open the type of agency and school that would make it in a small, blue-collar town. Within a year of that interview, I opened Riana Model & Talent and introduced the "real people" concept. We got so busy that Powers closed down within eight months of my school and agency's opening. Ah, personal power and success are your best revenge!

I remember when Alexi was hoping to be signed by a producer or record label. I promised her that I would do whatever it took to help her. We moved to Edgewater, NJ, right outside of NYC, on sheer faith alone. I knew she had the secrets of the five Ds to succeed, and since she was young, she had the Watch Me! mind-set. Also, as her mother, I believed in her talent, and I was ready to act as her agent and stand behind her dream.

I got a full-time job as a psychotherapist and gave notice at my counseling job with adolescents and at the addiction rehab center where I did therapy for women from the prison system. I closed my own counseling project, Inner Vision Counseling, a nonprofit agency located in Ventnor, NJ. I changed my whole life to support my daughter's dream until she was old enough to pursue her career on her own. Keeping your word and promises to the best of your ability shows your depth of character and integrity. It is especially important for your children to witness. Many children who experience broken promises from their parents act out with anger or turn inward with depression and find it hard to trust people when they get older.

I was dedicated to helping Alexi see this project through to its completion, and would manage her to the best of my ability while working a 70-hour workweek. Alexi moved to North Jersey in March 2003, while I worked on selling the big family home in Ventnor and finished off my last three months of counseling commitments.

Once I moved to Edgewater with Alexi in June, I still returned to South Jersey to perform weddings on weekends. I promised Alexi I'd live one year in Edgewater until she was confident enough to manage her own talent career.

In June of 2004, I felt Alexi had the knowledge to live and work in NYC, and possessed the skills needed to promote herself as a model, actor, and singer. She was ready to handle her own career because her dedication to her goals and dreams was solid. Alexi also had a keen business mind that was nurtured since she was a young girl. I now needed to get out of her way so that she could fly on her own. As much as I missed living with her and being a part of her exciting life, I returned to South Jersey and reopened a counseling center called Therapy by the Sea in Egg Harbor Township, NJ.

I was dedicated to wanting to write this book for years, and once I knew my daughters were fine, and I found a home and got settled, it was time for me to start writing.

I know the Watch Me! mind-set to live beyond your dreams has worked for many people I have coached along the way. As a counseling technique, it has been very successful for many of my clients. Whether they were addicts, suicidal, self-cutting, bulimic/anorexic, in difficult life transitions, or in toxic, abusive relationships, most of them have been helped by the Watch Me! mind-set and approach to goal setting.

Even children as young as five years old need to be told their thoughts and dreams are important, and that they can succeed! Children can get depressed when they have no hopes or dreams or their parents berate them. I have used the Watch Me! mind-set with schoolchildren of all ages, and this method has worked for them too.

The mind-set works with all people of all ages and cultures and with all levels of education to encourage their greatness. In the 13 years that I have counseled clients, I have discovered the same motivational techniques that I used years ago to inspire my actors and models work well with my coaching and therapy clients.

People used to ask me, "Isn't being a model and talent agent so removed from being a therapist?" "No," I responded, "Not at all. It is extremely similar. Models and actors often love to perform for the attention they didn't get as children, or they performed as children and found they loved the attention."

The Watch Me! mind-set was a part of them as children, but they often lost sight of their dreams, goals, or dedication along the way. Their free, creative thinking often got crushed, along with their dreams to perform. However, with a new sense of inspiration that instilled the courage to help them go for their dreams using the five Ds, and using the other techniques, they found success in their chosen careers.

Counseling clients often came to therapy because they have lost sight of their goals, dreams, and desires, they are experiencing underlying unhappiness or depression, or they feel they have lost themselves and need some special care and attention to help them feel whole again. Once refocused, recentered, and rededicated to living a life with purpose, actors or therapy clients often find success again.

This bold motivational mind-set helps models and actors through rejection, harried and demanding schedules, false promises and disappointments, lack of sleep, and missed opportunities. It gives them the inner wisdom and fortitude to handle some of the unfortunate phonies or difficult and demanding people they meet along the way. The entertainment world is full of ego, and the more grounded, mentally focused, and faith-based they are, the easier it is to maneuver the path they are on.

A sense of dedication to themselves, their craft, their higher power or sense of spirituality, and to giving back to the world is what helps people succeed in life no matter their chosen profession. This doesn't mean working nonstop every day.

But it does mean living the principles of the Watch Me! mindset every day. Dedication to the craft or talent may mean writing one day, reading a book another, meditating to find clarity, or working out to keep the body strong on yet another day. It means doing *something every day* toward your final goal or purpose, even if that means spending all day in bed resting after a whirlwind singing tour in which you got minimal sleep. It is the conscious choice of setting daily goals, no matter what they are, that builds toward your dream.

Whatever it takes to help keep you centered, balanced, growing, learning, and loving with purpose is what matters. Vacations, well-deserved rest, and taking time for fun and laughter are all an important part of this process. If you do not take the time for fun along the way, you will resent the path you are on.

It means devotedly taking care of yourself so you have the mental and physical stamina to reach your higher purpose. Exercising at least three to four times a week, trying to get at least eight to nine hours of sleep each night or a siesta in the middle of each day, eating nutritious, unprocessed foods, and drinking lots of water are all a part of this plan for overall health.

Put yourself first. Your own personal, mental and physical well-being must all come first, or you will soon resent the time and effort you give to others when you have no time left for yourself. Many of my clients who are mothers present with "mom burnout." Running kids around as a taxi driver, attending their events, helping with their homework, cleaning the house, cooking the meals, and being either fully responsible for their care and financial support or working part-time to help with a household income are all exhausting!

It's no wonder these supermoms have no energy or sexual desire for their partner/spouse at the end of a day. Why do you think divorce rates are at 50 percent and women do most of the filing? Many women are dissatisfied, and do not feel taken care of or appreciated by anybody!

They begrudge their husbands, who watch eight hours of football on a Sunday because they feel entitled to their time off. Where's her time off? Many women feel extremely cheated. They have told me that at least when they are divorced, they have one less person to take care of. With joint custody, they are at least given two to three days off a week from mothering responsibilities and have some time for themselves.

It's a sad way to look at things, but unfortunately, often very true. If only husbands would realize that if they did half the household chores and shared the parenting responsibilities with their wives, they would probably have the satisfying sexual life they so desire because their women would appreciate them more and be less tired.

Many men have stepped up to the plate in recent years and have become great dads and husbands, splitting the housework that nobody likes and doing 50 percent of the child care. These are the men who are still in happy, functioning marriages. Congratulations guys, we women salute you! We know it isn't easy, and housework is not fun. Nor is working in the job market, where women earn a good 25 percent less than our male counterparts for the same if not heavier workload. But we are willing to help financially and work full-time if you are willing to help domestically.

We also love making love to you, as you are the men we admire and respect, and chose to marry for many reasons. And because you help out, we are more than willing and wanting to help you out too, and to make passionate love on our date nights over the weekends. These men are the true life partners we women crave; these are the men we feel are dedicated to making their marriages work, and their relationships with their women and children happy and rewarding.

Why do couples stop dating once they are married? Stopping what you did when you romanced your partner is what kills the passion and fun in a marriage. Too many couples focus only on the kids, forgetting about their partners and their marriage. Years later, the marriage falls apart because intimacy has been gone for years.

Dedication comes in many different forms. Full dedication to a balanced, healthy life for our loved ones and ourselves is essential for finding the energy to be dedicated to our relationships, talent, work, and higher purpose.

Devotion

Devotion is best described as dedication from the heart to yourself, your goals, your spiritual beliefs, and your higher purpose. When you have a sense of devotion, you have a sense of altruism, charitable affection, loyalty, and commitment. In terms of the five Ds, I am talking about having daily devotion to your higher power and sense of spirituality, so that you may discover and perpetuate your life purpose. This can be done with daily meditation or prayer, every day, twice a day. Start your prayer with an attitude of gratitude by thanking your God for all the blessings that you do have. Then ask specifically for the dreams that you desire, and ask to accomplish the specific goals you are working on that day, week, or month. Pray for the things you need to accomplish that day to help you stay focused on your dream path. Then pray for your children and loved ones' happiness, health, and success. Find two times a day during which you will have the peace and quiet to do this. I choose to pray the moment I wake up and the moment I go to bed. Many start their commute to work with their daily prayer to inspire a positive, motivated day at work. They pray once again as they head home to their families. This prayer creates your mood, positive mind-set, dedication, and devotion to your higher purpose each day. The power of spiritual devotion is one of the primary principles of the Watch Me! mind-set.

Dare to Dream!

This is the last of the five Ds, the very important concept of opening your mind to all of life's possibilities. Dare to dream as you did when you were a child, when the sky was the limit!

Our step-by-step goals, done one day and one goal at a time, set in motion the process we must take to reach our dreams. What is sad and true for most of us is that we are told that our dreams are nonsense, unobtainable, unrealistic, and impossible when we are children or adolescents. We are instructed by our parents or mentors to give up our dream for something more realistic, so as adults, we often do. Or, we are made to feel not good enough to have our desired career.

To help appease your parents, you could have a Plan B ready in case your desired plan does not quite work. Although Alexi wanted to be a singer, we did tour various colleges she might have attended if she'd decided to. We also figured she could attend school at any time in her life; she did not need to feel confined by the tradition of attending college right after high school. She did attend Hunter College for a bit at age 26 to study water engineering after installing many of her freshwater wells in Africa. She found she was often called on to explain to the class exactly what she had done to build her wells. She discovered that her real-life skills were at a higher level than the college program that was supposedly going to teach her how to do what she was already doing, building wells.

Now you know that despite your age or current life situation, you can live beyond your dreams by using the Watch Me! mind-set for personal power and success. I challenge you to live your deepest dreams. What were they years ago? What desire and talent is buried deep within you now that you have let the realities of everyday life take over and bury?

Sometimes when I ask clients this, they haven't dreamed for so long that they have no dreams or goals at all. They may have a lot of excuses for why they never started on their goals to live with purpose or to realize their dreams. I must teach them again to let go, to dare to dream, and to have a wish list of what they hope to accomplish in their lifetime.

Stop reading for a moment and list 10 dreams, big or small, that you have for your future. When you're done, prioritize them, with number one being the most important dream. Then pick the dream that you could start on today. Some dreams fall under a personal category (to lose weight or live a fit lifestyle) or a business category (to write a training book for your business). If you are in school, it could be a scholastic goal (to achieve a 3.5 upon high school graduation).

Write a B next to business goals, an S next to school goals, and a P next to personal goals. Then pick one personal goal and one business or school goal you will commit yourself to working on using the five Ds and the Watch Me! mind-set.

Set a time limit to reach these goals that is realistic and comfortable but not too lax either. Some goals you can achieve in two days or two weeks; you just might have procrastinated about them for months.

For example, let's take painting a room, cleaning out a closet, or getting to the gym three times a week. It's okay to have these short-term mini-goals because you often have to get through these smaller ones to clear your mind for the larger goal you *really* want to obtain, like writing a training manual. You cannot clear your mind to write if your partner keeps bugging you to paint the room. Get through the chores, the mini-goals, and to-do lists, and then get on with your higher purpose goals.

These goals actually connect to your innate talents and your lifelong dreams. These dreams may take many mini-goals to accomplish, which will eventually lead to reaching where you aspire to be. Once you reach that dream, then it is time to live beyond your dreams by setting new goals and visions of giving back to the world. See the next chapter to learn exactly how goal setting can make your dreams and beyond a reality.

Chapter 5

Just Do It!
Goal Setting for Personal
Growth and Success

~~~

SET YOUR GOALS EARLY ON in your Watch Me! program. Try to establish for yourself three important and clear personal and three business or school goals from the list you made in the previous chapter. You need to review your progress weekly and monthly, aiming for completion within six months. What you do each day will build toward reaching these lofty, dream-oriented goals.

When you reach any of your goals, you should reward yourself with something you've always wanted and then set a new goal in its place. If you have a weight-reduction goal under personal goals, for example, treat yourself to a new dress or sports coat that makes you look smashing!

If you've reached a sales goal at work and received a bonus, reward your partner and yourself with a romantic weekend away to celebrate. If your partner knows you must work extra hours for a few months to reach certain goals, and the reward is a weekend away for the two of you, she or he won't complain those nights you need to work overtime. You will receive support from those you love as you try to achieve your goals if you make those people a part of your reward system.

If you're in school and you got all As and a few Bs on your report card, treat yourself to a sharp outfit or new sneakers—something that makes you feel good, and when you wear it, reminds you of your accomplishment. Of course if you are young and not earning money yet, your parents will have to help with the reward system (read about this in the parenting chapter).

If you were able to reach some of the goals but not others within six months, celebrate the ones you met and rework the others. Some goals may take a year or two to complete realistically, not six months; and you can complete some within a month. I only suggest you check in at monthly and six-month intervals to keep tabs on your progress. Reworking your goals means analyzing where you are after six months and determining what you will need to do within the next six months. You will need to add new steps, procedures, or mini-goals to get the ultimate job done.

Delays may happen, but the necessary side steps you may have to take are still a part of completing the main task. As long as you are actively working on the goal a bit each day and making progress each week, you will reach your monthly and ultimate six-month goals.

Twice a year, you *must* dare to dream and declare your six goals. One time is on your personal new year—your birthday. The second time would be six months from your birthday. Be sure to be realistic and set at least six goals that will help you to reach your ultimate dream. If your birthday is far from now and you want to start right away, pick the first of a month, or an upcoming date you will easily remember.

This pattern of setting six realistic goals twice a year and a willingness to risk whatever it takes to reach your mini-goals will enable you to reach your absolute dreams.

For example, if you dream of being a professional singer, reaching this goal within six months is extremely difficult. Instead, set three business and three personal goals to help get you on your way to your ultimate dream. Once you reach those goals, go beyond and set new goals to bring you closer to your ultimate dream.

To achieve this dream, you could choose from this list of three business goals:

1. Get a professional press kit together and gather addresses where you will mail it once your demo CD is done.

2. Work with a professional singing coach weekly to get your three to five demo songs polished and ready.

3. Find a job to earn the money to book studio time to record your demo CD when your coach considers you ready.

4. Enroll in a dance classes to polish your moves and build confidence and performance techniques.

5. Write your talent resume. Make sure it is perfect and that it matches all your stationery in your press kit.

Three personal goals that could help you get closer to your dream of being a professional singer could include the following:

1. Choose to eat healthy and exercise every other day to be in the best shape possible for your photographs and interviews.

2. Choose to read daily inspirational readings and instructional books on how to succeed in the music industry. Take notes as you read.

3. Audition for your school play or enroll in acting class so you have credits on your talent resume.

4. Try writing your own songs or music. Work with friends who know how to write beats or tracks. These may not be your demo songs, but one may actually turn out to be a hit, and you are learning music production at the same time.

5. Get professional talent photographs done, both headshots and long shots, in a look that will promote you.

Okay, so there are 10 realistic goals for the want-to-be singer! All you have to work on is three personal and three business goals within the six-month period until you revise and set new goals or continue working toward the old goals that aren't quite complete.

Create a goal sheet (or use the goal sheets, which are best used together, at the end of this chapter). Make daily, weekly, monthly, and six-month goals for two sections: personal (which could include relationship goals) and business/school objectives. So in addition to listing three six-month goals under each section, list three goals a day, three goals a week, and three goals a month under each section. Some listed goals could be considered either business or personal for you. That's fine; list them where they make the most sense for you, as long as you choose at least six total goals for a day, week, month, and six months. If you have fewer than six major goals within six months, you are not working hard enough toward your ultimate purpose and dreams.

These smaller daily or weekly mini-goals add up to accomplishing your major goals before or at six months. Keep in mind that your daily goals can be simple, like making a dental appointment, going to the gym, or buying stationery for a resume kit. Many people procrastinate on the smaller items, which can add up to never taking care of themselves, in turn resulting in stress, anxiety, or depression. Procrastinating on the daily mini-goals is what leads to start-up business failures or the inability to create a business altogether. Without accomplishing the daily, weekly, and monthly goals, you will never be able to live beyond your dreams.

This goal-setting concept is one essential technique I taught my models and actors in my school. If they actually followed the goal-setting techniques, they became the actors or models they wished to be. Success will come with these techniques; Alexi is just one of many success stories.

Now, let's talk about some generic personal goals that could apply to you.

Personal mini-goals that will show excellent results within six months include the following:

For Personal Health and Weight Loss

- ◆ *Daily.* Eat nutritiously and avoid junk foods. Drink more water every day, and take a variety of vitamins for your age and health needs. Promise to get eight to nine hours of sleep every day. Go to bed early after a late night to catch up on your rest, and keep a regular sleep schedule.

* *Weekly.* Exercise no matter what, at least three times a week. Schedule it first before anything else. Schedule a massage biweekly to help you deal with stress and anxiety.

* *Monthly.* Monitor your weight loss progress with weigh-ins. If your progress is slow the first month, consider a personal trainer, nutritionist, or getting the support of a doctor who specializes in weight loss. Don't give up—get tough and stay determined!

* *Six-month.* Go down one to two dress or pant sizes and stay there!

For Students

* *Daily.* Do daily homework. Study daily for the hard subjects. Limit phone use to 20 minutes per day on weekdays.

* *Weekly.* Prepare for tests and papers early. Watch no TV or videos Monday through Thursday; just read or study tougher subjects before tests. Go once a week for extra help if needed. Show your teacher you care.

* *Monthly.* For your resume, sign up for clubs or volunteer activities as they arise. Ask monthly how your grades are. If they are low in one subject, ask to do an extra credit project before the end of the marking period. Get extra help or tutoring if needed.

- *Six-month.* Strive to get all As. A couple of Bs are okay, but As must dominate. Graduate with honors or scholarships. Finish thesis or doctorate, or reenroll in college to finish a degree stopped long ago.

For Job Seekers

- *Daily.* Make one call to get a reference for a new resume kit, and gather dates and facts to update resume information. Be sure to do job searches daily, without fail. When you aren't working, your job is searching for one, at least eight hours a day.

- *Weekly.* Finish typing your resume. Begin copying letters of recommendation, certificates, articles, and any other information that shows your skills and expertise. Start building your job application kit; create a presentation portfolio (a "brag book") that makes you stand out among all the other applications! Sign up on indeed.com and careerbuilder.com to have job listings sent automatically to you.

- *Monthly:* If after one month you are not getting any leads, seek a job coach to review your resume kit and fine-tune your interview skills. Start thinking outside the box and apply to other jobs you could do that may pay less but would hold you over until you find your dream job. Look for jobs in surrounding cities up to one hour away that you may not have considered before.

- *Six-month.* By now you should be in a career you love and feeling settled. If you still have not been hired, consider moving into a more lucrative job market or returning to school for a different career. You may want to consider starting your own business you can run from your home.

Relationship Goals

- *Daily.* Vow to put yourself, instead of the person you date or are married to, first. If you are happy, you will make your spouse, dates, or kids a lot happier because you will feel you are not giving up your life totally for them. I don't mean that you should put yourself selfishly ahead of everyone else and not consider their needs. Do be courteous and caring and take care of your children, but don't exclude your needs and the time required to be at your best. Schedule in daily goals for exercise, eating healthy, getting enough rest, dating, relaxing, and fun time for yourself throughout the week.

- *Weekly.* Schedule a weekly date night with your partner, a family night where you are all together, and a weekly time for your spiritual reflection. Get involved with a spiritual study of your choosing. Read books, listen to CDs, or find a discussion group, temple, or church you would like to be affiliated with, and go. Attend with your partner and family; if they refuse, go anyway.

- *Monthly.* Have a monthly family talk to clear the air, set new goals, and acknowledge your spouse or children for jobs well done. Set monthly goals with your partner you want to reach together. Plan a mini-trip with your partner overnight every two months.

- *Six-month.* Take at least a one-week vacation every year. Try to do a one-week vacation with your partner, and one with the children.

These are a few simple examples of personal and business goals, and I could think of many more. What is important to you for your personal growth? What changes would you like to make to feel better about yourself? Pick at least three goals you will accomplish daily, weekly, monthly, and within six months. Once you have determined your major goals, announce them on Facebook and to your loved ones. Promising to others that you will undertake certain goals will make you even more dedicated to the achievement.

Be determined that you will accomplish these goals no matter what, and just do it. If you have reached any major goal before the six-month period is up, celebrate and choose another goal, and keep growing and living beyond your dreams!

By using the five Ds, you will reach that dream, step-by-step, goal-by-goal, and day-by-day. Only you stop yourself. When others try to stop you or tell you that you can't reach your goal, look them straight in the eyes and say calmly but assertively, "Watch me!" Their opinion is not important to changing your goals or stopping your plan because you are confident that you are doing the work it takes to make your dream a reality.

An example of the Watch Me! mind-set in action occurred when I wanted to go back to school for my master's degree right after I had my children. My husband said that we didn't have the money and I didn't have the time; in other words, no.

I had the time, as our children were in preschool. And the money? I found it by going down to Gannon University and getting a work scholarship. Not only did I get a salaried job writing business manuals, but the position also paid for my master's college tuition and books. Don't tell me I can't!

I also wanted to earn extra money modeling, so I went to the only modeling school in Erie. The director remarked snidely that I was too old to model now. Oh really? At age 26? My husband said that too, so I had two people to prove wrong! Not only did I start modeling for the top photographers in Erie, but I was also encouraged by them to open my own modeling training school and agency.

I did just that in 1987. My husband said we had no money to do this, but I opened with my first month's rent and was determined to succeed. I put ads in the paper for real people models from ages 4 to 84 and then started designing and writing training classes.

Within a few months, the other modeling school's director had heard of Riana Model & Talent and called Harrisburg's department of education, which tried to close me down for operating without a license. I didn't know I needed a license to teach modeling and acting skills. I was just 26 with a dream! I was given a great state adviser who said he'd give me six months to make a proposal for licensure to the PA board of education. Six months to create a whole curriculum and school! I knew I could do it—whatever it took. I worked on my daily, weekly, and monthly goals and focused on becoming licensed within that six month period.

When the guidelines came in the mail, "How to be a Pennsylvania Post-secondary School," wow, I had my work cut out for me. I also had to present the training manual. I looked everywhere for a commercial real people training manual. There were none, so I wrote one. Within six months and after a lot of help from my state adviser, I appeared alone before about 25 people who were on the PA State board of education.

I had ready a full notebook on my proposed school and my 250-page illustrated training manual I wrote. It was my first book

I sold for profit, as every student had to buy it as their training manual for $50. Over nine and a half years, that was a great return on my first book! It was written within the six-month window that I had; I worked until 3:00 to 4:00 a.m. every night until it was finished. I took mini-naps to gain enough strength and energy to work during the day, teach night classes at Gannon University, and still take care of my children. I passed for licensure with no revisions needed! I was in business as a school. Hooray!

My classes started with four students, but within a few months grew to twenty-four with a waiting list. There were 10 courses for each person to complete, and a graduation project was required. Each class had to do something to help a needy group in the area. The school motto was "Help Yourself by Helping Others." I taught the Watch Me! mind-set early on to help my talent audition and perform professionally and to deal with any doubters they encountered along the way.

The talent did exceptionally well, and we had a wonderful reputation not only in Erie, PA, but also in Pittsburgh, Buffalo, and Cleveland. The students had a great rapport with each other, had a lot of fun learning, and most importantly, many reached their goals and dreams of being professional models, actors, singers, or dancers.

One of my singers, Roy, had a wonderfully smooth voice like Lionel Richie—boy, I loved to hear him sing! His story is an interesting one. No one believed Roy could be a professional singer, because he had a severe stutter when he spoke. But he sang without a problem! I had the challenge of trying to make the psychological connection between his confidence and smoothness when he sang and his anxiety levels when he spoke. He had an awesome, muscular body and a beautiful face, so I thought he could be a great commercial model as well. I prepared him for the

Los Angeles IMTA (International Modeling & Talent Association) convention, and his photographs were outstanding and his vocal demo was incredible. We both felt he was motivated and ready.

Roy ended up not only winning the singing competition against people from all over the world, but also getting modeling offers and an invitation to sign with a recording studio! Roy had it all under control; his self-confidence soared, and his stutter became almost nonexistent. While he was training with me, I taught Roy the Watch Me! mind-set in preparation to compete at IMTA in LA, and he certainly showed his doubters in Erie what he could do.

Unfortunately, Roy did not take his many offers in LA, as he was the oldest son in a large family that needed him in the Erie area. Roy was a very spiritual man and lived his higher purpose of taking care of his family, but at least he knew that not only had he proved his talent to his doubters, but also to himself. Roy returned to Erie a much happier, successful, and confident man. He realized his dream, and chose to live beyond it in a way he felt was spiritually appropriate and fulfilling.

Within my first year of opening my modeling and talent school, I won the IMTA Educational Excellence award at a competition in NYC. The following two years, I won the large trophy for IMTA School of the Year for independently owned schools. I had a 100 percent success rate for getting offers for all the models and actors who went to either the NYC or LA competitions with me.

We had a blast, but we worked hard ("work hard, play hard!" is another favorite motto of mine). I prepared the talent for their week-long competition in the same goal-oriented system I had developed. They had daily goals to prepare for our weekly meetings. They had many goals to accomplish each month. Some included preparing for their photography sessions with top-rated photographers from LA and NYC, as well as preparing their lines for my well-known acting coach, Joan See, from The Three of Us Studios in NYC. Many of my talent are successfully working in major cities today because of my school's curriculum, professional staff, guest instructors from major cities, the IMTA conventions, and the Watch Me! mind-set for success!

Another Watch Me! mind-set story is that of Michael. Extremely shy, he came to me saying he wanted to become a model. He was kind of rough around the edges, a blue-collar guy who worked as an auto mechanic. He was so afraid of being teased by the guys at the shop that it took him five months to sign up for my talent school.

While he was considering whether to train or not, I explained to Michael that he really needed to consider becoming an actor, as his muscular body was too large for men's high fashion clothes. I told him he had a *Baywatch* kind of look—long, blonde, beach-boy hair, and a strong, solid body. I felt for certain he would be perfect for that TV show! When I said he must consider acting, he quickly refused, saying that he was way too shy and had never done it before.

As he was thinking things over, the guys at the shop found out he was going to take acting and modeling lessons and they started mocking him. He told me all the nasty things they said, and then he said in a defeated tone, "Ah, just forget this."

I then told Michael about the Watch Me! mind-set, and if he had an open mind and was very serious about being successful in acting and modeling, he could do it, and I would help him reach his dream. Well, Michael went from zero to a hundred! In preparation for LA's IMTA, I arranged acting classes for Michael in NYC, got him a well-known photographer to shoot his pictures, constantly helped him psychologically to become strong and confident, and trained him in everything he needed to know.

To help defray his costs, I took private karate lessons from him for several months for a film I was booked to do. We also arranged that when he was placed in LA with his new manager or agent and getting work, he would pay me a 5 percent commission over five years, which was very standard for a referring agent.

Well, Michael did get a top LA manager, and before he moved off to Hollywood, he had a huge celebration party to entertain all his doubters, including the guys from the auto shop. He picked me up in a large white limo; he was in a tux and I was in a gown. All the models looked fabulous that night. What a great party!

When I had given my speech about how proud I was of him and how far he had come, we were both in tears. He then mentioned that I had taught him this new attitude and way of thinking called the Watch Me! mind-set, and he used it to help him muster up his courage to perform. He said the experience over the past year had helped to make him a much more confident, happier man.

Within a short time of moving to LA, Michael appeared on *Baywatch* just as I had hoped he would, and in numerous other films and TV shows! He had done it! I was thrilled for him. There is a sad side to this story, though. Within a few short months, Michael said his manager told him he didn't have to pay me anything for a referral fee, so I never saw a dime, and Michael conveniently got lost. It saddened me greatly that he did not choose to honor my small 5 percent commission fee for all that I had done for him, but I was not about to sue for the money, or hire an investigator to find him. Michael forgot the biggest lesson of all; the spiritual component of the Watch Me! mind-set.

I knew that karma would soon catch up with him, and Michael's fate would be decided by his current and future choices. He got caught up in fame and chose not to honor his word to me, and not to use his newfound talent for a higher purpose and a better way of being. For years, I just sent prayers and blessings his way for success. I had no idea how he was until, just as I was writing this book, out of the blue, Michael wrote me on Facebook and we talked by phone.

He said he'd had an unfortunate run of bad luck and had hit a really bad point. Again, honoring our friendship, I encouraged him to get back to a spiritual place and refocus on building his life with a Watch Me! mind-set. This time, however, I suggested he do his work honorably and with a higher purpose. I sincerely hope he turns his karma around.

To expand my school, I developed a model and talent camp held at a college campus two weeks in the summer. The students were dropped off, and a week later, graduated with top-notch photos, modeling and runway techniques, and acting, promotional, and fashion modeling skills. I also taught exercise and nutrition, communication and manners, makeup and hairstyling, wardrobe, and how to work and survive in the business. All in one week! We worked 12 to 14-hour days, and every person came such a long way in one amazing week.

At graduation, parents and friends were astonished, many of them in tears at seeing how their daughter's or son's self-esteem and confidence levels had grown so quickly. That camp also afforded the opportunity for real internal growth for many of the students. We talked about life, love, fear, challenges, and changes—it was more than just a modeling school; it was more like a Watch Me! mind-set camp. It was an opportunity to make a real difference in many of the students' lives, and I loved it.

This camp was a clear example of taking daily goals seriously and reaching a lofty goal of graduation with many skills in just one week. This one-week goal led to monthly goals to create comp cards and auditions for bookings. Also, many had a six-month goal to prepare for and attend the IMTA convention.

After my second book in this series, *Love Beyond Your Dreams: Break Free from Toxic Relationships to Have the Love You Deserve*, is complete, my goal is to hold weekend retreats in Atlantic City, NJ, for singles and couples looking to better themselves and their relationships. The retreats will offer a lot of quality information in one weekend and provide the opportunity to form quality relationships with like-minded people. When two people have the Watch Me! mind-set, they can have an extraordinary relationship. For married couples, I will do a renewal of vows ceremony as "their graduation."

Some readers may be concerned about having enough money to have the business of their dreams. All my business ideas proceeded without the money or budget to carry them out. I started with a dream, a prayer, and a mind-set that I could do it. Hard work and the five Ds were part of that plan I accepted early on. I didn't need a large sum of money to start a business; through 30 years, I used purely the Watch Me! mind-set and paid as I went along! Keeping the spiritual component in mind, I made sure that all the people involved made enough money to be as excited about the project as I was.

Start small and conservative, with a great marketing and public relations plan to spread the word about your business. Attend your local chamber of commerce meetings and networking organizations. Join Facebook and LinkedIn, and offer to do business-oriented speeches for various organizations. Set up a booth to offer your product at a trade show if the cost of the space is reasonable, and if not, ask another vendor to join you and split the costs.

Personal promotion and networking is important to an individual and his company, because people like to do business with people they know, like, and trust. I also do all my own marketing and printing on my computer. Most of what you need to do to start your own business takes primarily your own creativity, imagination, and energy. Ask your friends to be "your marketing team" and to honestly tell you what they like or don't like about your product or idea. Fine-tune as you go along.

To anyone telling me I can't do something, I say, "Watch me!" Their doubt is my driving force. Then I set up my goal sheet and take my risks. You can do it too! I feel life isn't worth living if you don't take well prepared risks! Why play it safe? It can lead to boredom, monotony, and depression over someone else calling the shots or owning you. It's like selling your soul to the devil, because you don't own it anymore when you allow another person to control you.

I have always had goals to succeed at things that are important to me. By not living my dreams, I would have suffered, and my inner fire of passion would have burned out. You can see the light of energy burning in people who live with the Watch Me! mind-set. They are excited about their new projects and the joy it will bring to their lives. Creation brings inspiration, bliss, and joy as one begins to live with a higher purpose.

I don't try to control others or their choices, and I've always encouraged growth and success. When I dated someone, I was always his best cheerleader and always celebrated his good work; but often, he could not do that for me in return. I always felt a good relationship is about balance, mutual encouragement, being each other's best friend, and having both independent dreams for yourselves and mutual dreams you want to reach as a couple.

Many of my female clients over the years have felt the same as I do about being controlled and issues of balance. Why be ordered around when you pay half or more of the bills and do half or more of the child-rearing and household chores? And recently, many men have presented with this same anguish in my therapy office.

Without a new balance, relationships and marriages will have trouble surviving. Do I believe marriages can work? *Yes.* Many of today's younger men understand equality and don't insist on traditional roles because many have watched their own mothers struggle.

They want to be an equal contributor and a best friend. Most women want an equal partner in life, a man who isn't intimidated or jealous of their success, and who is thrilled to celebrate mutual successes. I write more about this in chapter 8, "For Couples: The Evolved Relationship—Being Your Best Self for Your Partner and Accepting Nothing Less."

I do encourage every couple I marry to engage in premarital counseling because we are all products of our past. We need to respect each other's frailties and unhealed wounds. See more about this in chapter 6, "Learning from Life's Lessons: Finding the Good from the Bad."

I wish I'd been older than 21 when I first married, and that I'd had couples counseling before marrying. I was stuck in between the *Ozzie and Harriet* "happy housewife" generation and the new age, in which the majority of women earned a college degree in 1980. It was too limiting for me to find satisfaction in only cooking and cleaning a house, and I had a BA in broadcasting and wanted to use it. I hadn't worked hard and graduated with honors for nothing!

After my daughters were born, I entered Gannon University as a master's student, but because my husband was so upset I wasn't just an at-home wife and mother, he refused to help at all with our daughters. It was very difficult to attend college, work, and be a new mom without help, so something had to go. I decided to put the master's degree on hold, and instead I modeled personally and started my talent school. Soon after that, I left my husband, filed for divorce, and had to support my children and myself.

Although we had joint custody, I paid the child support to their father for 12 years and provided a nice home for the girls and me overlooking a beautiful lake. It wasn't easy, but I was free! And to be free to pursue your dreams is worth everything. You cannot put a price on having freedom and peace after you leave a toxic relationship.

It is worth repeating that I have forgiven the father of my children, which has been very healing to both of us. This was my toughest test in forgiveness, but my spiritual journey could not be complete without forgiving my first husband and choosing to remember the good times instead of the difficult times we had.

I worked at the model and talent school around the custody schedule I was given. My daughters grew up around the business and were a great help. They knew every actor and model, and became very confident and social. Since the age of three and four, they made good money modeling and acting too. It was a hectic schedule for me, working about 80 hours a week for about nine years to earn enough money to support us. It was a hard but glorious time.

In 1995, my school and agency merged with a New York firm, so I made the move for the first time to NYC. Within the year, they reneged horribly on their agreement, I was feeling extremely burned out, and my work was no longer fun. I had reached my first dream and knew it was time to reinvent myself again, so I decided to leave the model and talent business for good in 1996. I moved to the Jersey Shore. Now the timing was better to complete another dream of mine, to get my master's degree in applied clinical and counseling psychology.

I set new goals for a different path, revisiting a dream I'd wanted to accomplish since junior high school. Organizing my university classes and overall plan, I figured I had to graduate by the time Stephana wanted to enter college, as I couldn't afford to pay two tuitions.

One adviser told me, "This is a four-year program, so plan on four years."

I said, "I must complete it in three, and I will do whatever it takes to do so."

She replied, "No one can finish this program in three years and be done with their thesis as well."

In my mind, I replied, "Oh yeah? Watch me!" I sure did finish in three years, and I was the first to graduate—and with honors—in August of 2000 for the new master's in psychology program at Rowan University in New Jersey.

I went on to my next set of goals: to have my own counseling center that specialized in helping women in transition and couples in crises. In 1997, I had started Choice Counseling under the supervision of Dr. Z. Benjamin Blanding, my fabulous mentor and adviser.

I created a free counseling program for teens in the Ventnor/ Atlantic City area, which was the basis of my master's thesis. My thesis project, *Ventnor Teen Vision,* helped over 400 area teens, with 30 receiving intensive group counseling over a 10-week period of time. Five pre- and post-test assessments proved that the creative arts are essential in raising teen self-esteem and grades while lowering high-risk behaviors such as dropping out of school and drug and alcohol use.

The project with the kids started in August and lasted six months (notice how many things end in about six months, due to my goal-setting approach). It took another six months to write the thesis with statistical charts and graphs, and 88 professional sources.

This thesis became my second educational book; it's 125 pages long and is a project I am most proud of. Today I see these prior "high-risk" kids succeeding in school and holding jobs in our area. I was very happy to be part of the process of giving them the confidence to reach their dreams. They, too, have learned the Watch Me! mind-set!

Once I graduated from Rowan, I opened a nonprofit corporation for counseling in Ventnor, NJ, called Inner Vision Counseling. A lot of people didn't understand the business name I chose, but it was primarily based on the internal thought processes and vision one has when using the Watch Me! mind-set for growth and change. I was the executive director and a therapist. It was a self-paying counseling center, offering a sliding scale for those in need. The motto was "Holistic personal growth for mind and spirit." I was trying to emphasize an all-natural, holistic approach toward health and wellness, along with talk therapy.

At this time, I had two radio talk shows. It was great fun and challenging to answer client questions right there on the spot, and doing this type of radio show was one of my dreams. Another long-term goal done! It was a great free marketing tool and helped to launch my business.

It is always important to state your goals to friends and family, no matter what their reaction. This makes them solid in your mind, and their disbelief or put-downs will only drive you further to succeed. Just smile when they say something negative and confidently say, "Watch me!"

It helps some people to have a more solid business plan written out on paper. For a new business, you can make financial projections about what you are committed to earn within the first six months, first year, and then five years. If the business is not new, making some goals or projections for an increase over previous years may be important. Your personality type can influence what type of goals you want to see in business.

If you need financial support to start a business, then a bank will need to see a well-prepared plan. Many colleges and women's centers offer a free service to help you develop your business and financial plan. Take advantage of these services and work using your goal system to prepare what they ask you to do.

Be as professional as possible, creating marketing products that work! Pray or meditate on the plan, using visualization to see it come to fruition, and use the daily goals to do the work needed to realize the dream. Be sure to add a spiritual higher purpose to the new business, or send partial proceeds to a charity.

I can get too stressed by rigid financial projections. I tend to work hard, one day at a time, and I often work from a creative vision, seeing the end result I desire in my mind while doing what is necessary to meet that vision. I do compare the prior year's income to the current's year income, consider market trends for promoting the business, and invest where appropriate.

For example, I am about to launch my free app, *My Relationship Coach*, for all smartphones and iPads. For a certified relationship coach, I am at the forefront of this type of promotion, and I look forward to offering coaching to clients from around the world! Remember, it is important to list other results you hope to see other than just revenue, like attaining your higher purpose goals.

When goal setting for business using the Watch Me! mind-set, ask yourself what you can change from last year's sales or marketing approach to increase your numbers. How could you get those in the community to know you better? Become very active with your chambers of commerce and local networking groups.

Try to be creative and think outside the box. One of my favorite mentors, Gene Vassal, the prior sales manager of WFIL Radio in Philadelphia, told me as a young girl, "Hon, ya gotta have a gimmick!" He was brilliant at marketing and promotions, and I was eager to watch and learn. Most of the jobs I have had I created from a need I saw in my community—like the model and talent agency in Erie, PA, the custom wedding ceremonies done on location, and the singles networking group in southern NJ. Do something different that doesn't exist yet. Brainstorm ideas with people of all ages who are creative and intelligent. There is nothing like a great business marketing discussion!

Once you launch your plan and business, if it is a good one, expect others to soon follow with similar businesses. If the market becomes flooded, either raise your prices or phase out this business and develop something else you want to do more.

Any business plan should include financial planning, marketing, promotion, public relations, sales kits and presentations, and short and long-range goals. Your business should also fill a need within your community. You have to develop your gimmick early on. What will make you and your product different from all the rest? This becomes your marketing piece. What spin-off business could you develop that complements the core business? I developed the singles networking group to build my therapy practice, wedding business, speaking engagements, and my book's promotion.

These businesses all interrelate; one complements the other. What can you do to make your original idea more exciting for both you and your clients? What ancillary services can you provide? How can you modernize an older concept to stay ahead of the promotional and marketing curve?

Next, how do you personally fit your career and product image? I do not look like the typical minister or psychotherapist, which is part of my outside-the-box, contemporary approach. My wedding services are more spiritual than traditional religious ceremonies; therefore, my more contemporary image fits my product.

As a therapist, I am not psychoanalytical but more of a life coach, and I am extremely motivational, holistic, and solution-focused. My personal energy matches that approach, as does my office and waiting-room environment, the books and tapes I lend out, and even the way I dress for sessions. Your whole presentation is a package.

You must ask yourself why a client would choose you or refer you to others. What makes your service unique and personable? Most business is done on referrals, so what do you do to keep in touch with your current customers and encourage them to refer you to others? Therapists are limited in marketing their practice due to licensing laws, but I try to provide little special touches for comfort.

I have chocolates throughout the waiting and therapy room, special hot coffees and teas available, aromatherapy, dim lighting, candles, toys for the kids—altogether it's a very pleasant waiting-room environment. Think of the little things; they add up to a big impression.

When can you say, "Thank you," again to your clients? Try it at holiday time, birthdays, the anniversary date of their working with you, at the beginning of each season, New Year's Eve, and so on. Try referring their businesses to others. Return their messages promptly, and let them know that you care.

On my Web site for weddings, I list the hotels and restaurants that have referred my ceremony services to future brides. I also hand out a list of references to each bride who visits my office. We refer each other; and, in turn, all our businesses grow. Of course, make these alliances with business people and companies you trust and believe in personally, so you can be sure they will make your referred clients happy. I usually do a mass mailing to all my referred clients every January, as well as to new clients I haven't worked with yet in the wedding business.

My shiny red marketing folder includes business cards, brochures, photos of my ceremonies, quotes from happy couples, my certifications, and a thank-you letter. I then follow up with a phone call to clients within two weeks of sending the package, so they can hear the voice and personality behind the marketing kit. What could you do to help expand your referral alliances?

Depending on your business, sometimes it takes more of a personal touch to cultivate these relationships. You may need more than a mailer, a phone call, or a networking meeting; you may need to take clients for lunch or to a show, or send a small gift on their birthdays. For some businesses (not mine), offer a commission on a sale that they sent you. Follow up with a thank-you card for their referral. Most importantly, do an outstanding job for the client they've referred to you. When you make their clients happy, you can count on them referring you again!

Be ready to promote and speak about your products wherever you may be. I always have business cards with me for all my businesses. Tell people about your new products and services, and when they ask in a general way, "What's new?" tell them! Seek opportunities to speak formally about your product or service to large groups. Ask someone you have an alliance with to set up a large group meeting, and in return, give them an extra bonus or free product for hosting the event. Make it a win-win for everyone involved. Be sure people understand exactly what you do. Have a Web site that freely educates, provides value, and promotes your product or service in various ways.

Be sure people are comfortable in buying from you. Have a sales agreement, warranty, refund policy, or free replacement of a product if it's faulty. Back up your product and believe in it! Know how to use it; show how to fix it. Your belief in the product will come out in your tone of voice, body language, and excitement about the product or service.

If you're selling a service, a big part of the sale is *you*. Dress appropriately to represent your service. Clients will buy from you if they can see how your product or service is working for you. For example, I know a woman who was promoting her weight loss book, and she was close to 300 pounds herself! This is a huge disconnect between her image and her product—would you buy her book?

I also know a professional counselor whose office was disgustingly dirty, cluttered, messy, and smelly—would you feel comfortable receiving treatment there? I would think, *why does he not have his own life in order?* When I see adolescent clients, I am often dressed in jeans, show them pictures of my daughters, tell their stories, and am totally down-to-earth and real in my approach to them. I know their music and like their fashion. This makes them feel comfortable, willing to open up to me, and most importantly, able to trust me. *Be* your product or service—this is extremely important to your success in selling it.

Be honest and honorable. Keep your word. If you say you are going to call, do it. Try to pick up your ringing phone within two rings, and have a pleasant tone when saying hello. Make your pricing fair, but not the lowest or the highest among your competitors. People will think the lowest price reflects a substandard product or service. Provide extra service and one-of-a-kind features for your higher price. Don't be embarrassed about your fees or be afraid to discuss price; after all, you believe in your product and know it is worth what you are asking.

Review your business development plan often. Constantly keep an open mind for a spin-off business that complements the main service. Ask those you trust for ideas you haven't thought of in how to promote your business. Brainstorm with those you've made alliances with. Use your time wisely, do what works consistently, yet make time for new approaches. Your daily, weekly, monthly, and six-month goals should keep you driven, not stressed out. Goal setting that is too intense could lead to procrastination and a fear of moving forward out of your comfort zone. Make smart, calculated risks over time so you feel fully prepared to take on the new challenge or business.

What about procrastination and laziness? Excuse making, or blaming others (the spouse, the kids, the dog, lack of time) for not being able to reach your goals or do what you cherish is a common form of procrastination. *Stop* making excuses and realize that *you* are the only one sabotaging your dreams, no one else. Find and enforce your boundaries. Put time aside to focus on the work that needs to be done to reach your goals.

Stopping procrastination begins with envisioning the desired results of reaching your goals in your heart and mind. After announcing your intentions, you would only embarrass yourself if you didn't do what you said you were going to do. Announcing intentions keeps you focused on finishing until completion. An example of this is when I closed the model and talent agency and announced in the Erie newspaper my plan to become a spiritual psychotherapist. I didn't know how, when, or where I was going to do this, but nonetheless I was determined to make it happen using the Watch Me! mind-set, lessons, and techniques.

Lo and behold—I am a psychotherapist and a minister, and I practice holistic, spiritual psychotherapy with all my clients! Touché! If you can dream it, you can *be* it. Just set the goals, announce your dream, and don't let anyone try and stop you, no matter what! Remember the importance of tying your personal and business goals into your ultimate higher purpose goal. Your higher purpose is to serve others, and this blessing from God or your higher divine power will be the difference in your reaching ultimate success. I realized my dreams to help others in my counseling center, and then moved beyond them to create another dream, by developing an app which will allow me to coach world-wide.

Another example of announcing your goals is when I had announced the progress of this book in a school seminar. I happened to run into a lady who attended that seminar a month later and she asked me how my book was coming. Was it the fact that she questioned me about my progress, and that I wanted to live up to my announced goals, that then made writing and finishing this book my top priority? Who knows? I just know that there are no mistakes in the spiritual world, so seeing her that day was supposed to happen, and it motivated me to finish on time.

Okay, so what is my next goal? Here it is, being announced to you readers! I would love to promote this book and the second one in this series by doing speaking engagements, whether live or on TV and radio. I want to promote the Watch Me! mind-set for personal growth and for establishing a more evolved relationship with your partner. I would like to bring this motivational system for success to many throughout the world by offering Life and Relationship coaching by phone, Skype, and FaceTime for individuals and groups, through my app, *My Relationship Coach*, and by offering weekend retreats for singles and couples.

These activities would help me to fulfill my ultimate business and personal goals and my higher purpose goal of helping those in need to find the motivation to change; to heal from their inner pain, anxiety, and depression; to help them find the spiritual connection that gives them courage and a new way of thinking, to help them find the determination and devotion to live their dreams, and to have the sheer joy and happiness of being their best selves by living the Watch Me! motivational mind-set.

Also, giving partial proceeds from the book to my arts scholarship fund and to Alexi's EPIC charity are just a small way of giving back to the world, and investing in my daughter's dream of seeing her charity continue to grow. All of this combined attains my higher purpose goals as a woman, mother, relationship coach, therapist, minister, writer, talent agent/manager, and motivational speaker.

Why not stop here and write out your next three personal and business six-month goals, and describe how reaching those goals would fulfill your higher purpose, destiny and dreams? Clarify these goals in your mind, envision your success, commit your goals to paper, and then announce them to others.

I leave you with a motto that Alexi created for EPIC: "What have you done today?"

Start today to change your life! Start by filling in the goal-setting sheets on the next few pages.

Goal-Setting Sheet
© Riana Milne, MA, LPC, Certified Relationship Coach

Define where you are now:

Create your vision of where you realistically want to be in six months and in one year:

Write down the goals you need to achieve to reach your vision:

Personal

1.

2.

3.

Relationship

1.

2.

3.

Parenting (of Children or Elderly Parents)

1.

2.

3.

Just Do It! Goal Setting for Personal Growth and Success

Job/Career/School Goals

1.

2.

3.

Six-Month Goals (Birthday and Six Months Later)

Business/School:

1.

2.

3.

Personal:

1.

2.

3.

Tips

- ◆ Remember that what we focus on, we get in life.
- ◆ Focus on your blessings and what is right, *not* what is wrong!
- ◆ Replace negative self-talk with positive over thirty days.
- ◆ Focus on solutions, not problems.
- ◆ Stop judging, blaming others, and finding fault. Take responsibility for your actions!
- ◆ Find what you can appreciate in the tough times, and know that change is for the good!

Mini-goals for Personal Growth

Goals for Today

1.

2.

3.
And if I have time _____

Goals for This Week

Business/School:

1.

2.

3.
And if I have time _____

Personal:

1.

2.

3.
And if I have time _____

Goals for This Month:

Business/School:

1.

2.

3.
And if I have time _____

Personal:

1.

2.

3.
And if I have time _____

Goals to reach within Six Months:

(list three to six goals for both Business and Personal)

1.

2.

3.

4.

5.

6.

Chapter 6

Learning from Life's Lessons: Finding the Good from the Bad

⁓ ⁓

W<small>E ARE ON THIS EARTH</small> to learn many valuable lessons. Many of the best lessons come from horrific events, events that we curse the gods for when they are happening. "Why me?" is our favorite question during the toughest times. Believe me, I used to ask this many times.

Sometimes when I feel I have it bad, I put things into perspective: I'm alive, fairly healthy, have two fabulous daughters, live in a safe place that I enjoy, love my career, and am well educated. So many people have much less than I do. I suddenly feel guilty complaining at all!

Yes, I have struggled dearly. My marriages cost me a great deal of money and emotional pain. With the first marriage, I was left with over $220,000 in debt that my husband and his father borrowed from my parents that I had to personally pay back, and a bankruptcy at age 26. My last marriage left me with debts of over $250,000; I've had to work many jobs to even make a dent in that amount. Each time I have recovered but have had to pay dearly for my freedom. Using my Watch Me! goal-setting techniques and a lot of hard work, I am happy to be totally debt-free today.

I had to handle the bankruptcy with my first husband because he was "too depressed" to handle it. He sat at home, overindulged in food and other substances, and withdrew from the world. I worked in downtown Philadelphia, got my kids to child care and back, cooked the meals, took care of paperwork, and put the kids to bed. My husband's poor business decisions made the bankruptcy total $750,000. I was appalled that the chocolate company, and now us as a couple, owed so much money. I didn't want to be bankrupt. I felt so guilty and ashamed. The Philadelphia attorney said, "Let me handle this for you, and then let me handle your divorce—there is no way you alone can pay off this debt."

I was young and naive and believed in love. My girls were so young, only three and four at the time, so divorce seemed out of the question. My husband wanted to move back to Erie, work in his father's restaurant seven days a week to get back on our feet, and pay back my mother and my father, who lent him over $220,000 for his various businesses.

I reluctantly went back to Erie, PA, but cried all the way back. I hated it there, but it was a chance to pay my mom and dad back. I felt I had no other choice. I was in the middle of a war between my husband and his father, and my own parents. It was a horrible feeling, and what made things worse was that my father was sick with cancer when I moved back to Erie. The little house my husband moved us into had rats in the basement, and a jealous lover's murder had happened there a few years before on the back steps. The spirit of that house never disturbed me, but the thought of rats sure did.

After the bankruptcy, I set stronger boundaries. I told my husband that if he ever asked for a loan again, I was out of the marriage. Within three months of the move, he came home to announce he was going to be a photographer. "With what money?" I asked.

"My dad's two friends are each willing to give me $5,000; that's all I need. That also pays for the professional course I will take to be certified."

"*Give* you the money?" I asked, feeling hopeless. "It's a loan, I'm sure, and I said *no loans*." My heart sank. *Here he goes again,* I thought, *using other people's money to be a big shot.* And I knew he wouldn't finish the course, because he never finished his course at his first college, or Penn State. He quit both schools. He said he was taking the loan anyway, no matter what I had to say about it. That was his choice, and now, I had to decide what to do about it. I knew I couldn't take being in debt anymore, so money or not, I was determined to leave this toxic marriage

That was May of 1987. I set my goal to gather enough money to pay my first month's rent to live on my own by my birthday in September. I started modeling when my husband made that announcement, opened the training school and agency in July, and moved out by September 1st with the girls. I was through. I had nothing, but I filed for divorce. Things couldn't have gotten any worse—I had a severely sick father out of town, I was flat broke, I had two kids and no help, and I was just starting a modeling business with no money or ability to get a loan because of our bankruptcy. I had to muster up all my courage and develop a Plan B.

Plan B. Everyone needs a Plan B just in case Plan A doesn't work, or even to help make it work. I needed income to make my new model and talent business fly. I had to feed my kids on my custody nights. When I didn't have them, I ate scrambled eggs, cereal, or soup, but they always had a balanced meal. I was in survival mode for the second of many times in my life.

My Plan B was to get a night job, run my school and agency by day, and take modeling jobs for other income. I decided that a master's degree in business had to be put on hold, as it was best to devote my energies to my modeling school and agency full-time. I really felt it had potential if I had the time for it. So I quit college but soon became a nighttime instructor at the same university, Gannon. Not too bad for the ego!

I taught courses called How to Sell Anything Successfully, How to Market and Promote Your Product, and Telephone Sales Skills. The university heard I was quite an impressive teacher and hired me for various teaching assignments for the senior graduating students. One class was Business Image and Etiquette. At $42 per hour, I would teach anything! Gannon University, and then the Erie Chamber of Commerce, hired me to teach various courses around town. So at age 27, I became a professional speaker.

One speech I remember in particular was for the surgeons of Saint Vincent Hospital. It was a class on patient communication skills. I knew they were thinking, *What could this young woman possibly teach to top-shelf surgeons?* as they whispered to each other as I approached the podium and prepared to speak.

Okay, I thought. I'm just going to be honest. I opened the speech with the question: "I bet you are all wondering, 'What is this young lady going to teach me about how to be a doctor?' Am I right?" They all started laughing, because I knew what they were thinking. "I'm just going to talk to you as a patient—one who wishes she'd had the guts to speak up about her experience in the hospital as a patient. Before we are done, I just may have a few tips and suggestions you'll like. So give me a shot, okay?"

After that, they were courteous and attentive, and several walked up afterwards and said that mine was the best lecture they had heard in a long time. I had been in an intimidating situation, and I just used honesty, humor, and the fact that we all are human and can learn from one another as the bonding element. Being honest and real can always help make any situation feel better.

So what does all this have to do with finding the good from the bad and having a Plan B? Well, Plan A was to remain married and raise my children. Plan B was to have a life free of debt, to make it on my own without someone else calling the shots, and to create a career I loved and could excel at. Each step I made (daily and weekly goals) once I moved out brought me closer to the life I wanted.

Being forced to take on the night job got me more teaching assignments with the university and then the Erie Chamber of Commerce. Speaking and teaching for a college were great references toward the licensing of my talent school with the PA board of education, which I would appear before in early December.

I was able to fund my business without a loan, and I made enough to feed the children. I didn't have much more, as I was barely hanging in there, but I had done it! I was also writing the school training manual until 3:00 a.m. every night. I remember my daughter asking me, "Mom, why are you sleeping right before I come home from school?" It was to catch up on my rest from the night before and to have enough energy to teach for three hours at night after working all day. That one-hour siesta got me through teaching.

The model and talent manual became my first book. It was over 250 pages, had illustrations, and was purchased by every modeling student within my school, earning quite a bit income over the years.

The bad that I endured brought about a lot of good—an internationally award-winning model and talent school and agency, teaching for a university, and becoming known throughout the community as an excellent lecturer as well as someone who gave back to the community through my talent school's charity projects. Our projects were always televised, so they ultimately brought me more business and a lot of goodwill. Parents could trust their kids with me, and the community liked me.

What was best? It was proving how far I'd get in Erie with the name of Riana and my *own* maiden name, not my married name. The Watch Me! mind-set had taken me exactly where I wanted to go. It kept me focused on my goals at the hardest of times and kept me determined when so many thought the school and agency would fail.

Even though my business was growing, the child support that I had to pay for joint custody kept increasing too. I was only one of two ladies obligated to pay support in Erie. In 1993, many of Erie's blue-collar factories were downsizing or closing, and modeling school was an extra for a lot of families. I slowly saw many of my booking clients closing their businesses. I decided I would have to live where I could get a better-paying job to meet all my bills. It was horrible for the kids and me that I had to move, but I had no choice. I was forced to be "the man" of the family and had to go where I could earn more to pay the support my ex-husband was demanding. I lived up to all my financial and parental obligations despite the hardships and was proud to do so.

I had to leave Erie for another reason, as well. I was told by a relative of my current boyfriend that a "contract was out on my life." This relative showed up at midnight, in a severe panic after "coming from a meeting" (so this was no story). I had filed a contempt of court order against my ex for not meeting his obligations in the divorce agreement. At the last minute, my attorney bailed out for no apparent reason, saying he couldn't represent me.

It was obvious he had been threatened. I told him his bill was paid, I did what he asked, and said he must represent me. The case was held in the judge's chambers. I had no jury or witnesses to what happened there. The result was a joke, a mere slap on the wrist for my ex-husband. It was all adding up.

I felt I'd had enough persecution in Erie and decided I must move if I were to remain sane and alive. In case something did happen to me, my will was in order, and I did have a life insurance policy that would benefit my daughters, so nothing more could be done.

I went to the New York IMTA convention, competed for International School of the Year and won, and looked for a job. I had offers in marketing from Calvin Klein and in sales from a top broadcasting company. Another business offered to open up a branch of my talent agency. I decided to take the offer to merge with my Erie school and agency, as that would serve my models and actors best.

That I had become internationally known as a talent agent and school director was what prompted the NYC firm to invest in my Erie business. The Watch Me! mind-set had bought me a ticket out of town and two talent agency locations; this was even better for the Erie talent, who were serious about moving to NYC or LA. I was able to help them while helping myself.

When I moved to NYC in September of 1995, Stephana was just about to enter 8th grade, and Alexi was going into 7th grade. They both decided to stay in the Erie school, where they were enrolled in the honors programs, instead of moving to NYC. Even so, I came back to see them almost every weekend to attend their sports events and school plays, and to get them what they needed. We spent a lot of quality time together.

As the New York office was just getting off the ground, the parent company had internal financial problems only eight months into our deal and had to make drastic and quick changes. They were claiming to be broke, and the new talent division was closed. What a crime! Our models and actors were both beautiful and talented, and all very real and down-to-earth. We were getting bookings for soaps, other TV shows, commercials, print ads, and film parts. I was really upset that I did not receive any notice or further compensation. Ugh! Another financial challenge. Another quick Plan B was in order.

I went back to Erie and closed the school by posting that thank-you note in the paper that stated I was moving on to pursue becoming a spiritual psychotherapist. I was burned out with the talent business; after working such long hours over nine years, I'd had enough. I didn't want to move back to Erie, and I needed to finish the year on my apartment lease in NYC.

I took in a roommate to make rent and started searching for a job. I worked from 7:30 a.m. to 1:30 a.m. daily, writing up cover letters and various resumes. I had seven resumes: for the model and talent business, marketing, PR and promotions, broadcasting, teaching, sales, and for being an executive secretary. I was writing cover letters and faxing all day long, as e-mail and job search engines didn't exist at the time. I treated searching for a job as a full-time job.

I had found that executive assistant jobs paid better than my other options. I was very close to being hired to assist the CEO of a major hotel chain, the CEO of a major cosmetics company, and one of the wealthiest female CEOs in fashion. I had two or three interviews for each position. I ended up taking a maternity-leave position as an executive assistant to Ralph Lauren. His longtime top assistant of close to 25 years was a wonderful woman who supervised me and taught me the ropes.

Ralph was a fabulous man, very classy. I always admired that whenever his wife or children called, they always got through, no matter what meeting he was in. He was quite particular, a quality that accounts for his success in fashion today. The maternity-leave job just about ended when my NYC rent was up for renewal, so it was then I moved to the Ocean City area of New Jersey—move number 16 in my life.

A Plan B isn't always ready the moment you need it, but focusing on your next best move will help keep your focus off the "why me?" pity attitude. Using your Watch Me! mind-set and spiritual techniques is very important as you form and initiate your Plan B. We all could ask ourselves, "Why me?" numerous times throughout our lives. We were given life, but no instructions or guarantees that it would be easy. Your Plan B may be the exact detour you need, and it just may take you exactly where you really wanted to go. So have faith!

Change is hard. Unexpected change with financial hardship is even more difficult. No one asks for major interruptions in life. When clients come into counseling, most are shell-shocked because of a forced and sudden transition: a new divorce, the unexpected death of a loved one, a newly discovered affair, a job loss, and so on.

Because of the emotional shock, many are stuck in the devastated pity-me stage and need someone to vent to. Most clients just need some empathetic healing while exploring some realistic solutions. Usually their friends and family are tired of hearing their complaints by the time these clients come to me. They are simply scared and stuck, and aren't able to see through their pain enough to form a Plan B. They haven't the energy or insight at the moment to try to find a good situation out of the bad one they've been given.

I tell them it's hard to see the lesson in what's happened, but ask that together we try to find solutions to their current situation. By coming up with a lot of possibilities, and with my encouragement and their willingness to take risks, we can form a Plan B. I use my motivational and inspirational coaching skills as we work as a team to rebuild their lives, one step and one goal at a time.

Every stage of your life cycle has challenges and gifts, and each phase is temporary. Ultimately, a new stage will begin once you initiate the change. It is important to live in the present, in the here and now, and be open to what presents itself as you are going through change. If you are keenly aware, certain people or opportunities will emerge that can help you reinvent yourself.

The death of my dear friend Michael Marcucci at the age of 16 always reminds me that life is indeed a gift that should be treasured. Difficult times are your tests, your lessons to be learned. Tough times are temporary, and how long they last is ultimately up to you. If you embrace the challenges, try to learn the lessons from them, and are always aware they are temporary, it will be easier to get through them.

You will grow and become stronger with each test and be ready for the next challenge's arrival. Wherever you are in your life cycle within the Earth school, know that you are there for a reason. Meditate to find the reasons and the solutions to your problems. Use positive self-talk to discover the path you should take. Closely examine all your choices, then write your goal-planning sheet, make decisions, and act! Procrastination is poison to your soul, and to your mental health. Remember, "God helps those who help themselves."

One counseling client of mine, Kate, was in a loveless marriage. Her husband Bob came to see me one time without her. He said he only remained married because he felt sorry for his wife. He admitted to no longer loving, respecting, or desiring her. He claimed he wasn't cheating, but he had lost 40 pounds, enrolled in acting classes, took long walks, and went for bike rides or kayaked on weekends. He would do anything but spend time with his wife or family. Bob had already stopped taking family vacations, eating dinner with the family, and attending the kids' sporting events. He admitted his foot was halfway out the door.

Kate complained that "he treated her like a kid." Her preference was to just sit at home and watch soap operas and take care of the kids, who were about 21, 17, and 13. Kate moaned that she never got her turn to have a career either teaching or in art. "Either Bob or the kids came first, never me," she whined. Every week she complained of feeling sick, either with migraines, stomachaches, or joint pain. I insisted she be tested for fibromyalgia, chronic fatigue syndrome (Epstein-Barr virus). I also suggested that at 45, she was likely in perimenopause and could be a great candidate for NHR (natural hormone replacement); I encouraged her to see her gynecologist. Kate took none of these suggestions early on. I suggested vitamin remedies to help with energy and well-being, but she refused, saying she didn't like to take extra pills, but she did take Zoloft (an antidepressant), which she claimed "didn't work anyway."

When I suggested exercise, Kate said she "couldn't exercise because of her asthma," but that she felt fat and unattractive. She walked all hunched over and wore baggy, unattractive clothes. She looked much older than her years and appeared to be carrying the weight of the world on her back.

Kate repeatedly whined to me, "I don't know what I'll do if he leaves me." I told her she'd better face some realities and get a

Plan B in place. She had to face the facts that Bob refused to be in couples counseling with her, and that they hadn't made love or gone out on a date for about a year. She saw that in many ways Bob had already started a whole new life. He supported the family on his own and spent time with his children, but it appeared that he might soon move out for good.

Bob told me he had stopped approaching Kate for sex months ago because she always refused or was "sick." "She had a ton of excuses, she never wants to do anything, and so I've gone and done things by myself," he said. "I have finally begun to start living, and I'm not about to change that for anything." I couldn't blame him.

I totally understood Bob's point of view, and it was up to me to give Kate a dose of reality. I had encouraged her to start being more of a friend and a wife to Bob, instead of being a nag and acting like a child. She did start exercising, and it took several sessions to convince her to reenroll in college to finish getting her teaching degree in elementary art. She loved the courses she was taking, had lost weight, and was walking straighter and prouder. Kate was smiling more and seemed happier. She promised she had stopped nagging Bob, and had started talking to him more like a friend. She had found ways to thank him and genuinely compliment him. He had started talking with her again.

I was concerned, however, when Kate told me, "If Bob sees that I can take care of myself and get a job, he'll leave me." Kate may only go so far and stop. She is very stuck in her self-pity mode because it worked for so many years. But she may be *forced* to go with a Plan B, whether she wants to or not. She may find Bob gone one day and herself all alone with the kids, needing to support herself.

Does Kate really prefer to stay stuck in her loveless marriage, where she receives no friendship or respect, just to be taken care of? Perhaps. I know Bob won't tolerate how she's been acting for too much longer. With his comment, "One foot is already out the door," it sounds as if he already knows when he will leave.

Maybe it will be when their second child goes off to college, but mentally, he has already left. It is in Kate's best interests to grow as quickly as she possibly can while she still has his financial support. It would be a lot harder for her to pay for college after Bob calls it quits. If Kate could risk growing and changing by continuing to try the techniques of the Watch Me! mind-set that were beginning to work for her, she might just find herself a lot happier, with or without her marriage.

When my daughter Alexi was 17 years old and hoping to sign a record deal, we decided together that her Plan B would be to attend college. We visited several campuses, and she liked the University of Delaware. She was interested in several careers, from fashion design to marketing and PR, and of course, the music business. Her Plan B had changed several times, and it will continue to do so as she matures and experiences different things along the way. But she always has one prepared, which helps her handle the risks she takes to grow within her career and in her life. As she is in the process of moving from NYC to LA for her television career, Alexi will retain her NYC condo and continue to work for her many NYC fashion and television clients until she feels she can permanently move to LA. She is willing to take risks, but they are very well organized with a Plan B in mind.

Throughout life, you must adjust your Plan B constantly, especially during or after a crisis. You must be open to the lessons this experience is teaching you and then create a plan to reinvent yourself as you adjust to the changes the best you can. You need to become proactive, not reactive, to change. Ask yourself the following questions during the difficult times:

1. What good can I learn from this, and what is it teaching me?

2. What is my next financial move? Do I need a part-time job, to ask for more hours, to cut back on expenses, to pay off all debts, or to consolidate loans to save money? Try several ideas.

3. How can my children help? Can the family come together as a team? If they can't help financially, can the kids take on more responsibilities so that I can take on a part-time job? Even the youngest children like to feel they can help, so show them how; it makes them feel important. Then praise them for being an important part of the team. Be real with your children and tell them you need their help. They will be amazingly supportive if you just ask. If they are 14 or older, they can babysit, cut the grass, rake leaves, or get a part-time job to have their own spending money. It's important to teach young people the value of money and the responsibility of having a job.

4. Do I have a hobby that will help me earn money part-time? I sold floral crafts, took my clothes to consignment shops, wrote some magazine articles for money, wrote and sold my model and talent training manual, and created some adult classes for the university that I felt I could teach. Use your imagination and think outside the box! We all have many talents. How can you use yours to earn some money to get you through the toughest of times?

5. Can I improve my skills? If you are a woman looking to improve your skills, contact your local women's community center, as they have many training programs that they offer for free or at a reduced rate. If you are not computer proficient, sign up for their free computer courses. While in the program, read a book on how to be an executive secretary.

6. Can I learn another language? If you are bilingual, this is an enormous talent that can lead to many job opportunities. Businesses everywhere are looking for bilingual people in every field, and many will train you in your responsibilities.

7. What is it I've always wanted to do? What small step can I take to start on that goal or to create my own business? Anything is better than doing nothing, no matter how small.

8. Instead of feeling sorry for myself, how can I empower myself? Get more rest, eat healthier, and exercise. Now is the time to take care of yourself so you have the energy to accomplish your goals.

9. Can my extended family help? Perhaps your parents or siblings can be supportive in some way, even if that means babysitting your young children while you take on a second job.

Be prepared. These challenges will come, even to those like Kate who thought that she would always be taken care of, and that her life would always be easy. Change is inevitable, and the more you can look at it with an open mind and the courage to start a Plan B, the sooner you will find a way out and recover from your pain. Work is good therapy, so working on your goal plan will help you to feel empowered. Know that finding the good from the bad is an important part of your healing process.

It is important to shed unnecessary emotional baggage to free ourselves of toxic people and ideas that no longer work for us. It is the spiritual way to cleanse ourselves and create space for new experiences or people to enter our lives.

Meditate or pray on what you must do, and take deliberate action to rid yourself of old ideas that do not work anymore. This will help you to regain the energy you need to positively move forward in your life.

Release and let go of the old, and the new will enter your life. Find the good from these hardships and challenges that you had perceived as bad. With spiritual faith, understand that the hardships were all necessary, as these difficult lessons were supposed to happen to launch you into your next stage of greatness!

Chapter 7

Achieving Balance in Life

~⁓ ⁓~

PICTURE, IF YOU WILL, two equilateral triangles. These triangles represent balance in life and within yourself.

Life Balance
Self, Family/Partner, Work

∇

Balance within the Self
Mind, Body, Soul/Spirit

∇

Life Balance

The first triangle is for *life balance*; the first side is *self*, the second is *family* or *partner*, and the third is *work*. These three elements should be perfectly balanced in an equilateral triangle for you to feel happy and at peace.

If you spend too much time with a partner or family and forget yourself, or if you become a workaholic, you lose balance. The *self* side becomes shorter, and you feel imbalanced in life.

Imbalance of *self* can be experienced as anxiety, depression, anger, resentment, extreme fatigue or illness, and overwhelming stress. If your *self* side equals your *work* side but your family is short-changed, your spouse and children may feel angry or complain that you are never at home. Many children will lash out with high-risk behavior.

If *work* is out of balance, you may feel discontented about not reaching your career goals. You may not feel effective or appreciated on the job, or you may feel burned out from a lack of personal satisfaction. If so, reevaluate what job you have and consider finding something more creative or rewarding.

Or if *work* is the larger side of the triangle, you may be working too many hours and your partner could become resentful, the kids might feel they don't even know you, and your entire ego might be wrapped up in your work. A person in this situation usually works seven days a week and would be lost without his job. His entire ego is enmeshed with his work, and down the road he often loses his wife and children's love and respect.

Where does your balance lie in your personal life? Which side is too long, and which side is too short? What must you do to bring your life back into balance with three equal parts?

Balance within the Self

The second equilateral triangle is for balance *within the self.* It should consist of three equal types of activity: mind, body, and soul or spirit.

Mind activity is what you do to continue to learn and grow mentally. Reading, going to school, learning a new language, creating a new business, or anything else that challenges your mind fits in this category.

Body activity is what you do to take care of your physical self: a good, nutritious, and balanced diet, exercising three to four times a week, getting enough sleep (eight to nine hours per night), and grooming yourself with pride. This includes showering, keeping your hair styled, dressing impeccably, and anything that shows your sense of pride in your physical self.

People often don't show up for the world. They will pick times to dress up and look nice. I tend to say, "Dress as if . . ." Dress as if you already are the president of the company, the chart–busting singing star, or the successful business owner. If you feel it, you become it! And part of feeling you have reached your ultimate goal is dressing as if you have already become the successful person you dream to be.

Soul/spirit activity is your inner light that shines with the confidence that your higher power is with you each and every moment. Developing your soul means learning and growing in your spiritual study with meditation, prayer, reading, group discussions or lectures, attending temple or church, or whatever it takes to feel as if you are a spiritual, loving human being. When this side of the triangle is too short, the other triangles fall out of balance too, as this side falls under the *self* side of the *life balance* triangle.

Studies show that meditating for 15 minutes daily brings incredible benefits, lowering cortisol, blood pressure, heart rate, stress, and anxiety for many hours after the meditation. I meditated before an eye surgery, and when I was put on the blood pressure monitor, my rate was an incredible 82/53—a rate I had never seen before. I had asked the nurse if something was wrong with the machine, but she said no and then asked if I'd done anything that might account for the rate. This was my second surgery, so she had a prior BP rate of 107/93 on my chart; that was still a healthy rate, but certainly much higher than this new one. I told her I had

149

meditated for 20 minutes at home prior coming to the hospital, but that was well over an hour ago. She confirmed the studies and said that *all* people should meditate daily for overall physical and mental health and for speedy recovery from any surgery.

Keeping yourself spiritual will help keep all the elements of your life peaceful, calm, and balanced. When you meditate, mentally review your two triangles and think how you can adjust them where needed. When you feel the serene, inner light or peace within yourself, others will feel this and see it within you too. You will attract others with the same spiritual mind-set, bringing happier people into your life sphere.

When someone emotionally unhealthy tries to enter your life, a sense of knowing that this person is not right for you will emerge. You will feel the red flags of their anger and negativity right away. You will decide in a gentle way that this person could disturb your sense of peace if you allow him to get too close to you. You could release him with love or simply keep him as a distant friend. In the past, if a relationship was turning angry or toxic, I would gently say, "I love you for many reasons, but I feel we are not right for each other. I want to say thank you for the time we shared. Good luck, goodbye, and God bless."

By doing this, I never end my relationships with an angry tone or situation. If you loved that person and are breaking up, thank him for the memories and your shared experience. Good karma and God's blessings will come to you if you wish him good luck.

I know this is challenging for most people to do. Instead, they want to blame and punish their partners. But with this negative, toxic feeling inside your body, you are the one who will suffer. You may never get the apology you deserve, or the explanation you want for the person's behavior. You cannot force someone to do the right thing, but you have an empowering choice in how you decide to respond to a situation. Let him go in peace, and watch what happens to your life. You will be blessed.

These two balance triangles are the new way to look at life using the Watch Me! mind-set. The old way was by flying by the seat of your pants, which means not taking the time to look, question, and analyze your balance in life. Without doing this, you can end up feeling anxious, angry, depressed, resentful, lost, and lonely, often without knowing why. There is no structure to your personal life or the family unit, and your relationships will all suffer.

Don't get me wrong; your triangles will move out of balance because life's challenges and changes will cause them to shift. If you are aware, however, of what the balance should be, and look at your balance daily, you can readjust before getting totally out of kilter. Let your spouse and children know about the triangles too. Sometimes those we love see our imbalances way before we do. Listen to them and think about whether you have lost your focus.

Children and teens are very bright and perceptive, and they love their parents. They may be angry when they scream at you, "You're never home—you work too much!" but they are giving you a powerful message. All anger exists for a reason; even the three-year-old having a temper tantrum has a reason. What are they trying to tell you, and why aren't you listening? (See more on this in chapter 9).

Teaching your teens about the balance triangles will help them with their stress and anger levels. Their brains don't mature emotionally until about age 23 for women and 26 for men. So angry teens express that their lives have become unmanageable in the only way they know. Many parents enroll their kids in too many activities and still expect high grades. Their school day is a 10–12 hour workday, and when teens get exhausted, they get frustrated easily. Add to this peer pressure, worries about being "liked" or not by the person they admire, part-time jobs, and pressures to get good grades and perform well in other activities, and it's no wonder they are overwhelmed. Help them to find a calming balance.

In today's stressful, workaholic, and highly competitive world, we must shift to new paradigms of balance to survive and still feel a sense of joy. We should realize what really is important in life—not the material things but time, health, family, sharing and giving to others, learning and growing, laughter, and inner spiritual peace.

Learning to take risks so we can always better ourselves and grow becomes easier if we have a sense of balance. Change is often scary, but usually good. It helps us experience life "to the max." When all is said and done, it's not the toys we take along with us but our memories of what we have done and experienced with our loved ones, family, and friends, as well as the impact we've had in the world.

What matters is the experience of reaching our higher purpose in life and living our dreams and beyond while enjoying the simple times along the way. In the end, we'll remember how we gave back to the world and those we loved. No one who is sick and dying says, "I wish I'd worked more." Learn that lesson while you are healthy, and "live as if you were dying."

When you live your life with purpose and in a spiritual way, you do not fear death. If you have divine faith, death is just the next stage of being. There is a certain amount of peace in the end when you pass from the Earth school knowing you have touched the hearts, minds, and souls of many others during their journey, making a real difference in others' lives.

Let's look at other balance triangle examples:

Balance Triangle for Creative Artists

The three equal sides for those in the arts are *free-flowing creation, collaboration, and work.*

Free-flowing creation looks like work to many, but not to us creative sorts! This is the time several of you get together and present creative ideas to one another. As a recording artist, you may write all kinds of beats, lyrics to a given song or work with a choreographer to try various unusual dance moves. It feels like play even though you are accomplishing work. We love being in the free-flowing creation zone—it is when our best work comes to life!

Collaboration is when we work with other professionals to solidify our piece. For the singer, it is working with the writer, producer, and engineer to put together your CD. For the actor, it is working with the makeup artists, stylists, director, and the entire film or stage crew to create the finished product. For the writer, it is working with your publisher, editor, cover designer, and printer to create the book in its final form.

Work is the organizing, outlining, finishing touches, contracts, phone calls, marketing, PR, and all the other tasks, mini-goals and follow-up required to launch a product or service. These are all necessary to successfully market your creative product and get it out the door to those who would enjoy it. You can see each side is equally important. Without one, you do not have the other. They are all independent and yet interdependent on each other. When in balance, both the creative process and your product will be a success!

Balance Triangle for Business Owners

The three sides to keep balanced are the *organization,* the *employees,* and *sales and marketing.* No matter what type of product or service you have, it must be marketed so someone will want to buy it. Whether it's a hat, fishing tool, a piece of gum, a tire, a basket, or a painting on a grain of rice (I bought three in Mexico!), a customer can be found for it.

With the grain of rice, the Mexican man had a book of designs; I picked one for one side and had my name printed on the other. Then he had four choices of necklace vials into which he put the grain, which expanded so you can read it. I bought necklaces for the girls and me to remind myself that everyone has a special talent; you just need to discover yours!

The *organization* is the owner, board of directors, management, and the decision makers of the firm. They can either make or break a company. They must share the same vision and work for the higher purpose of the firm. Unfortunately, when businesses get too big, money becomes "the higher purpose," and soon the greediness is exactly what brings down a company. Those in the organization must be without ego; they often make the mistake of looking down on "the little people" who are actually doing the hard labor and building the product. Without a happy staff, the executives in the organization don't have a business to run.

The *employees* are the meat of the firm, the creators of the product, or those who sell the service. It is because they are often mistreated, underpaid, and not appreciated that the firm crumbles. Everyone must work as a team to keep the firm in perfect balance. Without balance, greed and resentfulness creep in. The executives must always ask for feedback and suggestions from the employees. They are the front line—the ones who know. They hold a lot of power, and a smart business owner knows this and does whatever it takes to keep the balanced triangle paradigm always in mind.

The TV show *Undercover Boss* is a great example of a boss being among his staff to appreciate their daily work and the dedication they have to his company. It's a wonderful example of trying to keep the business triangle in balance.

Sales and marketing are essential to getting a product or service into the hands of the buyers. Marketing examines what makes the product or service unique so someone will want to buy it. Promotion and public relations involves face-to-face sales and educating people about your product. People will buy something if they see the value in it, if it is different, if they like and respect the person or company promoting it, and if they can come to believe that the product or service will work for them.

All three elements of the corporate triangle need to be in balance and in touch with each other for a business to be successful. A business cannot prosper without a great production staff, a creative team that implements original marketing and promotions with sales, and caring and involved executive supervisors.

Life Balance Triangle for Couples

This triangle consists of three sides: *you, me, and us.* I see a lot of couples whose major problem is either the lack of balance and the resentment that it causes, or a lack of communication. Often when couples do talk, it's with anger, blame, disrespect, and a lack of true listening skills.

Me is your part in the relationship. The questions you need to ask yourself are these: Are you willing to listen and be open-minded? Are you doing your part of the chores and child care? Are you keeping yourself physically appealing for your partner? Are you continuing to romance and appreciate your partner? Are you keeping your own personal life in balance?

You is how you perceive your partner in the relationship. If you see him or her as angry, controlling, moody, addicted, shut-down, depressed, anxious, or absent from your relationship, then you must talk openly about your concerns. If your partner refuses to listen, then you should start coaching or counseling on your own. This shows that you are concerned enough to seek help. Hopefully, this will inspire your partner to join you after a session or two.

Us is your relationship as a partnership. What are you doing for the good of the relationship? Do you discuss your financial concerns and goals? Have you made a plan for your future and retirement? Do you have wills to protect the other person in case something happens? Do you take time to date once a week, share the chores, have a romantic and passionate sexual relationship, do nice things for each other, and vacation as a couple a few times a year?

An emotional or physically abusive relationship is severely out of balance. This way of treating partners is all about control and domination. Victims are rarely getting their needs met and often try too hard to please abusive partners to get them to calm down. It is very important for a victim of domestic violence who is verbally, emotionally or physically abused to get counseling help to learn self-esteem and empowerment strategies, and to understand the cycle of violence. When adults engage in any form of abuse between themselves or toward their children, this triangle has shattered, as no balance remains.

This holds true for a relationship where one partner is addicted to a substance or destructive compulsive habit, and the other person becomes codependent just to survive the relationship or family dysfunction. There are many addictions that destroy partnerships and families. Once of the most common is alcohol abuse. Here are some signs that a drinking problem could exist:

- When you have alcohol, you drink until you feel buzzed and then keep going.

- You feel fear and frustration if you don't have alcohol.

- You're compulsive in your drinking, actions, and temper; you find it hard to delay gratification.

- Your life is built around alcohol (having fun, choosing where you go out).

- You can't stick to preset limits at an event; you can't stop at just one or two drinks.

- Alcohol often replaces or accompanies another addiction.

- You engage in binge drinking at parties or on weekends because you feel "you deserve it."

- Friends, family, or your children have told you that they think you have a problem.

- You start drinking alcohol early in the morning.

- You have a few drinks a day more than two days a week.

- Your personality changes to sarcastic or nasty when you drink; you argue and often don't remember the fight.

- You drop your personal responsibilities; you may overlook personal hygiene, stop cleaning your home, and miss work.

- You generally feel depressed as to where you are in life and become socially isolated, staying at home and drinking alone, or you go out drinking with friends, frequently leaving your spouse at home.

- Your primary relationship is in jeopardy.

- You have experienced blackouts or loss of memory.

- You have suffered legal or other consequences of drinking, such as being charged with driving under the influence (DUI), or being involved in an alcohol-related fight, domestic violence, or any other situation that has affected your reputation.

If you have experienced one to three of the above, there is an 80 percent chance that you currently have or are developing an addiction to alcohol. Many of the signs of the addiction to alcohol are the same as those of other compulsions and addictions.

The mid-life crisis occurs in people from the mid-to-late 40s into the late 50s. People reevaluate their lives and goals, and this can create despair and depression or delight and celebration. If they feel they have not accomplished what they set out to do in life, then despair often leads to depression and an addiction, as people self-medicate to numb their pain and fears of the future.

Erik Erickson wrote about the life stages in psychology. His theory of the *eight psychosocial stages of development* is characterized by a different conflict or transition that must be resolved properly by the individual in each life stage.

When conflicts arise, the person is faced with various choices and ways of coping, and either successfully overcomes the crisis or handles it in a maladaptive way. Positive changes in the personality occur when a crisis is resolved properly; then the person has the emotional and intellectual strength and fortitude to deal with the next stage of life.

In stage seven, *middle adulthood* (ages 40 to 65), the presenting conflict is *generativity* (the ability to care for another person) versus *stagnation*. The most important event at this stage is parenting. An adult comes to understand that the only source of true happiness is to increase the goodwill and higher order in his world. Therefore, the theory suggests that he must either nurture children or maturing parents, or become involved in giving back to future generations. A negative outcome can occur if an adult cannot deal with his emotional issues and challenges and his choices lead to stagnation, inaction, inappropriate acting out or addiction.

Maturity is stage eight, and it occurs in late adulthood, from ages 65 to death. The most important event that occurs is accepting your whole life and reflecting on it in a positive way. Achieving integrity means fully accepting yourself as a positive person and one who has contributed to the greater good. If you have done this, you will be able to accept forthcoming death with peace.

Accepting responsibility and undoing any past harms is essential to achieving this self-satisfaction. The inability to do this results in despair, anger, or depression. A positive outcome is a sense of fulfillment about your life and the acceptance of death as a part of reality and without fear. Those who do not attain wholeness will face death with fear.

I believe that those who turn to alcohol and other harmful substances or addictive activities such as gambling, overspending, overeating, or sexual addictions in an attempt to self-medicate or escape their reality subconsciously feel they have faltered in a serious way. The Watch Me! mentality can certainly help people overcome anxiety, depression, addiction, and despair and get back on the right track, but people must break the self-pitying, blaming role and do the daily work it takes to become a responsible, accountable, and evolved individual who lives with integrity.

We all must readjust the balance as we live life. It is easy to get knocked off course and head into a downward spiral. This is why quiet contemplation or meditation is important. It gives us the time to think and make changes where and when we feel we need them the most. This is also the time to refocus on the Watch Me! mind-set, and to visualize the next round of goals we must set for ourselves to regain much-needed balance in our various life spheres.

When you feel stuck, I know a good psychotherapist and life coach! Talking your problems or situations out with an outside source is often very helpful. It is natural to first turn to your spouse or best friends to discuss your issues, but remember that they will always have a biased point of view or be afraid to tell you the truth. They don't want to lose your friendship, so they will often tell you what you want to hear.

A good relationship and respect for your coach is like having a good marriage. You must feel comfortable enough to tell her everything, and trust her enough to know that sometimes her opinion or suggestions may hurt a little, but she must be honest and real with you.

Remember the answer to depression, anxiety, and stress is not in a psychotropic pill, although there are times when these meds are truly necessary to balance brain chemistry. The solution often begins with simply living with the principles of the Watch Me! mind-set, having a more balanced life, setting realistic goals for change, and experiencing supportive coaching or talk therapy. Psychiatrists often insist on counseling support before prescribing medication.

There are great natural products that can help ease anxiety, stress, and depression while you are sorting things through with your therapist. Why not try this approach first? Many are noted on www.webmd.com. There have been many studies on the benefits of SAMe for improvement in mood and St. John's Wort to help ease depression. Melatonin can help you sleep naturally, while ginseng can help keep you calm. Of course, check with your doctor before using these or any other natural remedies. In our "hurry up and fix it" society, everyone wants the pain to go away with one simple pill. But with medication, you are often masking the symptoms and not dealing with the real problems.

I have always believed in a holistic approach to health first and foremost. No doubt medication is essential at times, especially for the truly mentally ill and psychotic. However, far too many adults are put on psychotropic medications, which sometimes even escalate their problems. There are often negative sexual side effects from antidepressants. Talk about something to be depressed about!

The next time you feel out of balance, meditate on it and try to come up with various possible solutions to solve your problems. Consider whether you have left the Watch Me! mind-set behind, forgetting to use it when you got overwhelmed with life. Go back to the basic techniques you have learned, as well as brainstorming new goals.

Try forming a pro and con list for each possible solution. Try those mini-goals and approaches that seem most realistic. If you still feel stuck, seek the help of a life coach or therapist. If you don't like the therapist's style, say so and ask for a referral to another therapist. We all have a different style or approach. Most of my clients love the motivational solution-focused therapy I use, but I have had a few clients leave for a slower, more psychoanalytical or traditional approach. That is just fine, as all clients should feel they can be open and connect to their therapists.

I will tell a client if I feel I am not the best therapist for him or her. Sometimes the problem is severe, and I feel that the person may need a specialist in a certain modality or a psychiatrist for medications before entering talk therapy. These clients should not be offended if they are referred to another professional. Our ethics dictate that we should try to send the client to the best professional if we are not qualified to handle their situation.

If medication is suggested for you, it is okay to ask if there are all-natural substances you could try first. That is your right. If you find these remedies to be helpful, that's terrific. If not, you can always try the stronger psychotropic meds available for your condition. Whether or not you use medication, or regardless of the nature of your underlying concern, continue to use the Watch Me! mind-set system to strike a balance in all your life, self, couple, and work sphere triangles.

Ask for help from your family and friends. Study and read motivational and spiritual books for personal growth and healing. Ultimately, is it *you* who must be willing to change. No therapist, pill, doctor, book, or outside force can make you *want* to change.

Only the strength within your heart, mind, and soul, which can be developed with the Watch Me! mind-set, can bring about the balance in all your life spheres that you desire or need.

So, what are you waiting for? Start drawing those triangles!

Chapter 8

For Couples: The Evolved Relationship—Being Your Best Self for Your Partner and Accepting Nothing Less

"WHAT SHOULD I LOOK FOR in a woman?" a very dear male friend asked of me. It only took a moment for me to sit down and write what I felt he should look for. I was astonished that this beautiful, intelligent, and successful man did not know this answer, even though he was nearly 50. He was alarmed because a young man had asked him this question while he was giving a speech, and he could not answer. Everyone of course, will have their own definition of what a love partner should be, or what a healthy and "evolved relationship" should look like. As a woman, therapist, and a motivational relationship coach, here was my response to him (please note that "she" could be replaced with "he" for the women readers):

- She should offer unconditional love no matter what I struggle with; she is my partner, friend, and confidant. I can count on being able to turn to her in tough times without ridicule or fear.

- She should be my best friend; someone to laugh, cry, and dream with; and someone to get some honest feedback from to help me with my decision making and personal growth.

- She always offers an opinion because she cares, but ultimately, she lets me make the choices I need to make for myself. We both realize I am responsible for my own growth and strength, and my own choices.

- She needs me for love and friendship, but she isn't needy. She is strong in her own right, yet she turns to me as her man. She respects and honors me, as I do her. We are true soul mates. I feel loved as a man should, and it makes me feel powerful and strong, but I never try to overpower or control her.

- I am attracted to her physically, and I desire her, as she does me. Although I crave her, this relationship is *not* based on lust or sex. Rather, as a good friend of mine once said, sex is "the dessert to the great meal of togetherness."

- She is spiritual; we share similar beliefs about faith or religion and the importance it plays in our lives. Although we may be of similar but different faiths, we also have a respect and openness to other people's faiths.

- She is very kind and a pleasure to be around. She is not rude, negative, mean-spirited, or judgmental toward others.

- She is able to communicate her feelings well, whether good or bad, whether we agree or disagree. We are entitled to our separate beliefs, and she never makes me feel small for having different opinions than she does on any subject.

- She is socially confident and outgoing. People like her as much as I do. But she is her own person and doesn't necessarily follow the crowd. I am proud of her individuality, as she is of mine, and I am always proud to be with her.

- She is as fabulous a mother to her children as I am a father to mine. She has true unconditional love and friendship with her children.

- I love her energy; she is generally positive, rarely angry, and she shines her inner light into the hearts of others. She manages her moods well and is patient. ("Love is patient and kind"—Corinthians). She realizes her gift is helping others, and this is her higher purpose that she strives to meet. She is a *good* person, and I and others know it.

- She is of good moral character, and I trust her. She has had challenges throughout her life that did not break her, and that have made her even stronger in faith and character. I admire her values, and she lives what she speaks. She is a living example of her word. She is never afraid to tell me the truth, as she lives in the truth.

- She is intelligent and uses this wisely, in a way to serve others and to succeed in life.

- I have great passion for her as a lover and a friend. I feel excited to be near her, look forward to the next time I see her, and know my life would be empty without her. She is beautiful inside and out, and I feel blessed to have her in my life. I would feel truly empty without her.

◆ She takes care of herself by eating healthy foods, exercising, and getting enough rest. She dresses nicely, and I am always proud to be seen with her.

So what does it mean to have an evolved relationship? Evolved people have a strong spiritual base from which they conduct their personal lives, their work, how they raise their children, how they treat other people, and how they make everyday choices. This spiritual base centers their self-esteem, confidence, and ego strength. People like this would desire partners who understand the foundation of the Watch Me! mentality and use similar concepts to it.

What a partner chooses to say or do affect others because our world is a universal oneness; in other words, we are all interrelated, and as Buddhist philosophy often states, "what we do individually affects the whole."

Similarly, the golden rule from the Bible says, "Do unto others as you would have them do unto you." Our everyday choices affect the world around us. An evolved person understands this and lives each moment knowing that what he says and does has a positive or negative effect on others, and he prays to make the right choices every day.

He is not on this earth to judge another, as that is not his place. He is not arrogant and would not use another person for his own selfish pleasure or gratification. He is not here to control another, only himself and his own choices, and he understands each person has the full right to control his own life.

His ego is strong enough that he does not look to compete and bring others down. Just the opposite is true; he does everything in his power to make another feel strong. This does not mean it is his responsibility to make another happy. He does not look to change another, and he realizes that people must change themselves to be happy.

He lives each day with purpose, and asks for guidance to make the right decisions that will fulfill that purpose. He is kind, peaceful, and reflective. He doesn't respond to situations with anger, although he will experience pain, fear, sadness, and disappointment. Anger is a result of pain, and he is smart enough to know that experiencing pain means he must take action because something is not working in the way that it should. He knows he will make mistakes, because he himself is a work in progress, but he has enough character to quickly and sincerely apologize for his errors.

Evolved men and women share their love and peace wherever and whenever possible. Their sense of calm and spiritual knowing can quiet an anxious soul and raise a depressed person from despair, all by reminding another of his greatness and need to reconnect with his own soul.

Being evolved takes constant reading and studying. Our humanness gets in the way of our greatness. Our Earth school challenges rise up to try to defeat us, often making us slip into fear, inaction, uncertainty, and insecurity. By studying daily, whether from the Bible, The Torah, Buddha's teachings, or today's popular self-help books about spiritual awakening, we can keep centered, balanced, and focused regarding ourselves and other people, especially our partners.

Marriage and commitment are about sharing your life with another person, but not *losing* yourself in that person. It is about being the yin and the yang—intertwined with one another, yet separate. It involves appreciating one another's goals and differences, sharing your dreams, and listening and supporting one another's needs and goals but not being responsible for them.

Many of today's marriages and partnerships fall apart because of one person's lack of ego, sense of accomplishment, or inner peace. This toxic, unhappy, and controlling person tries to bring the other person down to his level of misery because misery loves company. If the other partner is happy, stronger, and trying to live her life in an evolved way, the toxic person will do everything in his power to destroy this. Because of his poor ego, he can't stand the other partner being so happy and successful.

Often, to handle his misery, the toxic partner tries to self-medicate with alcohol, drugs, spending sprees, sexual affairs, gambling, overworking, or overeating—anything to take the pain away for awhile. When the high of the temporary fix wears off, and the pain of his reality comes back, the toxic partner again seeks the quick fix of an illusion of happiness.

Once the toxic partner is fully addicted, the healthy partner really starts to suffer. Often in a marriage like this, an affair will ensue, as either partner may look outside of the marriage for friendship, peace, and love. But an affair is another temporary fix to numb the pain of the marriage that is not working.

If you become codependent and get swept up in trying to "fix" the toxic partner, or if you plan your life around someone to attempt to make him or her happy, your soul will suffer. You will lose your own ego, purpose, greatness, and pride. This happens during an abusive relationship whether the abuse is emotional, physical, financial, sexual, or verbal. If the healthy partner tries to escape the pain of the dysfunctional relationship with an affair, then she is merely adding to the destruction.

Often, over time, the healthy partner becomes dysfunctional too, losing herself to try to please the toxic partner. She tries to remain balanced and spiritual, but ends up living a double life. Anyone who has a spiritual base will not be able to live with the toxic person for long or with this type of personal deception.

Ultimately, something must change, as the spiritual laws of karma suggest, and a decision must be made. Either both partners must commit to working through the marriage problems together or the healthy partner must separate from or divorce the toxic partner for a chance of a healthier and happier relationship. It is important for both partners to admit their role in the broken marriage and disclose what lessons they have learned; otherwise, each partner will carry the dysfunction into his new love relationship. The severely toxic individual may take a long time to apologize or may never realize or admit to his faults. Nor will he admit to the level of destruction he caused in the relationship, so be prepared. You have to be strong enough to move on without an apology from the toxic partner.

Remember, an affair is not the *cause* of a marital breakup—it is the *result* of a marriage not working. By the time an affair happens, the partner who is looking for love or escape in another person has usually experienced years of unhappiness. Serial cheating could be the result of a sexual addiction, usually stemming from past childhood trauma that has never been healed.

Often the traumatized spouse punishes and blames the broken marriage on the outside party involved in the affair. That person is not responsible; the cheating spouse is responsible because of weak boundaries, impulsivity and lack of integrity in your relationship. It is essential to get to the core of the lies and deceit and why the affair happened. There is life after an affair, and the marriage can actually survive and be better than ever if both parties really want it to work and rededicate themselves to living the truth.

People and situations change constantly. Who you marry in your early 20s may not be right for you when you are in your 30s or even 40s. If your partner is making you suffer, if he refuses to grow up, and if his toxicity is poisoning your inner soul and ego strength, then it is essential that you move on.

Why? You were born into this world as one of God's angels. You have all the potential to be great and evolved so that you may reach out to others to serve them. If your partner has made you feel weak, toxic, sick, unhealthy, afraid, small, lost, insignificant, or not good enough, then you must seek help to regain your personal sense of power. A good coach or therapist can help you with this.

Below is a copy of the article I wrote for the *Current* newspaper of South New Jersey. The editor told me he was running a health and fitness section, so I assumed he wanted me to write about the ingredients of a healthy relationship. He said, "No, instead I want you to address what happens to people's well-being if they are in an unhealthy relationship." That was easy; I deal with couples in toxic relationships all the time!

I had five calls that evening the article came out, with people saying, "Riana, you described my relationship perfectly, and I can't take this anymore! I need to see you immediately!" Here is a copy of the article:

Help! This Relationship Is Making Me Sick!

Is it true? Can your relationship make you physically ill? Absolutely! In "toxic relationships," our entire physical, emotional, and mental well-being is disturbed. This relationship makes you feel as if you're walking on eggshells or as if your partner is Dr. Jekyll and Mr. Hyde, as you never know *who* you're going to get! If you have intense fear when your partner walks through the door and you wonder if he will be drinking, ignoring you all night, screaming and lashing out in anger, or ridiculing or blaming you, then you are in a toxic relationship.

Over time, negative stress releases toxins throughout our bodies. When we are being abused, our bodies go into fight-or-flight mode. Eventually, the immune system wears down, which makes it difficult to fight off colds, flu, and other diseases; this could bring hidden viruses to the surface like Epstein-Barr virus or chronic fatigue syndrome.

Other physical ailments can include migraines, stomachaches, and extreme fatigue. Those in toxic relationships suffer with symptoms of depression, anxiety, panic attacks, emotional withdrawal, and low self-esteem. These issues affect your ability to perform intellectually, socially, and professionally in the workplace. It can severely affect your ability to parent well.

Another form of toxic relationship is one with a commitment-phobe. Such a person is initially very charming, romantic, and pleasing, but the moment you get too connected, this person panics and either starts sabotaging the relationship with irrational arguments or flees altogether. He soon resurfaces and begs for forgiveness, using tears, flowers, or other tactics to win you back. It is a vicious cycle, and the innocent partner rarely wins.

The mentally healthy partner often becomes consumed by analyzing what she did wrong and worries about how to improve herself and make her partner less angry. She tries to do anything to get back the addictive sexual passion these relationships have initially.

Can such a relationship be fixed? Each person brings into a relationship dynamics from the past. Much depends on how his parents raised him and whether he was a child of an alcoholic or suffered other trauma or abuse; this all plays a part. The abusive partner must enter into psychotherapy to examine his past and what he must do to fix his dysfunctional habits and faulty coping mechanisms.

However, often the toxic partner refuses counseling because he doesn't think he is doing anything wrong. This denial is extremely strong and can last throughout his adult life. He may enter counseling for a brief period of time, just to win the partner back after an affair. But rarely will the partner change his basic abusive tendencies, and the dysfunction is bound to cycle again.

The partner who was originally healthy but now feels *she* is going insane has two choices: either to enter into therapy herself to learn appropriate ways of dealing with the abusive partner, or she must love herself more and become strong enough to move on to a new, healthier, more peaceful, and loving relationship.

* * *

An ideal relationship is one where both partners have full lives of their own; one partner is not overly dependent on the other as a source of happiness. When you become codependent on another person, you look to him to make you happy. Happiness and a sense of self-esteem can only come from within, when you develop and nurture your spiritual purpose and you do the work to further that purpose.

If, for example, you have to work a nine-to-five job to support your family, and it is not a job that you particularly like, then you have two options: do volunteer work to fulfill your spiritual purpose or, during your off time, work toward a new career that will meet your spiritual purpose and support you at the same time.

What does your work have to do with relationships? A lot! Our work takes up more than half of our waking hours each day.

If we are miserable at work, or if we become workaholics to ignore the unhappiness of our lives, our relationships greatly suffer. Remember, inner peace and happiness is also about balance; it's about being each other's comfort at the end of a day.

It is important to be one another's best friend to share our hopes and dreams, to celebrate our accomplishments, and to discuss our fears during the tough times. But do *not* look to your partner to solve your troubles, take away your challenges, control your decisions, tell you what you can or cannot do, or rescue you from your daily unhappiness. That is *your* responsibility, and if you need help, get it.

Where do you find such an evolved partner? Let me be the first to tell you, it's very difficult! Spiritual wisdom says, "Become the person who you want to attract in life, and when you become that person, your partner will come." In the process of your own personal growth, and as you become more evolved, you will find many suitors who do not seem quite right for you, so you must be patient.

Here is an activity to try that will help explain this:

Write down all the qualities and characteristics you hope to have in a partner. Make a long list. After the list is done, prioritize it from most important to least important.

Now, when you are done with the list, ask yourself, "How many of these qualities do I have myself that I can offer a partner?" If you want a financially well-off partner, do you have savings and are you out of debt yourself? If you want someone who is fit, are you in good physical shape yourself? If you desire someone attractive, do you dress appealingly and groom yourself well? If you want a spiritual person, are you spiritual yourself? If you want someone who will appreciate and love your children, are you able to love his?

When I was single in my 40s, I initially thought I could date a man who had never married or had children. I soon discovered, after dating several men without children, that some had this sense of entitlement and selfishness—a "me mentality"—that I found very overwhelming. I don't think it was anything they did consciously; it was more that they knew nothing different.

They hadn't learned about the unconditional love that a parent has for his child, and they lacked the ability to negotiate a decision so both parties could win. They hadn't learned the incredible need to be patient, as a good parent is with his child. They hadn't experienced the incredible responsibility it takes to raise a child, nor did they understand the unending sacrifices it takes to make a child feel happy and secure.

I learned that I must look for a man who was a father and who took his parental responsibilities as seriously as I did. I do not mean to say that those without children are selfish; many do get involved with charities and in helping children who are not their own. Those single people who teach, coach, or work in some capacity with children, the sick, or the elderly do learn a sense of unconditional love and patience also.

Define your list of what you feel you will need in your potential partner. You should have this list memorized, so that when you see a red flag emerge, you can talk about it with your partner or stop dating that person altogether. For example, if honesty is a character trait at the top of your list, and you catch your partner in a lie, you must discuss it immediately. If you discover a significant lie, you must immediately drop that partner, because dishonesty is habitual and a very toxic quality.

An example of a significant lie occurred after one of my best girlfriends had been dating a man for a while. Into the fourth month, he called her to meet him at the park. Sitting on this 52-year-old man's lap was an infant. My friend asked, "Whose baby is this?"

He responded, "Mine." This eight-month-old was his! He had been denying his own child! He had never told my friend he was a father of a newborn daughter. He also told her he hadn't had a significant relationship for close to 10 years. Later, he said he'd been engaged to the mother of the baby and had lived with her for nine years. My girlfriend felt so deceived, and rightfully so.

She called to ask my opinion on this, and I said that he was such a good liar, she could never trust him again. This man said he hadn't told her because he was afraid she wouldn't give him a chance. He was so selfish that he took away my friend's ability to *choose* whether she wanted to date a man with a newborn baby. At 52, she did not. She was looking for a partner to retire and travel with, which he'd known from day one. More importantly, she wanted a man who she could trust!

Chemistry and Love Addiction

Is chemistry for another person a real thing? Absolutely! When you feel chemistry, you know it. Your heart races, you sweat a bit, your breath deepens, and your body reacts sexually when you think of your partner. The feeling shoots through your whole body. Chemistry happens in an instant, usually beginning when you first look at one another. The world stops, and nothing else matters.

Attraction to another is formed quite early in life. Research indicates that between the ages of approximately five to eight, the person a child has her first crush on becomes her type for life; this is called a "love map." Think about it; you can probably recall the first and last name of your first crush. A boy often prefers his mother's eye color, hair color, and skin tones, and a daughter prefers her father's coloring. I know my love map still applies to me!

Chemistry is really L-Phenylalanine (PEA), an amino acid that is released throughout the brain and body. Dopamine and serotonin levels rise when you are sexually excited. Sexuality does begin in the brain, even though beauty is in the eye of the beholder. These "love chemicals" are released throughout the infatuation stage, which scientists say is enough time for a man and woman to connect and perpetuate the human race. How long is that stage? It can last for just the first meeting, and it can also last a lifetime.

I had a relationship where the rush was instant. We started dating, and three years into the relationship, he was still blushing when I met him, as it was obvious he was happy to see me! The sexual chemistry never went away for me either. It was one of the hardest relationships for me to get over. When that relationship ended suddenly, I was just numb. The tears just flowed, and I felt like I was dying. Emotionally, I was. I had to call off work for two days, and as I lay there taking some time to think and mourn the loss of the relationship, I also prayed for strength to move on. Eventually I did, and I know I am better for it. I had to reinvent myself once more using the Watch Me! mind-set and create new goals to start a new life without him. Soon after, I began to write this book.

How do you move on from a relationship in which there is still so much chemistry? Usually, something else extremely severe gets in the way, to the point where all that is left is the sexual chemistry. There is normally some form of abuse, either self-abuse or abuse directed toward you, the healthy partner. My ex-boyfriend developed a drinking problem, his work ethic suffered, and he lost his pride and ego strength. He began to tell me that "I frightened him" because I had such personal confidence and power. I didn't understand that. How could I have frightened him when we were so close, had become best friends, and had dated for three years?

What I had to admit was that his ego was not strong enough, and he was not a father either, so he could not understand my leaving town to help my child, Alexi, fulfill her dreams. He looked upon it as my leaving him for good, not temporarily as I had seen it. I will always love him as a friend, and for what we shared together. I was going through a very tough time when we met right after my second marriage, and he was the strong one at first. The trouble with the relationship began when I started to personally overcome my financial obstacles and I finally got ahead. When I became strong, he became weak, even though I tried to help him by confirming my love in many ways.

Eventually I needed to realize I could not change him. I could not convince him that we would be okay. I had to understand that *he* was not all right within himself; I could not help him stop his destructive habits or become stronger, as I had no control over his sense of ego or personal happiness. I had to release him with love and move forward in my life.

It must be clear that we are not responsible for another person's happiness or ego strength. We cannot "make" anyone do or feel anything. They must feel emotionally good, be confident, or have a strong ego for themselves. In many relationships where chemistry and passion is a priority, the strong attraction and fabulous sex are the last element to go if there are other problems. But eventually, a couple discovers that their relationship cannot last with just passion alone.

There is such a thing as sexual addiction to a person. The L-Phenylalanine (PEA) rush is so strong that any withdrawal of love feels like a heavy crash, and often a severe depression sets in because all the feel-good chemicals have stopped flowing throughout the brain and body. Not only PEA, but also dopamine and serotonin levels crash because the love partner (who causes the high) is suddenly gone from your life. These chemicals explain why so many people return to their lovers even when they know the relationship is terribly dysfunctional. They have a hard time enduring the pain of the withdrawal, the crash of internal chemicals. This will go away in time, but in any addiction, going cold turkey is difficult.

Many theories suggest that love addiction is the hardest addiction to overcome. When the chemical rush is flowing through the brain and body, you can't think of anything else. You awaken thinking of your partner and think of him throughout the day and when you go to bed. Little things remind you of him, and you find yourself smiling over these thoughts. Just thinking of him sends your body into an excited sexual state. You yearn for him, want to talk to him, see him again, touch him, and make love to him.

If parents think their teenagers cannot experience such a strong love, they are dead wrong. There is no such thing as puppy love. Teenagers' hormones are already in an excited, growing state, so a love interest becomes incredibly addictive for them. A girlfriend or boyfriend becomes their whole world. Remember that kind of love? Never negate a child's pain over a breakup. It is severe for him!

How do you recover from love addiction? You can use the basic techniques of the Watch Me! mind-set. Although everyone is different, these suggestions may work for you:

1. See a relationship coach or therapist to discuss your past relationship patterns and why you may have difficulties moving on. Therapists should examine your childhood history to see if you are an adult child of trauma or an

alcoholic (ACOA) and if you have suffered from abuse, abandonment issues, or other patterns that you are trying to fix in this current relationship.

2. Stay busy! Start focusing on you again. Of course, you should never lose sight of your own personal needs, growth, and accomplishments during a relationship in the first place. If you have, know that this is part of the problem. Join a gym, take up a new hobby or sport, try going out to new places, make new friends, or start a new career or improve a current one.

3. Bond closely with your girlfriends or guy friends. Never drop your friends because you are in a new relationship; you must still make time to be with them too. If you have a breakup, they will be there for you. Ask if you can call them for extra support, encouragement, and feedback.

4. Read a lot of books on how to gain spiritual strength and self-control. I recommend many of them in my References and Recommended Reading section and on my Web site, www.RianaMilne.com. Audiobooks or CDs are excellent for your commute to work, helping to put you into a positive frame of mind before you start your workday.

5. Redecorate your home. Clean it thoroughly, and make it peaceful and serene. Eliminate harsh lighting by adding dimmers, buy some beautiful bedding, use aromatherapy, and buy fresh flowers weekly. Plant flowers in your garden. Buy beautiful music that is relaxing to you. One of my favorite artists is Luis Miguel; I don't understand a word of his Spanish love songs, but they are so relaxing yet energizing to me.

6. Travel alone or with a good friend. Traveling alone forces you to make new friends with people you don't already know. It forces you to get out of your shell and experience other cultures, food, and new environments. Also, you will have the quiet time you need to mediate or write, whether it's a journal or a book. Journaling is a great way to explore your feelings and help yourself to heal.

7. Try speed dating, singles groups, or online dating. My daughter Stephana met her amazing husband Charles on Match. com. I have heard some disappointing stories about online dating, and I believe many people are burning out from this type of approach, as there has been so much deceit, as well as serial dating, going on. However, it will get you into the practice of dating again. Just be careful, follow online safety rules, and take things slow; don't rush into another relationship. Be sure to get a last name and Google search that person to find out more information. Tell a friend his name, phone number and online name before you meet.

8. Meditate in nature. Walk on the beach or in the woods, or take a drive in the country while listening to some good jazz music. (The feeling of the wind blowing on my face and through my hair while driving my convertible gives me an incredible sensation of freedom and peace of mind, which is my "therapy.") Stop for an afternoon glass of wine in the warm sun. Take a good book and relax. Nothing feels better or more serene.

Healing Relationships

We all need time to be alone. Our alone time revitalizes and replenishes us, and helps restore our internal balance. Solitude is necessary for meditation on necessary changes and how to best go about them. But when our intention is to hide from the world, withdraw from others, feed an addiction, or refuse to make changes necessary for growth, too much isolation is not physically, spiritually, or mentally healthy.

Hiding can be a form of procrastination, and it removes us from actively living our lives and dealing with our problems. Fear often immobilizes us, but pushing ourselves to deal with our problems instead of isolating ourselves and procrastinating is one of the best gifts we can give ourselves. Isolation should be used for meditation, rest, and rejuvenation we need for the changes imperative for personal growth. In this way, isolation can empower your personal success in work and relationships.

Analyze and contemplate where your relationships are with your partner, children, friends and family. Who do you need to forgive from deeds done in the past? Who have you neglected or harmed in some way? Who deserves a phone call, e-mail, or letter just to let them know you are thinking of them? Who have you hesitated to tell, "I love you," or "You mean so much to me"? Examine each of your relationships and do what you must to achieve inner peace.

Following a conflict, have a friendly, loving, honest, and open discussion with your partner. Tell him how you are feeling using "I feel" messages instead of blaming statements like, "You did," or "You made me feel." Start by saying you love him but are concerned about what you have been feeling lately. Ask if this is a good time to talk, and if not, could he schedule some time to do so. Begin your discussion with two of the wonderful traits your partner has, and the reasons you chose to marry him or be with him exclusively. This will help him drop his defenses, as usually his fears put him in a defensive mode. When you are done talking, ask what you might have done to hurt his feelings or disappoint him in some way. Hear him out and really listen.

When you both have had your chance to tell your side of the story, try to empathize with what he has told you by placing yourself in his shoes. Explain that you understand how your actions would make him feel and then apologize.

If the discussion leads to an argument, or if your partner raises his voice, ask if he would like to take a break and discuss the topic again later, after you both have had time to reflect on the issues. If you feel heated, go take a walk to help relieve the stress. Let your thoughts fly free in your mind. As you calm down, look for the good from the bad, and remember all the wonderful qualities your partner has. Remember why you married him and what it was like in the beginning for the two of you.

With this in mind, revisit the conversation with love, not fear. Stay calm and control the volume and tone of your voice. Remember, it takes two people to yell and have an argument. If you refuse to get upset, there will be no argument, but if you both cannot solve the issue, do seek a relationship coach or couples counselor.

Teach your partner the techniques in this book. Better yet, buy him a copy for a gift of love. Tell your partner that your relationship means the world to you, and it is important for you both to be working toward an evolved relationship.

The elements of this relationship include communicating openly with trust, and having emotional safety, a deep and lasting friendship, respect, honesty, and compassion. All are essential qualities in experiencing a love life with a common and higher purpose.

Use the Watch Me! mind-set and the techniques to always approach your partner in a loving, calm, and peaceful way, and be determined to settle for nothing less in return!

There is a reading I include in every one of my wedding ceremonies that I think is a perfect way to end this chapter on love and the evolved couple. It is a shortened summary from the Letter of Paul to the Corinthians, from the Bible:

> Love is very patient and kind, never jealous or envious, never boastful or proud, never haughty or selfish or rude. Love does not demand its own way. It is not irritable or touchy. It does not hold grudges and will hardly even notice when others do wrong. It is never glad about injustice, but rejoices whenever truth wins out.
>
> If you love someone you will be loyal to him. You will always believe in him, always expect the best of him, and always stand your ground in defending him. Love goes on forever. There are three things that are most important—faith, hope, and love—and the greatest of these is love.

If you love your partner and want a lifelong loving relationship, live a faith-based life of integrity, honesty, peace, and balance. Never stop dating and romancing each other, and never take the other person for granted. Cherish him as the treasure he truly is.

Chapter 9

For Parents: Raising Successful Children and Teens by Teaching the Watch Me! Mind-set

M ORE OFTEN THAN NOT, parents walk their teenagers into my therapy office and say, "Fix my kid—he's driving me crazy!" I first talk to the parents and hear their horror stories of how their teenager has wreaked havoc in their home. I sit there listening politely and ask questions to clarify. Then I bring in the teen, "the culprit," and ask his side of the story. Below is an example of how the Watch Me! mind-set and principals can help families such as these.

I immediately tell the teen, (let's call him Tim), that I am on his side. I can tell by listening and watching the parents that they are angry at each other. They sit on opposite sides of the room; the mother's body language is very tense and closed, and the father has a hard time looking me in the eye.

Very often, the mother is submissive and the father is authoritarian, overly strict, and domineering with the entire family. I ask Tim if there is a lot of anger in the house. He replies, "Yes, they scream at each other, and they scream at me all the time. I never do anything right, they put down my friends, they ground me for everything, they are on my case the minute I get home from school, and they spoil my younger sister, who in their eyes never does anything wrong!"

No wonder Tim is so angry and rebellious; he's the only one who has the guts to say that something is wrong with this family! I tell him that I understand why he is angry, and ask if he will work with me to help educate his parents in living a different way. He is surprised I am not lecturing him and telling him he is out of line. I show him respect and commend him for sharing his feelings with me. I ask Tim what he would like to see changed, and at first, the answer is always, "I don't know," which he says with a lack of hope and a sense of defeat.

Then he blurts out, "I'd like to have time with my friends. I want my parents to trust me and get off my back. I want them to stop bugging me about my grades and homework. I want them to stop putting me down for how I dress and the music I like to listen to."

"Okay, we can do this," I say encouragingly. "One, you have to get them back here each week, and two, you have to trust that I am on your side. Can you do that?" If he agrees to do this, then this family will move forward and be able to change.

I tell him, "When I am in with your parents, we are not talking about how bad you are; I am often telling them what they must change in how they parent you, okay? There is a lot of parenting education going on in these sessions. Sometimes, I may rarely talk to you, but your being here is part of the change." Tim agrees.

186

When I bring the parents back in, they are expecting me to agree with them that their son is totally defiant and out of control. Instead, I ask how their marital relationship is. I ask if there is a lot of anger and yelling in the home. Dad responds that "everything is fine—there isn't much yelling."

Mom, gathering her courage, negates this. "There is a lot of yelling. John yells at me, and then Tim. The yelling starts as soon as John gets home. I try to keep the peace and get Tim doing his homework, and Tim says I am all over his case." She is. Mom takes her frustration out on Tim because she is too afraid to confront her husband.

Further probing reveals that John drinks too much alcohol, and is a child of an abusive father. John emotionally and verbally abuses Mary, the mom, and he hit her on two occasions long ago when the kids were young.

Her heart grew cold then, but she felt stuck in a marriage with two young children, so she became submissive in order to tolerate her situation. John feels his wife doesn't love him anymore because she is no longer interested in sex; this makes him angry and emotionally and verbally abusive, and he turns to alcohol.

Often abuse runs through the generations, and Tim has already turned to alcohol and drugs to escape from all the anger in his house. He admits to me he smokes a little pot and drinks occasionally. His parents aren't sure if he is using. John defends Tim by insisting that, "all teens drink a little alcohol."

Welcome to family therapy. It is *never* about fixing just the child or teenager; it is about reparenting the whole family and rebuilding the marital relationship. If your children are acting out in defiance, then something is wrong with the family system. I understand that children do not come with "care labels" when they are born, and the majority of us did not get any education on how to create healthy and happy kids. Parenting is a tough job.

I have worked in many schools, with kindergarten students through 12th graders, as a student assistance counselor (SAC). It is the counselor who sees the emotionally upset, bullying, angry, or acting-out defiant student. This is the only position within the schools that has federal confidentiality protection. Children can come to me with their concerns about themselves or their families, which will be held in confidence unless I must report the information to the Division of Youth and Family Services (DYFS) because the child is in danger. Children share a lot of the information about how their parents are abusing him, or about their fears when their parents drink too much and then fight. Needless to say, I make many DYFS calls for the child's protection.

What I hear within my office sickens me. Parents and grandparents abuse their children by hitting them with belts, switches (tree branches), or electrical cords; I even had two brothers in one school whose grandmother hit them on their genitals with metal trucks. Dad is often nowhere to be found, Mom is a drug addict who ran off with her addict boyfriend and became homeless, and this aging, sick grandmother has been left to raise the mom's three young boys, the first two diagnosed with ADHD.

As an SAC, I held many groups for all grade levels and during one of the girls' friendship groups, a student raised the concern that her dad was in jail. Slowly, all five girls shared that they had a relative in jail. These girls were known to be defiant and troublesome in the classroom, often the bullies picking on other children.

So the group wasn't just about friends getting together; it was also about teaching these girls *how* to be a friend and not a bully. So many children have dysfunctional lives at home that they must return to every day. One boy shared with me that he watched his stepdad cut up "the white powder" that Mom has to take around to "their friends" every day. This young child is dressed in the finest hip-hop designer clothes, but he is smart enough to tell me what his parents are doing is wrong!

Parents can be very quick to blame the schools for not teaching their children properly. I see how hard the teachers work day after day in every school I've been employed in. Almost every teacher I worked with was excellent, and the parents have no idea how loving and concerned they are about each child. As the SAC, I was called upon to help children with critical emotional and mental health issues. Two different children I had in one school year were caught playing with their own feces in their classroom bathroom, with one smearing them on the desk.

There was a third-grade girl who still messed in her pants. Another student's well-known PTA mom, reeking of alcohol, picked up her daughter from school intoxicated. The little girl told me that Mom and Dad scared her when they drank, and that Mom drove drunk with all the kids in the car. I had another elementary-school child who induced vomiting for several weeks up to six times in one day to gain attention and to try to go home.

I had kids defiantly telling their teachers, "Shut up," and "You can't make me!" An elementary boy who moved schools every year had entered our school angry and looking to fight. He came in from a tough LA inner-city environment, Compton, and had witnessed several murders on his street. Another young child looked extremely evil and emotionally vacant when her mood changed to angry. Schizophrenic? Possibly. She was referred to a mental health hospital, and they did put her on medication.

All this occurred in one suburban New Jersey, K–6 elementary school. I was laid off, along with ten other district SAC counselors, when the schools lost their funding for us crisis counselors. My students were in tears when they heard I would not be there for them the following year and my teachers were extremely concerned. Many children often do not feel safe in our world, in their neighborhoods, in their home, or with their parents; and many come into school very angry.

School districts fund football teams, but they won't fund the desperately needed SAC counselors. And without the children having the emotional support they need to function, these schools will fail to perform academically every year. It frustrates me that no one at the district or government level is smart enough to see the correlation. SAC counselors should be mandatory for every school!

I had a 16-year-old girl in a north New Jersey high school go home on a Friday afternoon to find that her whole family had moved out on her. The electricity had been cut off, and the food was gone. All that was left were her things in her bedroom. The new stepmom, the father explained to me, didn't like his daughter, as she had her own children. This student's mom was in another country, Jamaica, and her dad was raising her. He said she got too out of control and was old enough to raise herself now. I found a shelter for her with the help of the DYFS's attorney in Bergen County; I had to go to the top to get immediate action.

This is what is happening in our schools today, and our government officials are worried about New Jersey Assessment of Skills and Knowledge (NJ Ask) and High School Proficiency Assessment (HSPA) scores? What about the wars in our homes and on our streets, the ones our children and teens are fighting each day when they go home?

Even if certain children within the classroom have "normal" families (less than 50 percent of families have both parents at home, so two-parent families are no longer the norm), these children are still affected by the angry, mentally ill children that are in their classrooms. All these children want is love, respect, safety, and someone who cares.

They melt like butter when they are with me because they know "Ms. Riana cares." I listen, I try to help, and I am real with them. They know I think children are brilliant and talented, and I do my best to teach them to believe in themselves. However, I can only imagine what these troubled children go home to each day. It is distressing for me; I see their hope and smiles in my office, yet I also witness their angry meltdowns, defiant lack of respect, and temper tantrums that can be triggered almost instantly.

My male student from Compton ended up being an excellent dancer. Last year, I took all the frequently suspended kids and formed a dance troupe. They put together a dance routine with my help, and we practiced during recess time. They were to perform for their entire grade. I had one rule: if they got suspended again, they could not perform. We started with nine students; only one student didn't make it. He still hung with us, though. When the dance troupe did perform, they got incredible cheers not only from their classmates, but also from all the other children in the school who had witnessed their dress rehearsal the day before. When they were done, the observers rushed the stage to high-five them. My dance troupe was amazed; all of a sudden they realized, they were a hit and had a talent that others enjoyed. The other kids liked them!

I'd always felt there is nothing like the creative and performing arts to raise children's self-esteem, and my master's thesis project had proved it. The dance performance was the beginning of the talent club I created, which was held for three years after the original performance. It was an honor to be part of the club, and we had about 24 acts for each show. The kids were on TV and in the newspaper, and they felt like stars in their school and communities. The once-angry, acting-out kids were now the talented, fun kids who others admired! Kids wanted to be their friends, and they began taking a leadership role in their school, watching out for the other kids. The turnaround in their behavior was amazing!

I feel that competitive team sports are not as good for a child's self-esteem as performing is. Why do I feel that way? When I was in sports, although I had a record in the Penn State Hall of Fame for swimming (100-meter breaststroke), I never felt I was good enough. As a child, my swimming times were always compared to those of the other kids, and I was repeatedly told I wasn't doing my best. My two brothers excelled at swimming and water polo and became an All-American. This is fantastic for them, and I am proud of their success, but I felt like a mere shadow growing up in between them. Children do compare themselves with their siblings, so find something for each child that they can excel at and that will fuel their self-esteem.

Within a family system, to handle household dysfunction, the children often take on many different roles: the family hero, the mascot, the victim, the rebel, the scapegoat, and the little lost child. There are other roles, but these are the best-known ones in family systems psychology. I felt like the lost child, the quiet and shy one who held her feelings deep inside, expressing them only in my poetry and other writing.

It wasn't until I won a $500 scholarship to modeling school in the eighth grade that I felt that I could do something well. I poured my heart out into that essay, and I remember one of the judges telling me I really had the gift to write. In modeling school, you only compete with yourself and your own growth. My self-esteem rose, and I started modeling for various Philadelphia department stores and then did promotional work for the top Philadelphia radio station. By age 15, I was working with celebrities and loved it. There was some competition with auditions, but no one in the business criticized me or told me I wasn't good enough if I didn't get the part. I felt great just being my best self.

To this day, I hate to compete and dislike team sports. I only inspire my own individual growth and encourage others to do the same. In team sports, usually only one to five kids excel per team and get the coaches' attention and accolades from the other students. In field hockey, I played fullback but often didn't get to play. I remember feeling so dejected at not being chosen; I hated it.

I was excellent at disco dancing, another individual, creative activity that my family rarely came to watch. My first husband and I were the runner-up in the PA State Disco Dance Competition in 1980. We had no set routine; the music just told us what to do as we flew around the dance floor in romantic unison. I remember my parents coming to watch the state competitions. It was the first time they saw me compete in dance, and they were quite amazed at my talent for performing. So parents, if your kids are not athletically inclined, don't force them to play a team sport just because you did! It could hurt their pride and self-esteem, and set the course for later failures. Instead, introduce them to individual sports such as tennis, golf, dance, or karate.

As for those kids who enjoy team sports, you should encourage them, but don't become an obsessed parent on the sidelines. Parents who force their kids into hours of practice, whether it is for cheerleading, basketball, baseball, or football, may see their child come to hate the sport. It is the same with practicing a musical instrument. After playing the piano for eight years for 45 minutes every day, I came to hate it. I begged my dad to let me quit, and when I finally did, I never played again for years. I now own a black baby grand, and I would love to play again for enjoyment. I have such a mental block, though, that I cannot play one song! I do intend to teach myself to play again.

Parents who force their children to do anything are harming their mental well-being. And those who try to live their lives vicariously through their children or who look for personal self-esteem through their children's accomplishments are causing them great harm. Of course, I love to see my daughters succeed, and when Alexi told me she wanted to quit singing in 2004 to focus on acting and modeling, it nearly broke my heart. After all we had been through together to get her singing career off the ground, and she was really doing well with it! But I would never force her, and I said I respected her decision.

I told her I thought she was really good at it, and I hope she will revisit it one day again. But her happiness was more important to me, and I wanted her to follow her own path. Even more significantly, I never wanted to lose our very special and close mother-daughter bond.

We have to trust and respect our children. We have to be real with them, talk openly about our feelings, apologize to them when we make a mistake, and treat them like the treasures that they are.

Ideally, you should start the techniques I offer below when your children are very young to build resilience, emotional intelligence, and survival skills over their lifetime. However, you can also start at the age they are now. I got many of my ideas from reading about parenting and from books that taught how to inspire the love of learning in children. I am also going to share what worked so well with my children. These suggestions will help you to cultivate a very positive and loving relationship with your children early in life, which will last as they grow and mature.

The Early Years: Birth to Age Five

1. Talk to your children often when they newborn, as if they understand you. Be expressive.

2. Play lots of music in your home and watch TV rarely. Dance and exercise to music with your baby. Sing, laugh, and play together with educational games and toys. Put your children in a playpen rarely—I used them for the kids' toys, not the children! Buy them chairs and swings that move to encourage exercise.

3. Take them out for daily walks and exploration. Talk to them about what you see—flowers, trees, birds, animals, and everything. Babies' brains are like sponges; they learn so much and grasp everything. Instill a sense of adventure; take them shopping, to nature parks, for car rides, and to the beach. Act as if they are much older, not infants who don't know anything. The more you talk, the more quickly they will learn and talk back to you.

4. Read to them a few times a day with a dramatic and excited voice. They will learn that reading is a fun game and an exciting thing to do.

5. Read the many books offered from *The Glen Doman Method of Education*. I read several of the books while I was pregnant 30 years ago. They were about teaching children who had brain damage how to learn. Their methods worked so well with these children that they began studies using the methods with normally functioning children. Use your computer search engine to get the most up-to-date information on this method of learning. In 1982, what I read made sense to me, so I gave their methods a try. I went to the Better Baby Institute (now called the Institute for the Achievement of Human Potential) and training center in Wyndmoor, PA, and bought the supplies the books suggested. You can buy

the items online today at www.iahp.org. I purchased the math dot cards, reading strips with words printed in red, and cards with inventors' pictures on them. They said to treat learning like a game, to start slowly and simply and give lots of praise for any learning the child does. It should never be forced upon the child or used as a punishment. Learning must be fun! Here's what I did:

a. Start with a large word strip and the word the child knows you by ("Mommy" and "Daddy"). Add the family pet's name, "Grandmom," "Granddad," and any sibling. These are the words the child hears often, and they are associated with love. Show the cards one at a time and say the word excitedly. Do this twice a day, but only if you can make it fun (if you do it grudgingly, it won't work). Soon, your child will be asking you to play "the word game." Slowly add in other cards with harder words. My children were reading Sesame Street and Dr. Seuss books by the age of two—trust me, *this works!* Your child will be happy to have playtime with you, and as you praise him for learning the words and repeating them to you, he will feel a sense of pride from learning. This is all established many years before the child sets foot in school, and the love of learning lasts a lifetime!

b. When he has conquered about 30 words, move on to the math game. There are square cards with red dots on them. Start with the first five cards. Simply show the card, and say, "There is one red dot—one." Go to the card with two dots, and continue. They have cards up to 100. Your child is absorbing the numbers in his mind and learning to visualize them. Progress to math games with simple adding. I remember taking trips to Grandma's Shore house and playing math games. At age five and six, my girls understood the concept of negative numbers, addition, and subtraction. Then they learned multiplication, all through these math games.

6. If you can speak a second language, do it. Children learn languages much more easily when taught young. Do not speak it in place of English, however, because they need to learn their English first.

7. No matter how many hours you work, schedule quality time with your kids outside of your home. We traveled to Pittsburgh, Cleveland, Buffalo, and Toronto, Canada, for day or overnight trips when we lived in Erie. After moving to Philadelphia, we regularly went to the zoo, parks, the Please Touch Museum, and the Franklin Institute. We loved those day trips! The children came to expect an adventure each weekend. Friday night was pizza and movie night with me, or they could have a guest sleep over. Saturday or Sunday was adventure day, but Saturday night was Mom's date night. I scheduled myself a break and explained it was important for my happiness to have time with my boyfriend. They understood and came to accept this. A happier mom, especially a single mom, makes happier children.

8. Turn off the TV, but if children do watch it, they should watch fun, educational shows. My children loved *Sesame Street* when they were young, so they watched that. As they got older, I told them they could watch creative shows.

MTV had just come out, and they loved watching the young singers and dancers. My girls grew up hearing a lot of R & B, dance music, jazz, and classical music. I did play some popular rock but didn't like heavy metal or punk music myself, so they didn't hear that. One of their favorite activities was to watch a music video, practice the dance together, and then ask me to film them. They had great fun watching the tape back on the VCR. I still have those tapes today. Obviously, Alexi's early acting, singing, and dancing fun became one of her future talents and chosen career.

9. Encourage your children to go out and play. My children built forts, created a play and sold tickets to the neighbors, went fishing at the creek, played kickball, rode bikes, and played hide-and-seek. Remember all those games? They teach social skills and the art of negotiation. If kids tried to cheat or got out of line, the group would encourage them to knock it off, and they did. Today you rarely see children playing in groups outside. What a shame!

10. Enroll your children early in school. I enrolled my girls in the Montessori program from age three through kindergarten, which I would highly recommend. Between what I had taught them before preschool and what they learned in Montessori school from ages three to five, they had already excelled before entering first grade. Early on, they qualified for the talented and gifted program. All it took was *my* time and dedication to my children's future growth. What you do from birth to age five is critical in establishing your child's future success. Those who think learning begins with kindergarten are really hampering their child's intellectual progress and future success.

How do you handle temper tantrums in such young children? Know the causes of the outburst. It could be hunger, emotional overload, fatigue, or their frustration at not being able to tell you why they are upset. All parents have been in the grocery market when their child has had a tantrum. I think it is part of parenthood, and it is frightfully embarrassing! Try to have someone watch the kids when you shop, or choose to shop early in the morning when they are at their best. Have them "help you" look for things, talk to them constantly, and ask their opinion; all this helps to keep them occupied. If the child still breaks down, stay calm and leave the store if you can, or just continue through the checkout line as you pray for peace. Talk slowly and quietly, as sometimes they stop so they can hear you. Take comfort in knowing that *all* moms and dads have been through this!

Ages Five to Fifteen: The Continuation of Positive Parenting

It is said that from birth to age 11, a child's basic personality and ability to learn and succeed has already been established. These are critical years. Although my children suffered from my divorce to their father at ages four and five, they still excelled. As a young single mom who was forced to pay child support on a very limited income, I had to work several jobs and lots of hours to make ends meet. Nonetheless, I still scheduled our quality time, and I made sure to emphasize the following:

1. *Travel.* We traveled every year to NYC to see at least one Broadway show. I wanted my daughters to see different parts of the world, so they would not be afraid to move wherever they chose. I let them help choose our trip and plan it. When I bought a time-share, I had the children pick

their trip first. Alexi chose Hawaii and Stephana wanted to go to Paris. We did travel to both of those places, as well as to Key West, Cancun several times, Monte Carlo, Nice, St. Tropez, and various American cities by the time they were 16. For Stephana's graduation gift, I bought her a seven-country tour of Europe that included London, Venice, Florence, and other cities. As soon as Alexi started singing and touring at age 19, she went to South Africa, Paris, Amsterdam, Italy, Germany, Sweden, Tokyo, and over 30 other countries! At age 22, Stephana became a flight attendant and then worked her way up to become a supervisor and trainer with a major airline, so I guess I instilled the love of travel and adventure in both of them! I recently took my girls to Greece to learn about their heritage. I had promised them the trip while they were young, and I could finally give it to them. We visited the island of Crete and the city of Athens. I am proud to say they each have been to more countries than I have, all before the ages of 22 and 23.

2. *Classes and sports.* Enroll them in various classes and individual sports like art, dance, music, theater, karate, tennis, golf, and others. Encourage activities beyond school so that they have an opportunity to learn to make other friends of different ages. Introduce each class for a period of time. If they do not enjoy it, don't push them. Encourage them to continue for a while, but if they seem unhappy, introduce something new. It is important they have at least one activity outside of school.

3. *Honesty.* Teach children early on not to lie. Children lie because they are afraid to tell the truth. I taught my girls

that if they told me the truth, they would not be punished when they made a mistake. I expected them to apologize, and then we would talk about the lesson they learned. I have told them repeatedly that we all make mistakes, and they will too. The important thing is to be honest about it and learn from it. Before starting this method, they were quick to blame each other for a mistake made. Being only a year apart, they tried to get each other in trouble. When I started this method, I remember Stephana trying to make eggs in the microwave on a Sunday morning; she dropped the bowl on the kitchen floor and it broke. Instead of blaming Alexi, she came running in to wake me up to tell me the truth and was very proud that she did. Never scream at your children, especially when they tell you the truth!

4. *A star chart.* This is a *must!* I started this when the children were four and five, and it continued in my house through the teenage years. The chart showed five chores I wanted each of my girls to do, without my needing to remind them. If they did their chores each day (use a six-day week), they got a star in that row. At the end of the week, if they reached 24 stars, they got a reward of their choice. For a period of time, it was picking out a new Barbie doll outfit. The item shouldn't cost a lot of money, and the reward could be a family outing to a movie, bowling, a day at the zoo, and so on. They don't need to be perfect (we aren't as adults), so they can miss a few stars.

The secret behind the chart is that it needs to be *positive*, not negative in any way. I explained to my girls that adults go off to their jobs every day, and their job at their age was to do well at school. When we all are home, we work as a team, to keep our house together. We all have a part, we count on each other, and all of our parts are important. This teaches your children responsibility, respect for their abilities, that they are an important part of the family team, and that you expect them to excel and participate.

Here is a sample chart for your child, using no more than five to six chores:

	Monday	Tuesday	Wednesday	Thursday	Friday	Saturday
Feed the Dog						
Make your Bed						
Set Dinner Table						
Pick up Toys						
Do Homework						
Be Respectful						

In this sample week, there is a chance to earn 36 stars, as Sunday is a day off. Assuming some mistakes, with six daily chores, the child only needs to earn 30 stars, or 24 total stars for five chores a day. The chores are abbreviated on the chart, but explain exactly what you expect from your child to earn a star. With the examples above, your expectations could be as follows:

- Feed the dog after school by 4:00 p.m., make sure he has fresh water, and then let him out.

- Make your bed each day as soon as you wake up, before school.

- Help set the table with silver and plates, and bring your own dishes over to the sink when done with your dinner.

- Pick up your toys each night before bed and put them in your toy closet.

- Come home and start your homework by 4:30 p.m. without my asking, after your snack.

- No yelling at Mom, Dad, or sister; do what parents ask the first time.

Chores should be age appropriate; so for teens, you could call it an allowance chart, and the jobs could be as follows:

Once a week, do your laundry (Thursday), vacuum (Wednesday), clean your room (Friday afternoon), cut the grass (Saturday), take out the trash (Tuesday), and empty the dishwasher (Monday). Let your teen choose the day for each chore.

Friday should be "payday," so a chart should run Friday to Friday. Mark the chart at the end of each day so the child sees his progress and the parent won't forget if the chores were done. This way, a teen earns his allowance money by the weekend, and will not ask you for money to go to the movies, to buy CDs, etc. Change the charts from summertime to school time, and change the chores as your child matures.

5. *Limiting technology.* Don't buy many video game systems. Limit their recreational gaming time. Kids will survive without it, and actually do better for *not* having one. I refused to buy one for my girls, because I did not want

them to become addicted to the games or to TV. Watching too much TV can become an addiction; people tune out life by turning on the TV. A show here and there is fine, but to watch for hours every day is not a good thing. I see so many children withdrawing into their world of video games out of boredom, loneliness, or just to escape from their families. Over use of technology can be a full-fledged addiction for many teens and young adults. The same is true of e-mail, Facebook, IM, or Internet games. Cell phones have become the new computers, and texting has become the latest addiction for teens. Take your children's cell phones away before homework is done and before bed. Limit their time on the computer. I have had more than a few addicted clients in my office who went from being addicted to video games as children to being addicted to computer games, porn, or Internet gambling as adults. Many older people and parents are addicted to TV, watching hours of it a day. Please realize you shut your children and your spouse out emotionally when you tune into your shows. Believe me, children feel the loneliness of this addiction.

6. *Daily quiet time.* Give your kids time to "chill" upon getting home from school. They hate the 20 questions routine from Mom and Dad, and so did I. School, in case you've forgotten, is exhausting. Their days are a 15-hour workday. Teens are up by 6:00 a.m., start school by 7:45 a.m., end by 3:00 p.m., may have a sport or after-school activity for two hours (or for little ones, be in after-school programs until 6:00 p.m.), get home by 5:00 or 6:00 p.m., eat dinner, and then have two or more hours of homework, until 9:00 p.m. That is a long day, and they do it five days in a row! Try to

remember your exhaustion when you went to school. Do get off their case. Give them quiet time when they come home, and calmly be available if they want to talk. You'll get more communication by being loving and supportive, and not nagging them with lots of questions or demands. Try to catch up on quality time and communication over the weekends. Plan one weekend night as family night.

7. *Gentle discipline.* Don't scream at your children or hit them. This teaches nothing but abuse. Talk firmly to your children or sit down and calmly talk to them about what they did wrong. Explain to them why it is wrong or dangerous. Tell them you worry because you love them. Children should know ahead of time the consequences for a rule broken. Both the consequences and the rewards should be displayed near the star/allowance chart. (Remove a privilege for a week if they did not achieve 18 of 30 stars.)

8. *Participation in business.* Ask your teens to help you in business. I often asked my daughters about music I should use in a fashion show, how to choreograph a certain dance routine for my models, and what logo or slogan I should use on a brochure. Give them a choice about what promotional idea may work, and ask why they think the one they picked will work. Respect their insight and intelligence. Both my girls are excellent in marketing, public relations and running businesses because they have helped me in these areas since they were children. I had them in my office doing paperwork and filing since they were 11. Tell a child he can handle something, and watch—he will excel at it. Give him a chance! I still phone my girls for advice, and they call me for advice or an opinion also. This shows

the mutual respect we have always had. Teach them the skills to handle your business, whatever it is. Don't shut them out; take them to work often. My girls knew the names of over 80 models at my agency, and if they didn't know someone, they asked his name. I wanted to make sure they were socially confident and business savvy. If I didn't give them that opportunity, who would? What you teach them from birth through age 15 is what they will carry with them the rest of their lives.

My daughter Alexi chose not to go to college, and she landed the position of manager at a very upscale lounge in NYC, earning $40,000 a year at age 21. With her confidence, business savvy, hard work ethic, and ability to learn, she excelled at that position. She beat out numerous college graduates with either a BA or MA for the position. Stephana, at the age of 19, was manager of a large, successful restaurant in Santa Barbara, CA, earning a fabulous salary with only two years of college. She went on to work for Midnight Oil in their NYC corporate office, where she managed the inventory for over 23 upscale restaurants and lounges. Sending your child to college is no sure avenue to success, but teaching them the important Watch Me! life skills is essential to their success over their lifetime, no matter what they choose to do in their career.

9. *Expressing love.* Tell them *you love them* every day. Tell them often *you are proud of them*! Any time is a good time to tell your children these two things. Children want to please their parents; they want to be good and make you proud. With a defiant teen, find something she is good at and praise her! Let her know she is loved and important to you.

10. *Being a positive influence.* Children believe what they hear you say and model what you do. If you scream in the house, they scream. If you are demanding of them as children, as teens, they will be demanding of you. If you tell them they are losers—guess what?—they will become losers! Parents, *you* have all the power to raise terrific kids. Learn what to do. Read. Treat them with love and respect, listen to their concerns, and show them that you really care!

11. *Healing ruptured relationships.* If you are extremely unhappy in your marriage after trying marriage counseling over a period of time, get out. Children are often better off in a single-parent home that is loving and peaceful, than in an angry home where the parents constantly fight. Don't put your child in the middle of your divorce. Don't ask them to carry messages to their other parent, and don't put the other parent down in front of them. Trust me, this only backfires on you. I was constantly bashed to my children by their father, for years. I could only say to my girls, "I love you unconditionally, and always will. I will do the best I can for you. You are both very smart children, and one day you will see the truth that I love you very much." That was the best I could do. My children did see the truth during their mid-teens.

    Alexi ended up leaving her father's house completely at age 15, and Stephana left college and her dad's house in Erie to come to my home in New Jersey, and then with my help, went to California. Alexi healed that relationship only after her dad apologized to her, and Stephana chose to break all ties with him for several years. He finally did apologize to Stephana and then came to me to apologize. Our family members did a lot of healing, and today, things are easier. Be the parent. Admit your wrongdoing and make peace with your children. Do what it takes to make amends. If you want to lose your children emotionally, then enter into the divorce war with your spouse. The two adults should enter into counseling and mediation to make the divorce as peaceful and loving as possible, and keep your children out of it!

Discipline

Some parents will now ask, "What about discipline? You say not to yell, hit, or scream, so how can I discipline the older child?" What most people don't know is that the word discipline comes from the Bible and the word "disciple," and it means, "to teach." Discipline is a part of the positive parenting approach. We do need to teach our children self-control and to make wise choices.

Discipline teaches children appropriate behavior and important values, and it corrects a child's misbehavior. Effective discipline helps children learn how to the following:

- ◆ Exercise self-control at school and home
- ◆ Be responsible for themselves
- ◆ Respect limits and boundaries of adults and peers
- ◆ Make decisions that are in their best interests but don't violate others
- ◆ Acquire a sense of security
- ◆ Understand the consequences of bad behavior

The most effective discipline helps children learn from the results of their actions while preserving their self-respect. It minimizes power struggles and allows for the possibility of compromise. It is important to be firm, fair, and consistent. *Avoid physical punishment.* Here are the dangers of using abusive physical punishment on your child:

1. You teach your child it is okay to control others by using intimidation and physical force, thus creating a child who is violent to others.

2. It is more likely your child will be rebellious toward you when he reaches adolescence. Abused children often are substance abusers as teens; teenage girls often engage in risky sexual behaviors.

3. You can seriously harm your child, possibly face criminal charges, and lose custody.

4. You make it less likely that your child will develop sensitivity to the feelings of others. Those who are severely hit often become bullies as children, violent as teens, and sociopathic as adults. One in 25 adults are sociopathic.

5. You discourage your child from resolving conflicts by reasoning and negotiating, which are important skills for their future success.

6. You increase the chances your child will be abusive to their own child one day.

7. You risk getting a visit from family and youth services, as *anyone* in the school who has knowledge that your child is being physically abused and hit inappropriately *must* by law report this to the authorities. In extreme cases, your child may be removed from your home and placed in foster care.

Summary: Keys to Effective Parenting

Focus on your child's positive qualities and constructive behaviors. Praise him often when he is doing well. Do your best not to take his misbehavior personally, and keep in mind that we all make mistakes, including your child. Explain clearly the house rules and what discipline he can expect if the rules are broken.

Good discipline could include removing his cell phone, gaming, computer, TV, or other privileges and sending him to his room or time-out chair.

Bad discipline is anything physically or emotionally abusive, such as hitting with a hanger, belt, buckle, electrical cord, or switch, or burning the child. It also includes frightening or threatening him, such as locking him in a dark basement or dirty attic, refusing to talk to him for a long period of time, or constantly yelling and screaming at him.

Smart Discipline Techniques

1. *Point out positive behavior.* Praise good behavior, and your child will want to continue to do it. Children by nature want to please their parents and teachers.

2. *Present a united front.* Parents (whether married or divorced) and grandparents must discipline in the same way, and must know the primary parent's house rules. Agree on the disciplines to be used in every household before an incident happens.

3. *Follow through.* Be sure to follow through on a discipline once the rules are set. If you don't enforce the consequence or remove the privilege, your child learns that your words

don't mean much, and he misses the opportunity to learn from his mistake.

4. *Be prompt and consistent.* Act as soon as possible so your child associates the misbehavior with his consequence.

5. *Take appropriate action.* Fit the consequence to the misbehavior, and have your child apologize to any offended party. If you must scold him, be brief and to the point. Children stop listening if scolding goes on too long. If you make a mistake, apologize promptly to your child.

6. *Offer choices.* Children generally respond better to being given choices than to receiving commands.

7. *Listen carefully.* Children learn from watching others. If you want your child to be polite, you should be polite to him and others.

8. *Be respectful.* Show respect to your child through your words, tone of voice, and body posture. Always focus on the behavior, not the child. If you tell him he is bad, he will be, thus fulfilling your expectations. Instead, tell him he is a good child who made a mistake he can learn to change.

9. *Show you care.* Hug and kiss your child often and say, "I love you," every day. Praise him for things he does well. Children who feel loved are more willing to repeat positive behavior and quickly want to correct bad behavior. Tell a child or teen he is great and he will become a great adult!

Remember, *you are your child's role model.* He learns from you ways of handling his anger and frustrations, and showing love and respect toward others. Children will carry your example forward in life, so *make it a great one!*

If you tell your child he is bad and stupid, he will be bad and feel stupid, fulfilling your expectations. Tell him he is smart and wonderful, and he will be smart and wonderful!

Some children cannot help being impulsive; they don't think about the problems their behavior can cause. These children may be suffering from attention deficit disorder (ADD) or attention-deficit/hyperactivity disorder (ADHD). There seem to be more cases occurring each year. I was a member of the school Child Study Team meetings and have heard parents say they don't want their ADHD-diagnosed children on medication. But parents need to look at their child's condition for what it is, a medical condition, similar to asthma or diabetes. These children need medical help in a prescription form to control their impulses, and they must be able to focus so they can learn. Many experts feel the foods our children eat are so tainted with pesticides, preservatives, sugars, and artificial ingredients that it may be linked to this condition. We do not know for sure what causes ADHD, but many experts feel there is a genetic component, meaning one parent is likely to have it as well.

I invited a holistic pharmacist onto my radio show in southern NJ, and he spoke about the importance of putting your child on an all-natural diet. Try to stay with "what God provides," as he said. That means fresh fruits, vegetables, nuts (including milk from coconuts or almonds), fish, and poultry like chicken or turkey. Stay away from packaged foods and large animal meats. Snacks should be natural too, like fresh-popped corn in olive oil or cut apples with peanut butter. I sent some parents and children to see this amazing Asian pharmacist, Dr. Stephen Chen, and his remedies did work for many of the children. But dietary changes must be adhered to every day. Stay up on the research about this.

Those children who cannot make significant changes with dietary changes and behavioral strategies within the home and school may need medication. I can tell you after seeing them first-hand in the schools that ADHD children usually do incredibly well with their meds and are much happier and more focused with them than without them.

They don't get yelled at as much, their work seems easier, their grades go up, they do better socially, and their self-esteem improves greatly. A parent not permitting his child to take the medication he needs is making him suffer and setting him up for continued failure in school and in learning. Sometimes the parent's ego does not want to admit that his child has ADHD, but the loving parent wants what is best for his child.

Parents, if you have a child whose teacher and counselor are suggesting he get a medical review for ADHD, please do get him to the doctor. We see your children for seven hours, five days a week, so we know them and can see that they are struggling. Be an informed parent; read all you can about the medication and its side effects. Help your child get what he needs!

We almost had a child transferred to a BD (behavioral/discipline) special classroom because his behavior was so extreme. For months, his mom refused to put him on medication. Finally, after spreading feces on his desk and all over the bathroom walls, and exposing himself to his classmates, he was sent to a children's mental hospital by DYFS for an evaluation. The doctor found what we suggested, extreme ADHD. He was finally put on medication, and he is a totally different child. He is focusing and behaving in class, participating, getting along with other children, and finally succeeding in first grade. His grades have greatly improved, and with medication, he can succeed in the regular classes at public school.

Don't forget about the potential effects of poor nutrition on your child's behavior. Children's lunches are horrific in most schools; they are mostly prepackaged or fried. What happened to the home cooking of the cafeteria lunch ladies when we were growing up? Where did they go? Check out your child's school cafeteria. If you are seeing prepackaged foods, please send your child to school with a healthy lunch from home.

Many children misbehave because they crave attention. Instead of paying attention to their bad behavior, find something good that they do that you can praise. This is the theory behind the star chart in my SAC office. I have all the acting-out, "bad behavior" kids on a star chart. They need 5 stars in a row to receive a special prize, and after acquiring 20 stars, they receive a "grand prize." They earn a star by getting a "good day" stamp from their teacher.

At the end of the day, I have all these happy, smiling, well-behaved kids running to my office, proud and ready to add another star to their charts. Their teachers are amazed at how well this works, and how these kids' behaviors have changed. Trust me, all kids want to do well; inspire them to do so, and they will.

Offering an incentive early on to change behavior is a great idea. Once the child feels the difference that being good in the classroom makes, his self-esteem improves, he makes more friends, his grades go up, and he genuinely *likes* school and being good! He receives praise from both his teachers and his parents. This is why I encourage star charts at both home and in school.

Other kids will misbehave to get their parents to give in to their wishes or demands. Parents have to be firm yet calm. If you said, "No guest this weekend because you failed your math test," then that means no, and there should be no further discussion.

However, you should give the child the opportunity to bring home a guest when he brings home an A on the next math test. Let your children know there are rewards for good grades and proper behaviors.

You should have a family meeting at least twice a year, right before school starts and right before summer starts, so that your children clearly understand the house rules and expectations. Rules should change as the child matures and shows enough responsibility to meet curfews.

Make sure kids know in advance the consequences for breaking rules. It is best to punish for a broken rule by removing a privilege. For teens, the best discipline is no phone calls (or cell phone) for a week, no computer IM or chat (only for homework), or no trip to the mall or movies with friends.

With children, removing TV privileges, video games, or not playing outside with a friend for a week would work. Do not change your mind during the stated punishment, or kids will think they can always convince you to change the punishment or its duration. Both parents, whether together or not, should have consistent household rules. Back each other up on the punishments given.

Speaking of computers, do monitor your child's usage, and try to have him do his computer work in the living room or kitchen. Cyberstalking and cyberbullying are real. I had a girl in my therapy office who almost committed suicide because of being teased so badly on MySpace. Know what your kids are doing on the computer. Let them use chat only when you are home, and only in a family area.

I have had children and teens watch porn on their fathers' computers because theirs had parental controls. Be smart and place this control on all household computers. A lifetime porn and sexual addiction could emerge if children are exposed too early to this type of thing.

Children who are prone to temper tantrums often need a time-out. I advise all parents of explosive children to make their home environment as peaceful as possible. Dim all lights, play calm, classical music (keep the TV off), use aromatherapy, and speak in calm voices. Without being obsessive, keep your home as orderly as possible, especially common areas and children's bedrooms. Tell a screaming child that he must go to his room to settle down, and when he is calm for 15 minutes, you will let him come out. Put on a timer the moment he goes into the room to lie down. If he leaves the room or asks to come out, start the timer again. Children will get used to the pattern if you adhere to it the first few times. Again, speak with a calm, yet firm voice, and don't yell or scream at your child (an adult tantrum).

It is important to teach your child early that he has responsibilities. I explained to my girls that they could not have a guest come over until their closet and room were clean, or their friends might get the wrong idea and think they were slobs. Also, we did not leave for our adventure day until they were dressed properly and had picked up everything in their room.

Try to have family dinnertime every school night. The more your family is on a schedule, the more relaxed your children will be. Children are calmer with routines.

Sometimes teens do well with a contract that all parties agree to. We make a wish list for the teen and parent, and negotiate what each is willing to do. For example, a 17-year-old boy who really wants to go out Friday nights by 7:00 p.m. with his friends and stay out until 10:00 p.m. can negotiate this with his parents. We can get his parents to agree to his night out if their son agrees to meet curfew, pick up everything in his room before going out, join the family for Friday dinner, and cut the lawn on Saturday by 10:00 a.m. Their son wanted to sleep until 11:00 a.m., so the parents agreed he could cut the lawn by noon. All was settled, the agreement was signed, and everyone was happy. Also, consequences were discussed ahead of time. If their son was more than 10 minutes late for curfew, did not pick up the cell phone if they called him, or broke any of the other rules, he would lose his Friday night privilege for two weekends. They agreed.

Positive Parenting

Traditionally, there are three parenting styles. The most common two we see are as follows:

1. *Authoritarian.* This is a strict parent who tells the child what he can and cannot do, punishes harshly and usually for too long, and does not care what the child's opinion or feelings are on the matter.

2. *Apathetic.* Parents do not spend a lot of time with the child, nor do they give her a lot of guidance or discipline. There is minimal direction, and the child is not given responsibilities. This usually happens with the overworked parent who has no energy to handle her kids at the end of the day. Or, during a divorce situation, one parent over-spoils the child and refuses to discipline at all.

Obviously, both of these styles are wrong, and if you use either, you are asking for rebellion and trouble in the teenage years. The best parenting style, the third style, is somewhere in the middle between apathetic and authoritarian. It is the style I describe in this chapter, *positive parenting*.

With the positive parenting approach, the parent requires his child to tend to his chores or responsibilities as part of the family team. The parent issues a direction and a time frame to complete the tasks. The child has input about the time and day she would like to do most of their chores. The parent is supportive but does not step in to do the chore or nag.

If the chore is complete as planned, a star or check goes on the weekly chart. When the child does make a mistake, she sits down in quiet to talk about it, away from the other children. Honesty is encouraged so that the child feels safe to tell the parent the truth, and does not try to lie or place blame. If she tells the truth immediately, there is a small consequence to the action, but it is not as severe as if she had lied. What the child learned from the lesson is discussed, and the parent talks about his feelings about why he is worried for his child, and it always ends with, "Because I love you and want you to be safe."

If the child or teen has bullied someone, he should write a note of apology to the injured party. Check the note, and tell your child you are proud that he is doing the right thing to correct his mistake. Ask why he has been bullying the other child, and if there is mutual teasing, call the teacher and the other parent. Tell them you and your child want to make amends, and ask the teacher to keep an eye out for the two of them or send them to their SAC counselor to talk things through and negotiate a plan. If your child is being bullied, have him tell the teacher, and ask for a counseling appointment right away. Children should not be bullied at school (this is now a federal law), and they must tell to get the support they need.

A discussion with your child or teen should never contain words that put him down or make his self-esteem suffer. It is all right for you to be disappointed, and for you to say so. Together, you can make a plan to ensure the negative event never happens again. Children just want you to be real with them, so talk about your feelings honestly and openly. Remember, kids model what they see and hear.

My houses in Erie and Ventnor were the homes that everyone wanted to hang out at. The kids talked to me freely and came to me for advice. I'd often hear them say, "I could never talk to my mom like this!" What a shame. I remember hanging out at one of my best friend's house in Lower Moreland. Martha Macht's mom, Jean, was a psychotherapist and my first inspiration for wanting to be a counselor myself.

I could say anything, and she really listened and made me feel important. I could ask her questions about boys and not feel ashamed or embarrassed. I often told my friend how lucky I felt she was, and that I wanted to be that kind of mom to my kids too. I think I have done that, and as a therapist, I have helped kids of all ages with their questions too. Open and real communication with your children starts when they are babies. It then feels natural for you to talk to them, and they to you, as they get older.

The form of parenting that I encourage you to use, along with the tips I have given you will help you to raise healthy, happy, intelligent children who love to learn and who will grow up to be successful and confident.

Teach them the techniques of the Watch Me! mind-set any-time the opportunity arises, like when someone teases them or doubts their abilities (young kids in the schools love learning this method when I have taught it to them). Kids are smart, and they want to learn how to handle things for themselves. Give them the opportunity to learn this when they are young, and they will develop it further as they mature and grow.

Instilling a sense of spirituality within them can happen if you attend church, but more frequently, it happens if you talk about

God, a higher power, or spiritual concepts in normal conversations. Remember, God is not punishing, so please never threaten them with, "God will punish you if you do this or that!"

Do not be negative when talking about God or your belief at all. Talk about your child's God-given talent and how happy you are to see him use it, how proud you are of him, and how he is doing work that God would be proud of. Tell him that it is good karma to treat others well, and that when people die, they become one of his angels, and so forth.

I adore working with children and teens because I remember the pain of growing up. I remember being teased and bullied, feeling like an ugly outcast, not being as good in sports as all of my siblings, and often feeling like a loner. I remember feeling so depressed in eighth grade that I felt suicidal. I didn't have the tools I needed to know how to be happy. I remember wanting to go to a counselor to help with my sense of depression, but it was "not acceptable" at that time to do so. I suffered a lot in silence, and writing became my therapy.

Later, it became one of my goals to become a counselor to help other kids like me. I specialize in adolescent counseling because I can relate to their pain as if I was experiencing it yesterday. Parents, if your child asks to go see a counselor, please take him as soon as possible. All my teens in therapy are so happy they came, and they rise from their depression, relieved to see their families functioning well again.

In the life stage of a teenager, according to Erik Erikson's *eight stages of psychosocial development,* teens 12 to 18 years old have the basic conflict of peer relationships and *identity* versus *role confusion.* They must achieve a sense of identity in school/occupation, sex roles, and religion, according to Erikson. If they do not handle the conflicts presented with their peers in a positive way, and instead fall into destructive habits, this could lead to a state of inaction or rebellion that could in turn lead to low self-esteem and possible lifelong addiction.

In the *intimacy* versus *isolation* stage of ages 19 to 40, love relationships are the key conflict and challenge. If your child cannot develop them successfully, he will suffer feelings of isolation and despair. Each relationship presented is a chance to learn, change, and grow into a better, more evolved partner.

Remember, children and teens can experience immense pain, anxiety, depression, and trauma over lost relationships as intensely as adults do. Furthermore, a teenager who experiences heartache over a breakup may need extra support from a professional counselor to deal with all these new emotions. At certain times, encouraging words from parents just don't seem enough. Get the help your child may need to learn how to be resilient and handle such emotional changes and challenges in his life.

I believe that older teens and those in their early 20s are supposed to break free of the family ties and test their own limits. This is how they will learn, by making mistakes and learning to correct them. Giving them the space to make their own choices encourages them to take risks and take on responsibilities. One of the worst things a parent can do is baby his teenager, try to hold him back, and protect him too much. He will then become a young adult who is lazy and may be afraid to leave home. Teach your young adult children the life skills they need to survive in the real world.

I am writing this book to help the parents who don't know what to do, or feel stuck raising their children today in this harsh, difficult world of broken families. Please try the techniques mentioned here, and see if they don't make a difference.

If you need counseling support, get it. You and your children will get through their growing-up stage, but you want a loving relationship on the other side of it. It will never be perfect, but respecting, listening, and loving your children unconditionally while practicing positive parenting techniques will help you all survive!

Chapter 10

For Teens: Advice from "Mom"

~~~

I FEEL QUITE HONORED to say that over the years I've had many young people other than my daughters call me "Mom." It is a badge of honor, and it describes the most important and satisfying job I have ever had!

I consider my daughters two of my best friends. They love me, challenge me, support me, inspire me, and are there for me. Together, the three of us make an awesome team. I am so proud of the job I have done in raising them that my heart fills with love and devotion whenever I think of our many experiences and the pleasures we have shared. Now my Stephana is pregnant, and I can't wait to be a grand mom!

When I think back to my own adolescent days, I remember feeling like I didn't fit in, being teased, not feeling good enough compared to my siblings, and withdrawing into my world of writing to express my pain. It was so disconcerting that the memories burned into my soul, and I feel as if I experienced it all just yesterday. When teens come to me with some of the same challenges I experienced, I understand and feel their distress too.

I remember experiencing extreme depression and suicidal thoughts in eighth grade. I recall the deep pain of having an intense crush for years on a boy who never paid any attention to me. One of my first dates was a no-show, and I will never forget how embarrassed and devastated I felt. I felt not pretty enough for him. Many of the kids teased and bullied me, calling me names because I had no shape and was very tall and thin.

The pain of not being in the cool group and feeling the isolation of being an outsider still makes my heart ache today. The numb feeling of "my love" breaking up with me for another girl still resides deep within me and emerges when I have an adult breakup. *I feel your pain, and I understand!* I want to help you teenagers see beyond your past and current fears and disappointments to your greatness and toward positive futures where you can excel, grow into your best selves, and be resilient enough to handle these types of emotional upsets and challenges.

Modeling and promotions was what saved me from low self-esteem. Mingling with people outside of my hometown and my school taught me to become worldly and was instrumental in my becoming socially confident. Handling responsibilities at my job instilled a sense of pride, and I put the money I earned toward buying my own car and some updated clothes. Being the third of three daughters, I often wore my sisters' hand-me-down clothes. I was teased terribly in school and church classes because my clothes were not up-to-date. I used to hide in the girls' room and silently cry with embarrassment at church. Only when I started working at age 11 as a babysitter, then at age 13 as a model, did I have enough money to dress fashionably.

My work became so much fun, I felt as if I had two separate lives: that of an outgoing, confident fashion model and that of a quiet girl at school and home. I had lots of guy friends, but many of the girls were nasty and cold to me. Looking back, I think perhaps they were jealous, but they made me feel as though I wasn't good enough for them. It's great now going back to high school reunions feeling successful, proud, and whole. I feel absolutely wonderful! Remember the statement, your own happiness and success are your best revenge? Reunions are a prime example. Today, most of my high school classmates are my friends on Facebook, and the petty, mean adolescent games are totally gone. Thank God!

My private life as a model became public when I performed on stage at the Philadelphia Tower Theater at the group Queen's *Night at the Opera* concert. Lead singer Freddie Mercury pulled me on stage to dance the encore with him when I was in my WFIL radio "Boss Chick" promotional model's outfit. The radio station had sponsored their concert, and we worked with them all day.

In the front row were four of the popular boys from my Lower Moreland High School. I panicked for a minute before I saw their reaction, which said, "Wow, Terri Milne is on stage, dancing with Freddie!" Well, it was all over the school the next day, and I guess the guys liked me even more, and the girls liked me even less. At that point, I didn't care. I was making $25 per hour or more as a model, great money for a teen back then, and I was working with top celebrities. My life outside of school was awesome, I was getting good grades in school, and I was building a great resume for my future. The hateful girls could kiss my butt! I was making a small fortune doing what I loved, and my future goals were clearly in sight.

I was in national magazines, in newspaper ads, on television, and doing promotional events with celebrities all over New Jersey and Philadelphia. I just couldn't wait to get high school behind me, go off to college, and get on with my life.

Alexi also worked during her high school years for a top modeling agency—Reinhard in Philadelphia—and she was permitted to work on school days for QVC and other top companies as model/actor because she kept a 4.0 average. Some girls in her Atlantic City high school bullied her too, but she dealt with it straight on, asking them if she'd done anything to upset them. It was jealousy as well, but she negotiated her way through it. She had no concern for high school dramatics; her sights were set on a recording contract and modeling/acting in NYC as soon as she graduated.

Teens, let me tell you, there are defining moments in your teenage years. You'll need to make important choices that will define your direction in life. Don't let anyone bring you down; sometimes you have to take the high road alone to get ultimately where you want to be. So the sooner you refuse to accept others' opinion of you, the sooner you can get on with living the life you want. Look outside of school for work you can do that you would enjoy. Start working as soon as you can, and put away the money for a car. Wheels are freedom! Buy a good used car and learn to be responsible for getting to your job on time.

If you don't have enough cash by the time you can drive, your parents may have to cosign on a loan. I did this for Alexi and put the car and the loan in both our names. I explained to her that this was the beginning of establishing good credit. It was extremely important that she paid her car loan on time, and that she paid it off as soon as possible. After she did, she was able to get her own credit cards and learned to be financially responsible, which was very important for her independent lifestyle.

A lot of teens in my counseling office want more freedoms as they age, and rightfully so. I am on their side. But what they must understand is that they have to prove to their parents that they are responsible and mature and can make good choices. Parents are afraid to let you go; they love you and they have spent many years protecting you.

Letting you go arouses their fear, and it is a negotiation process that takes time. I help my young clients come to terms with their parents' feelings and wishes while we obtain some new freedoms for them. We establish curfews and a chore list. Teens must learn they need to be a working part of the adult team if they want the freedoms of a young adult.

My adolescent clients come to understand that their parents are stressed out with finances, juggling schedules, working a lot of hours, and household chores too. If teens are willing to step in and help out, then a parent will want to reward them in various ways. Rewards, rules, and discipline must be established for you teens and discussed up front so that you know the consequences of making a bad choice or being irresponsible.

For rewards, I suggested in the last chapter an allowance chart. Just in case you didn't read that chapter, here it is in brief summary.

Together, you establish five to six chores you need to complete each day over one week. Some may be daily chores, like feeding the dog; some may be a once-a-week chore like vacuuming or doing your laundry. You will do these chores over six days, with one day off. Your parent checks off that you did the chore, and you'll need 24 out of 30 checks that show that your chores were completed *without having to be asked by your parents*. Your reward or weekly allowance will be established up front, along with payday (I suggest Friday, when most adults get their paycheck). You will like this system for two reasons: you will get your allowance for chores you have to do anyway, and your parents will stop nagging you. Not bad, huh?

You just have to deliver the chores without being asked or complaining. Easy. Next, when your parents see you can be responsible in completing your chores, they will also see you can handle some more adult privileges.

Staying out a bit later, having more time on the computer or phone, accepting dates, and staying over at a friend's house—these are just a few requests my clients have negotiated with their parents in my office. If you are struggling with a very strict parent, suggest to him that the family go to counseling because you feel you need an outside opinion on receiving privileges. If your parent refuses to go, start going to a counselor in your school. Counselors may have tips to help you. The important thing is to go yourself, and eventually, you may be able to get your parents to join you.

Many times a parent has attempted to drop off his child at my office and then leave to go run some errands. Counseling an adolescent is a family systems problem. A teen is usually angry about what is going on in the household. And parents, you are a part of both the problem and the solution, so you must attend counseling for the family to learn a new dynamic of interaction.

As a parent, I agree that it is hard to raise children; we do the very best we can and many times we falter. Kids, just know that your parents love you, and many times they are afraid themselves of what they are going through. Some parents forget what it's like to be a teen—remind them!

I remind them as a therapist; I tell them that you put in a very long and hard day at school, and the last thing you want is a lot of questions when you get home from school. You need something to eat, some quiet time to vent to a friend on the phone, and then you have to calm yourself down enough to do homework. Some of you have after-school activities or sports. In all, you are handling a 12–14 hour day, five days a week. It is exhausting, and parents need to be reminded of that. If they are nagging or questioning you, ask them calmly if you can talk later, after you rest a bit.

We discuss respect and empathy too. It is important for your parents to respect you, and you them. I try to have them remember the difficulties they had in high school so they might understand what you are going through. It is important you try to tap into what others are feeling, as that is the starting point of open and mature communication. Remember, if you act like a child with a bad temper and attitude, they will be reluctant to start giving you adult liberties.

We also talk about your parents supporting your efforts to find a job. While you are in school, I suggest working no more than 20 hours per week in a part-time job, and the majority of those hours should be worked over the weekend. Keep the weeknights clear for homework, as the schools today give you a lot of points for homework completed.

Try to choose a job that has something to do with what you want to pursue after high school. For example, work at a garden center if you hope to be a landscaper, or work in a teen clothing store if you want to go into fashion design. These work credits will be an important part of your college resume, as college recruiters like to see young people who have had various jobs and responsibilities before they enter college. In the summer, work a 40-hour-per-week job to save as much money as possible for the things you will need after high school.

Do join school clubs to get those credits on your resume, and take classes outside of school that may pertain to your future career. There are many classes held at local universities that young people can attend—for example, in writing, photography, poetry, cooking classes, financial management, and in business skills.

Think outside the box and go to these classes, again, thinking "credits" for your resume.

Also, I strongly encourage you to volunteer for local charities you feel very interested in. Some suggestions are to start a school fund and donate to EPIC, feed the hungry, assist at an animal shelter, walk for AIDS or breast cancer, help younger children at the Boys & Girls Club, clean up the beaches or your neighborhood, or create your own event. Young people are great in coming up with ideas about how to help. Our elementary students in my past school collected funds to help the Hurricane Katrina victims and donated to the school food pantry for families in need over the winter.

The more involved you are outside of school, the more well-rounded you'll become. You'll get used to working for a boss or other older adults, with older teens who may be in charge, and with people of other cultures and races. You'll also have the opportunity to learn a new skill outside of school.

For those of you who do excel in school activities and sports, good for you! Just know, however, there is a big world outside of your school and hometown. If you are the local football star, you'll find that when you get to college level, it's a whole new ballgame! Don't let your ego run away with you. Many adults know past friends who "peaked" in high school and never became more than the local star. What a shame. Life goes on, so don't get stuck in the hometown fame. Continue to challenge yourself and keep growing!

Getting good grades is essential to your future success. Don't let the cool kids bring you down; they are just into their reputation and nothing else. A high school reputation means nothing after graduation. After high school, you will be on your own, and what you do with your grades in high school will determine your success, whether you go to college or not.

Both Stephana and Alexi's good grades were important influences on their future successes. Alexi's initial talent press kits contained copies of her report card along with three great letters of recommendation from teachers who vouched for her hard work and character. We included a professionally written talent and academic resume. She had a whole page of work and volunteer credits as well.

She graduated with a 4.0, at the top 5 percent of her class, and she was exempted from 11th grade. Alexi also missed 60 days of her 12th grade year for her modeling career. The principal of her high school said that as long as she maintained a 3.5 average or higher, she could be on a work-study program. She never slipped below that 3.5, as her modeling career in Philadelphia was very important to her.

When the Grammy Award-winning singer I met in South Beach saw her press kit, he told me he decided to studio test Alexi over many other artists because of her grades in school and her record of responsibility and hard work. She now understood why achieving good grades was essential. He may have been a hip-hop artist, but more importantly, he was a businessman.

I always explained to my daughters that going to school was their job and that I expected and knew they would both do well. They both received top jobs in major cities due to their work ethic and grade history starting all the way back to high school.

If you are struggling with a public high school for any reason, ask to attend a charter school, an arts school, a vo-tech school, or a private school. Just be forewarned, there are jerks wherever you go, and you are going to have to learn how to handle them the rest of your life anyway. But you may feel more comfortable in a specialty school, so I encourage you to talk to your parents about it.

I suggest to my teen clients that whenever they want to approach something with their parents, they should do the necessary legwork and have their information ready. If you want to go to a modeling or acting school, for example, have the information on the schools available in your area, their tuition, length of program, and job opportunities after graduation. Know when you can have an interview and ask your parents to attend with you.

Be ready and show your parents that you are serious about this decision. When they see you are serious about something, they will respect what you have to say. Just saying, "Mom, I want to go to modeling school," without backing it up with actual information about schools would be juvenile. Tell Mom you are willing to pay for half because you have saved your money from working your job. Now she'll know you are serious!

Peer Pressure

I know teens hate the term "peer pressure"; adolescents don't want to think that they can't stand up to their own friends or that their friends could bring them down. I don't think your friends *mean to hurt you*, but I do believe they don't always make wise choices. So when they ask you to do something, you have to start thinking beyond the moment.

Will you get in trouble at home or with the law? If you're working toward your privileges with your parents, will this one bad decision ruin all you've gained? Is this kid really smarter than you, or is he just looking for a temporary rush of excitement? Can this act hurt *you* in any way? If so, you have got to speak up and refuse.

For example, if you are invited to a party and you heard that drugs or alcohol might be there, refuse to go. Blame it on your mom or dad, choose to go to the movies with a friend instead, go shopping, or stay over at a friend's house. Use your head and make a wise choice. Hopefully, you have an open enough relationship with your mom or dad that if you get to a party, and you don't like the scene there, you will walk away and call them immediately to come pick you up. No one has to know. Fake sickness to your friends and go home; do anything to get out of there.

Alexi did this once, and I really respected her decision. I did not ask her any questions, or call the parent of the person hosting the party. That would have created problems with her friends. We kept things between her and me, and I was proud that she made the decision to leave. I picked her up a block away from the party as she requested.

At another party Alexi attended in Erie, a young friend of hers drank too much and passed out. Alexi knew enough about alcohol poisoning to call 911. Many of her friends said not to call because they would all get into trouble for having alcohol at the party. Alexi had to make a quick decision. Her friend's life was more important than the peer pressure surrounding her. Later, all the kids found out that their friend would have died without Alexi's quick decision and her strength to go against peer pressure. I was really proud of her decision, and I'm sure it is one she'll never regret. Help your friends who are in trouble. Call 911 if you think it may save a life!

There are five challenging years of school: grades eight through twelve. Start focusing on your future and what you want to do beyond high school. Choose your friends carefully. If you get involved with activities like dance or golf outside of school, for example, you may find those friends to be healthier and more serious about their future. Those may be the kids who will make it in the end. Come on, you're bright, and you can see who's going to end up flunking out, getting into trouble, or going nowhere fast. It becomes so obvious who is bad news and who is a safe and good friend.

Having one or two great friends who are looking toward their futures is better than being part of a group of girls or a gang of guys. In these groups, people are always trying to vie for the position of the coolest by taking risks and being daring. These are the acts that will get you into trouble. Is it worth it? Will it help you after 12th grade?

Drugs and Alcohol

Being a drug and alcohol counselor (LCADC) and a student assistance counselor (SAC) in the schools, I suppose I should talk about drugs. Many parents have their heads in the sand and don't want to admit there are drugs all over the schools. And they've forgotten that their generation had drugs floating around the schools also! The drugs in my school during the '70s were pot, alcohol, and quaaludes. There was occasional talk of cocaine, especially in college. There was not crack cocaine or heroin in my high school that I know of, but it is all over the public schools today.

I recently had a beautiful, blonde 5-foot-10, 17-year-old girl with a heroin addiction in my counseling office. She was from a good family, and no one would have guessed her problem. She could have been a model, and part of her therapy was having her look in that direction.

I was able to get her clean in two months, which was almost unheard of with heroin use. Her grades went from failing to As and Bs, and she ended up dating the football captain and attending her prom. I got to her just in time. Heroin and crack are two of the toughest drugs to quit. Please never start.

Alcohol misuse is now carrying jail time. Never before have our jails been so crowded with "good people" who end up in jail because they were a fraction of a point over .08 in their blood alcohol test. A third DUI now carries jail time in the state of New Jersey, and once you have a record, your job opportunities are diminished. We all know that teenagers have been drinking at least since the 1950s. But the laws were minimal up until the 1990s, and Mothers Against Drunk Driving (MADD) has been a huge force in getting even stricter laws.

At proms, at least the kids are chipping in and getting limos, or having a designated driver. Please think of the consequences of drinking while driving. The best solution is not to drink at all. A drunk driver killed my best friend during our homecoming weekend, and it affected all of us students emotionally for the rest of our lives.

I had a counseling client who lost her best friend with two other girls when their Mercedes crashed; the fire was witnessed by over 30 of their classmates on a scheduled senior outing. I went to talk to the teens and their parents at a memorial service, and shared my story of the loss of Michael and Corrine. Bereavement is difficult to handle on your own. If you have lost a friend unexpectedly, please get counseling immediately. My spirituality, which had developed at age 16, was the only thing that helped me make sense of it all.

Bullying

Let's discuss bullying and the jerks most of us have encountered in school. One in four kids who bully will have a criminal record before the age of 30. Bullies usually learn aggressive responses from being treated aggressively themselves, or from witnessing fighting, yelling, or intimidation in the home. Very often, having empathy and concern for the bully can diminish his power and keep him from wanting to pick on you. The important thing is not to tolerate abuse in any form from a bully, a girlfriend, or a boyfriend.

At the first sign of trouble, approach the other teen and ask if there is a problem. Ask if there was something you did that upset him. Perhaps there was a misunderstanding? With this approach, you are coming across as friendly and calm yet firm; you are refusing to cower when he tries to intimidate you. If he's still angry and tries to fight you, give him a warning. "Look, I was trying to work this out with you, but if you are looking for trouble, I'm going to have to report this." Approach the other person in a public area, with the support of a peer mediator, counselor, teacher, or group of mutual friends.

If someone is harassing you in school for any reason and in any form, empower yourself by getting help. Tell your counselor at school or your teacher. Confide in someone you trust. If the bully does not stop bothering you, keep reporting the incidents, as there are no-tolerance laws in place now. Remember, you are building a case. Ask for a meeting with your counselor and the other who is causing you trouble.

Fighting the other person is not the answer, as you will only get yourself into trouble by getting suspended. After a second bullying incident, get your parents involved by having them approach the principal and ask for a meeting with the other student's parents. Don't lose your anger or cool with the bully; remember that he is trying to get you into trouble. Be the more mature one, and stay in control.

Bullying kids will be sent to a behaviorally disciplined classroom, to a "second chance" school, or to a juvenile facility if they establish a record of violence, bullying, or harassment. Be vocal, protect yourself, enlist the help of adult mentors and parents, and be proactive instead of reactive. Being proactive means acting *before* trouble happens, while it is just beginning or escalating. Being reactive means acting *after* the incident has already happened.

Also be careful with cyberbullying. If someone is harassing you through Facebook (you should have a private account, not public) or MySpace, tell the police, who have entire departments devoted to nailing predators looking for young teens. Many men will pose as older teen boys to entice you to meet them. The underground sex-slave trade is real and dangerous. Never go to meet someone you don't know. Many younger girls are kidnapped this way. Please play it safe and don't trust strangers promising you a modeling or singing contract, an acting career, or anything else.

Teenage Sex

Now I wouldn't be a good mom without addressing teenage sex. This is a tricky one, because I know your hormones are raging. I remember that stage! What is most important is protecting yourself physically and emotionally! In South Jersey, there are now AIDS cases in almost every high school. The largest group of people acquiring HIV is teenage girls.

Guys have this perceived rite of passage of "trying to get laid" as often and as soon as possible, so they can brag about it to their friends. Girls, you have to protect yourselves. And yes, oral sex *is* sex, despite what one of our presidents said. It can still ruin your reputation horribly when others talk about it in school. And a "bad rep" spreads really fast. Do whatever it takes, ladies, to protect yourself and your reputation.

My gynecologist told me that the HPV virus (venereal warts) is a rampant STD, with close to 80 percent of sexually active teens getting the virus. This virus can make you sterile and cause other complications. I once saw a young girl with small warts all around her mouth area, so this is no joke.

You also have herpes to add to this mix. Lovely. Sex now doesn't sound so romantic, does it? And you could top it off with an unwanted pregnancy. Then what will you do? All this, just for a momentary thrill? Ladies, wait until you "time-test" your boyfriend. Make him wait at least six months to be with you. If he is honorable, he will wait for you and still be your boyfriend.

Move slowly and make him respect your wishes. If he doesn't, he isn't for you. If indeed you become an established couple, then people are less likely to talk about you, and your partner will defend you from any rumors spread. He certainly won't be spreading the rumors about "his girl" either! Makes sense, doesn't it?

But all sex has risks. If either one of you was sexually active before being with each other, you both could be carrying diseases from your previous partners. If you love each other, get tested together before being intimate. I talk to my adult friends about this, and they think asking their future partner to do this sounds weird. I don't; I have had too many HIV clients in my office who were too afraid to ask for an AIDS test, had unprotected sex, and now have HIV too! Protect yourselves. Be strong and protect yourself—you could be saving your life! Again, if your intended beloved thinks your asking him to be tested is degrading, then he is not for you. *Next!*

Ladies, I have also seen some horrifying shows on television where young women are accepting verbal and emotional abuse from their boyfriends. Where is your sense of pride? Do not ever think abuse is okay, because it's not. If one incident occurs, there is bound to be a second. Insist your boyfriend get into counseling if he has a temper that he has trouble controlling. Boys who were abused often become men who abuse their girlfriends. If you feel you want to forgive him the first time, clearly state you will not tolerate it a second time; he needs to enter counseling or it will be the end of your relationship, period. And keep your word.

You may suffer a little when you break up with him, but in time, you will see it was the best thing you could do for your self-esteem and sense of pride. Gentlemen, the same rule applies to you. Abuse of any type—emotional, verbal, or physical—is never acceptable. About 10 percent of reported abuse cases are from men, so although it is rare, it does occur. You will meet someone else who will love you properly. If you need help, seek counseling to know how to become stronger and to get yourself out of the abusive relationship.

Summary

Now, let's summarize all this information as to how it applies to the Watch Me! mind-set. As teenagers, you are going through a critical time in your life. You are making decisions for your future, negotiating privileges with your parents, entering your first major dating relationship, and learning to develop trust. The choices you make are critical to your future success. Talk about a lot of pressure!

The Watch Me! mind-set lives within your mind and soul. Go within yourself for inner mental dialogue (self-talk) about what choices you should make when you are not sure. Using the techniques described in this book, you will gain the confidence to move in a positive direction. You'll know what is right for you, even if a friend puts you down for your decisions.

With practice and daily use, your confidence will become strong enough for you to do the right thing, especially during times of peer pressure. This mind-set also teaches you an inner sense of calm so that you can have reasonable discussions with your parents. You will learn how to forgive them and others, as well as to develop a sense of empathy; all this goes a long way in establishing mood control. The Watch Me! mind-set teaches you to look at a situation from a different perspective and to maturely discuss your points of view—versus jumping to conclusions and acting out impulsively in rage, revenge, or defiance.

You will see that the Watch Me! mind-set will assist you through your most difficult of times in the teen years. Study it, come to understand it, and work the principles daily. If you need assistance, see a life coach or counselor for support. Read as many spiritually motivating books as you can to keep learning and growing. Please know that your future is totally in your hands, no matter how impossible things seem. My father taught me that when I was in my teen years when he explained to me the secrets of the five Ds.

The Watch Me! mind-set tells you to go for your dreams and it shows you how reach them one step at a time. See Alexi's chapters in Part 2 to learn what she did as a teenager and young woman in her 20s to stay focused enough to reach her dreams and goals as a recording artist, model, actor, and businesswoman. She did it despite all the doubts from others, the remote odds of making it, and intense competition in this type of career.

If she can do it, you can too! Dare to dream! Make your goal sheet, fill it out, and review if often. Get going and don't be afraid! You just have to *really want it, believe that you will achieve it, and tie your goals and dreams to living your highest purpose in life and beyond!*

Part 2

$\sim$

It Works for Young People Too!

by Alexi Panos

Chapter 11

My Story: Discovering the True Meaning of Watch Me!

W HAT IS THE WATCH ME! mind-set all about? It took me a
good six years to discover the answer.

At 15, I was just like any other starry-eyed dreamer who
wanted what I thought at the time was the best out of life: success,
money, and fame. I was determined to take my talents in singing,
dancing, and songwriting and join the crop of young pop artists
in the music world. I started to map out my plan.

My first move was a literal one: I had to get out of Erie, PA, if
I was ever going to get anywhere. Given that my mom lived close
to a big-name producer in Atlantic City, NJ, who had auditioned
me the previous summer and wanted to sign me, I knew exactly
where I was going! Now, I had to figure out a way to convince
my father that he should let his 15-year-old daughter leave a great
school district in Erie to move to a struggling school district in
Atlantic City to pursue a career as a singer. I knew that no matter

how I phrased it, or what information I gave him to back up my decision, he would be less than thrilled. I was right.

Despite constant fighting and turmoil with my father back in Erie, I was determined to stop at nothing to get where I needed to go. I packed up my bags and decided I was moving to New Jersey! This is when the Watch Me! mind-set first came into play in my life. I felt that I wanted to prove to everyone who doubted my move and my dream that I could make it happen and make it my reality.

My move to New Jersey was the catalyst to many successes in the beginning stages of proving that I deserved to live out my dream. My first triumph was when I was exempted from 11th grade and able to graduate a year early in my new school district of Atlantic City.

My second was recording a song with Grammy Award-winning producers and writers who had numerous number one hits to their names.

My third triumph was actually working every day toward my dream, whether I was busy with voice lessons, studio sessions, dance, or songwriting. These various successes seemed to continue effortlessly as I kept my goals and the Watch Me! mentality in the forefront of my mind. It's amazing to what lengths you will go to prove a point to doubters in your life!

My next success, and perhaps the most influential, was the result of my mom's chance meeting in Miami South Beach with a hit-making music star who ruled the charts. With a little shameless promotion, my mom sold him on the fact that he needed me on the new label he was forming.

Two weeks later, there I was—in a limo on my way to Teterboro Airport, one of six people on a private G5 jet on their way to LA for the Teen Choice Awards! I was also going to be doing my in-studio test that week. You can imagine how any young girl from Erie, PA, would feel: I was about to meet the man who rocked the Billboard charts and face my dream head-on. Nervous with anticipation, I had arrived.

My journey with the label continued for three years after that date. I recorded multiple songs with different artists, began working on my album, traveled the world on tour, sang on stage in front of 30,000 people, and landed myself on two multi-platinum albums. Pretty impressive for a 19-year-old, but something bigger was missing, something that I was either too excited or too naive to see.

Not knowing what this "thing" was, but knowing that something didn't feel right, I quit. I stopped showing up at the studio, stopped writing songs, and stopped seeking out producers to collaborate with—I just stopped.

I had set out to achieve this goal, to prove to the disbelievers that I could, and I did. So why wasn't I feeling satisfied? I began doing a lot of soul searching, trying to find the reason for this sudden departure of my love for music. I discovered that what seemed so hard to find had always been right in front of me; I was just too engulfed in what I had created.

My answer was this: music, or any dream, should not be something that you pursue for fame or fortune. Even all the famous and rich artists that I had met during my travels weren't truly happy. They all had some sort of addiction that allowed them to escape from the misery they made for themselves. No, you shouldn't pursue your dream for money or fame because that can always be taken away, at any moment, and then all you're left with are broken dreams. Sure, you can achieve fame and wealth by pursuing your dreams, but if those are the *only* reasons you're chasing them, you'll never feel fully satisfied.

I believe your dreams are a part of your destiny. Whatever gives you life also breathes certain passions and paths into you. Only when you pursue these passions with the right intentions, and the knowledge that you do not ultimately control your path, will you become truly successful and happy. It's about living each day in pursuit of your intended higher purpose.

This is when my true understanding of the Watch Me! mindset came into play. Watch Me! is not about achieving success on the world stage or the approval of the masses; it's about *proving to yourself* that you can succeed in your destiny by living for your higher purpose.

It's about fulfilling your deepest desires and creative needs, expressing yourself, and being yourself. Watch Me! is something that you should be saying to *yourself* daily, not to others. It should inspire you to overcome your own negativity and self-doubt and prove to yourself that *you can achieve anything if you believe you can!*

After this reawakening, I approached everything differently. I felt clear again. I felt that I could now move toward any situation or goal with my true self in mind, with the right motivation, and with the knowledge of my higher purpose in the forefront. Now, I am working on many creative pursuits to fulfill my need for accomplishment—and not to prove to anyone that I can, but rather to prove it to myself.

Although my love for creating and performing music is abundant, it isn't the only thing that moves my soul. Returning from a musical tour in Africa, I was overwhelmed by the extreme poverty, lack of resources, and disease that was so prevalent in every city. I decided that instead of just noticing the problem and going back to my life filled with the everyday blessings of Western culture, I was going to do something about it.

Enter the birth of Everyday People Initiating Change (EPIC). I started EPIC with my friend Tennille Amor, a fellow musician who once lived in Africa. Tennille and I took our personal experiences from Africa and molded them into what has now become a cause that is supported worldwide. Through the fusion of goodwill, networking, and a lot of luck, EPIC now provides clean, sustainable water systems to those in need in the developing world. Like my path in my musical career, EPIC began with and is still fueled by small steps toward a bigger goal. However, now with a little hindsight, I've made sure to always keep the perspective of who I am throughout the process and to keep my ultimate motivations and vision clear.

Through my continuing efforts with EPIC and my creative and entrepreneurial pursuits, I use the Watch Me! mind-set and my own 10-step program to help me achieve my goals, step-by-step.

I believe that everything worth doing takes time and effort, but your dreams can easily come to fruition if your goals are clear, progressive, and taken one step at a time. Ultimately, these goals help you to fulfill your purpose and passions in life, as well as to discover more about yourself along the way.

Chapter 12

Let It Go: The Watch Me! Mind-set Begins with Letting Go

L IFE IN ALL ITS MYSTERY seems to hand us a myriad of struggles and hardships to get through, moment to moment and day after day. We are always striving for more but seem to get nowhere. Have you ever stopped to think about how much anxiety you put into all of your plans before you actually begin to execute them? Though your body has performed no physical action, your mind is already exhausted from the thought of it all! Of critical importance in letting go is knowing what to give up and what to pursue. Applying the Watch Me! mind-set to letting go essentially boils down to balance.

Apart from actions you apply daily, there are few things in your life that you truly have control over. Your actions include, but are certainly not limited to, learning, practicing, exercising the mind, and exercising the body. These are the things you can control in your physical sense of being. However, there is undoubtedly more than just the physical realm. This is where the essential life balance comes into play. As much as you can control the activities you choose to participate in daily, life always seems to take back the reigns of control and let you know that you don't have ultimate control over everything.

So keep in mind as you read about the Watch Me! mind-set that it isn't about having maximum control over your life. Nor is it about leaving it all up to chance, a higher power, or destiny to do all the work. It's about finding the right balance to carry out your passions and purpose by letting go of the things you ultimately have no control over.

Time

Time is a tricky little subject. We all seem to fall victim to the lack of time we create in our busy little worlds. We're always too busy, too late, too tired, too bored, and too stressed, but every human being has the same amount of time to work with. If we surrendered to the fact that we can't *ever* control time, would we then stop trying to manage it? Could we ever admit that time was there before us and will be there after us? And if we did give up our need to control time, couldn't we then focus more on managing our actions and ourselves and not time?

Time is just a series of moments in the present, strung together in a chain that includes the past and determines the future. This is why our present is so important to manage. This present will affect our future and our path. So why not start making peace with time? If you stop living your life for the chaos of the world, you will stop being a victim of time.

Our modern conveniences have only added to the stress and sense of lack of time in our lives. Put controls on how much time you spend on cell phones, e-mails, social media, television, and text messages. Don't feel obligated to take every phone call. Tell your friends the times you will be available to talk. Only you can manage your time, so choose wisely and stop letting technology be your priority. So much time is wasted on mundane tasks and busy work that makes us *feel* productive but doesn't really get us any closer to the finish line. Start monitoring how much time you really spend on such things, and then start regulating it!

Put Your Mind at Ease

When applying the Watch Me! mind-set, you may come up against what seem to be some pretty tough challenges. But keep in mind, life only gives you what you can handle, and none of it is given to you by accident. Remember, everything happens for a reason. Every hill you have to climb has another side that you can descend with great ease.

Life's challenges are never meant to devastate you; they are merely the lessons that are sent to you to enable you to learn and grow. They are all placed in front of you so you can learn something about yourself. So start taking all your negatives and find the positives in them!

Start surrendering to life and what it brings you. Try not to curse the negatives, but accept them with a knowing that they are there for a reason. With reflection, answers about how to solve these challenges will come. This surrender will ultimately bring you closer to discovering your authentic self and keep you navigating the right path.

Surrendering to the Divine

When I say "the Divine," I don't mean to push any religion of any sort on you. Everyone relates to their feelings or knowledge of the Divine in their own way. It can be an infinite amount of possibilities because it is everything. It is bigger than us. It is the ultimate flow of life. I personally don't subscribe to any religious beliefs, but I do believe in something greater than us that is ultimately in control. You can think of it as God, or destiny, or just the flow of life; whatever you're comfortable with, feel free to define it in that way.

When going through your journey, there are only two agendas to follow: yours and that of the Divine. Until you have ultimately surrendered your life's control to the Divine, you will find that your agenda will clash with its agenda.

When you force your life to move in a direction that disagrees with your ultimate destiny and higher purpose, life creates hardships or roadblocks. You can try and fight with all of your might to overcome these bumps in the road, but the universe will always win. When you face obstacles, you can either give up on life and live a meager existence, or you can give in to the Divine, which is in control, and try your best to reach your higher purpose and live beyond your dreams.

Although this concept of surrendering to a higher power sounds fairly simple, it may be the hardest part of your journey toward fulfilling your purpose. You must be willing to confront the darkest shadows of your past and see them through the eyes of the Divine.

When you thoroughly examine them, you will probably discover that the most challenging people or situations have become your greatest teachers in life, compelling you to move toward personal success and your ultimate destiny. For this reason, it is important to forgive them and put your negative feelings behind you.

Once you surrender to this notion that your higher purpose is your reason for being in this world, you will come to realize that failure doesn't exist. To the Divine, there is no such thing as failure, just redirection. This redirection comes when you may need a drastic wake-up call to readjust how you go about working toward your ultimate path and purpose. Life is a game designed for you to win, even though it seems impossible at times.

The Watch Me! mind-set is about telling yourself every day, "Watch me—today I'm going to live for my purpose, regardless of what anyone says, including my own negative and self-defeating thoughts!" Using the Watch Me! mind-set is the inner redirection and focus that keeps you motivated and inspired to win at *your* game in life, with the ultimate prize being success in fulfilling your higher purpose, living your dreams, and reaching beyond them to create new goals and dreams to pursue.

Chapter 13

One Step at a Time

~~

Now that you have a bit of insight into managing the present, surrendering to the Divine, prioritizing your goals, and ultimately letting go, you are now ready for the mental preparation needed to start your journey. However, now you need to take an active role in self-exploration and conditioning your talents to fully achieve your destiny.

Let's face it—we all have these amazing visions in our minds of what we see for ourselves if everything could only work out. Well here's the honest truth: Are you ready for it? It *can* work out if you're willing to *work* out! I'm not talking about hitting the gym, although that's never a bad idea; I'm talking about the fundamental workout plan of life, the ladder. Applying the Watch Me! mind-set is as simple as climbing these ladders of life, at your own pace, step-by-step.

I've mapped out an easy and progressive self-exploration 10-step guide to achieving whatever it is you want out of life. Within the steps, I'll ask you to do some soul searching through writing. You can do this in a journal or notebook, but keep in mind that this will inevitably be the book about you! Be thorough in your writing and above all, be honest. This is for no one but you. You can keep this journal as a reminder of your climb to personal success, and it will help in keeping you motivated, one step at a time.

Prior to this section, I have included what I consider to be crucial insights into using this 10-step system in your everyday life. Although there are 10 important steps on this ladder, it is the ladder itself that is the most crucial to your success.

This ladder represents your higher purpose, path, or destiny that was granted to you from the Divine. While climbing your own ladder, keep in perspective that the Divine is ultimately in charge of everything, and trust that your various paths will reveal themselves to you as long as you stay focused and righteous in your intentions.

My Favorite Color Is . . .

Step 1: Knowing Your True Self

Now I know this sounds easy, right? But *really* think about it: Who are you? What do you love in life? What do you hate? What are your talents? What do you desire? When was the last time you took some *"you"* time to think of all these things?

Well that's where this first step comes into play. I mean, what's the use of climbing up a ladder when you don't even know how high it is, or where it may eventually lead? So here's your first assignment: take a pen and some paper and start getting to know yourself!

Here are some helpful things to consider when writing:

1. When was the last time you were truly happy? What was it that you were doing at this moment?

2. What is it about yourself that makes you feel inadequate or afraid? Where or what does this fear stem from?

3. What are some of the feelings you'd like to feel more of in your life? What do you need to do to start feeling them more?

Knock, Knock . . . It's Your Ego

Step 2: Recognizing Your Strengths and Your Weaknesses without Your Ego Getting Involved

Okay, so you've done a little soul searching. How do you feel? Scared? Relieved? Elated? Whatever it is, I hope you feel a little closer to that secret *you* locked inside that shell of yours!

Remember when I told you to think about your desires? You know, those things that seem so far away and so unachievable? What do we call those . . . oh yeah, dreams! Well, what would it take for you to achieve those dreams?

Would you have to be an amazing athlete? A no-holds-barred business person? A talented musician? A skilled artist? Whatever the case, get to know what you're good at! Everyone has a talent; you just need to discover yours!

Write these down as a list, and don't be afraid to write as much as you can; stretch yourself and really dig deep. There's no room to be modest here!

Oh, and when that little voice (ego) undoubtedly objects to your positive thoughts about your strengths, pick that thought right out of your head and throw it on a piece of paper so you can see how mean you've been to yourself!

Phew! Not that bad, right? I know, at first it seemed a little hard, but once you started being honest with yourself, you really start to see that list grow. Congratulations! You've almost fully climbed to Step 2 of your ladder, but there's still one more foot that needs to come up.

The second foot is a little easier than the first to move up, only because we're all used to doing it so often. This is where you make a list of all your weaknesses. Now, I'm not talking about those last five pounds you have to lose, or the fact that you have an insatiable appetite for donuts that you just can't kick! No, I'm talking about character weaknesses: pride, self-doubt, frustration, shyness, lack of determination, or laziness. Does any of this ring a bell yet? Most people's lists will closely resemble each other's. We all have these little seeds of character weaknesses that will only grow given the proper nutrients. Start listing so you can find out what you should avoid feeding your soul to stop these weaknesses from growing.

When listing your weaknesses, remember to focus on character weaknesses and things that would eventually affect obtaining your goals.

I Fear Nothing . . . Except What I'm Not Good at!

Step 3: Recognizing the Fears That Stem from Your Weaknesses

Okay, so you've taken a *huge* step and actually written down all your strengths and weaknesses. Good job! Now, I'm going to need you to take a deeper look at those weaknesses and figure out what you're afraid of because of them.

Are you typically a lazy person? If this is one of your weaknesses, maybe a fear of yours is becoming successful and having to work all the time. Maybe you feel intimidated by the response you'll get from your public, because you don't feel 100 percent confident in your craft. Whatever the case, figure out *what* you're afraid of and *why*.

It's really quite simple. All fears stem from feeling inadequate to handle whatever situation you're in. Your inadequacies are what you see as your weaknesses. So by giving these weaknesses a label, and by recognizing the fear that stems from each weakness, you can then transform your fears into self-confidence by strengthening your weaknesses!

Rewrite the previous list of your weaknesses out, and add the fear that stems from each weakness. Don't be afraid to be honest with yourself!

I Want to Be an Astronaut, but I Hate Flying!

Step 4: Applying How Your Strengths and Weaknesses Will Affect Your Ultimate Dreams

Remember Step 1? That was the one in which you dared to ask, "What is it that I actually want from my life?" Well, I want you to go back to that, back to that dream that fuels your soul. Have you got a clear picture in your head? Good. Now, let's go back to that pesky Step 2, the list of strengths and weaknesses. How will these traits in Step 2 affect your pursuit of your ultimate dreams?

Are you dying to walk on the moon and uncover the hidden secrets of the universe? Not if you are deathly afraid of flying! How do you plan on breaking through sound barriers if you can't even clear 35,000 feet? This is where all of us dreamers need to become realists.

What is it about yourself that will affect your goals? You've got to face your fears! Hey, if it's a fear of flying, why not try a short, one-hour flight to start getting over it? Then progress to a longer flight until you can work up to a cross-country flight. Every fear can be overcome; it's just a matter of how much you are willing to take a risk to change and achieve your goals.

How bad do you *really* want this? If you know you're never setting foot on a plane, you can throw out the idea of ever being an astronaut! But why not test yourself and push yourself to that ultimate limit? Isn't that what the Watch Me! mind-set is all about? Why not take a look in the mirror and say it to yourself, *"Watch me!"* Push yourself and test why you are afraid of whatever it is—face your fears so you can overcome them!

Make a list of what will ultimately affect your dreams, good and bad, from the list of strengths and weaknesses. This is something of a progress report for you. You'll see how far along you actually are, and how much further you need to go to obtain your goals.

When it then comes to listing what will adversely affect your dreams, make sure to write what it is you can do to get over this weakness or fear so you can start climbing up the ladder!

I Love You . . . but I Can't Commit

Step 5: Committing to Overcoming Your Weaknesses and Solidifying Your Strengths

Does fear of commitment sound too familiar? That's right, folks, we live in the day and age of the ultimate fear: commitment! But when I say "commitment" what is it that first comes to mind? A romantic relationship? If so, change your focus young Skywalker—I'm talking about your life!

Why is it that we can talk until we're blue in the face about what we see for ourselves and what we know we are capable of, and yet we can also give every reason under the sun why it just hasn't worked out yet? It's about commitment. We all want to sound as if we are committed to our dreams, but how many of us *really* are?

To be *fully* committed to our dreams we must first know *what* we are committing to. How can we fulfill our dreams if we still view ourselves as having all of those weaknesses we wrote out in Step 2? Sure, we know you have strengths, but let's start by working through your fears and your weaknesses. You must be willing to take positive risks to change and grow.

Look at your last assignment where you wrote down what you can do to overcome your weaknesses. So, what are you waiting for? Do it. Go ahead. No, really, it's not that hard, I promise. Don't let this intimidate you. Take it one step at a time, but know that each step is a step closer to your goals and adds a new strength to your list. Doesn't that sound good? Imagine what you can do with a whole list of strengths? That will happen if you continue to work at them!

Strength in relation to your character is just like strength in relation to your body. To build up your muscle strength, you work out. You hit the gym, go for a run, lift some weights, master the stairs, and so on. But what would happen if you stopped? Sure, for a while you'd look great. But slowly your muscles would become weaker, your metabolism would slow down, and you'd be right back to where you started! So why should it be any different when building your character strengths? You have to commit to working on your strengths every day so that they are always just as strong, or (hopefully) stronger!

Refer to the list you created in Step 4's assignment. Pick out the first weakness you are going to commit to changing into a strength. Then write out your own personal plan of commitment for achieving this!

Next, write out your own personal plan of commitment for maintaining and improving your strengths. Is it pushing yourself to practice for an extra hour a night? Doing four more laps around the track? Reading up on your interests to keep your mind in the positive flow of things? Whatever it is, start committing!

I'm the Best, Because I Said So

Step 6: Be Confident, Not Cocky, in Your Strengths and Talents

Look at you! You talented thing! Why, you have all the tools to make it. Not only have you honed your skills, but you also, by golly, have mastered them. Well, almost. And this is the tricky part—*you will never fully master anything!* Sounds crazy right? But think about it. If you feel you've mastered something, why would you need to put any more time or effort into it? This is something that you *must* keep in mind while working toward your dreams. You are always a student, always learning, always striving for more because there is always more to accomplish and learn. This is what it means to live beyond your dreams. Set a goal, do everything in your power to achieve it, but then step it up a notch and challenge yourself to go further than you could've ever imagined.

In any industry, the cocky only go so far. It's the strong, insightful, and talented individuals who achieve and maintain success. The ones who achieve lasting success know where they are presently, but they always keep in mind where they came from. Success is about striving for your dreams by using your talents, but keeping in mind that something bigger than you is always in control, and you always have something new to learn. So have some humility—it looks good on you!

It's Not Quantity, It's Quality!

Step 7: Surround Yourself with Like-Minded, Positive People

Have you ever been around those people who suck all the positive energy out of you? You know, they're the ones who constantly complain about *everything* that's wrong with their life and why they can't do *anything* about it? Have you got those people in your mind? Those are the people to avoid! It's hard enough dealing with all the negativity we feed ourselves. Who needs someone else's drama?

This step is what really solidifies you because the company you keep ultimately defines who you are. Don't you think you would feel more motivated if your best friend got up every day with a positive mind-set? Or if you spent your free time filling your life with optimistic people, experiences, and conversations that would push you in a positive direction?

With all of the time you are about to dedicate to yourself, you'll want to be *very* choosy about who you spend your free time with. These people will ultimately help shape the path that you walk. I know it seems hard to take a step back from those friends of yours who have become so in need of receiving all of your commiseration and advice. But if they love you, they'll understand your need for personal time and energy to focus on your goals!

This step also comes in handy when finding a workout buddy to climb the ladder with. Why not find someone with the same goals as yours, or a similar goal that leads you both up a comparable ladder? That person will help to motivate you to get up and go on those days that you don't feel like going, to maintain a positive outlook on your journey, and to stay focused on your goals.

Remember, you need as many positive voices around you as you can find! So shed all of the negatives in your life: your inner fears, negative self-talk, toxic people, and harmful habits and things. Try looking up for a change.

I Have the Perfect Plan for Success, Which Will Begin as Soon as My Favorite TV Show Is Over!

Step 8: Get Up and Go!

What are you waiting for? You have all the necessary steps to make you who you've always wanted to be. So what's holding you back? At this point you should know yourself fairly well, so make sure you always check in with yourself to see that you are still on the path to greatness.

Are you still honing your strengths? Working on those pesky little weaknesses? Surrounding yourself with positive people? Are you keeping your life in balance? Are you still committed? Are you keeping an eye on your goal sheet? If so, congratulations! If not, reevaluate your goals, what you really want, and how much you're willing to commit to it.

Make a note of what you still need to work on. If it's something you just can't seem to overcome, put little reminder notes all around you: on the fridge, in your wallet, in your car, wherever they will serve as a constant reminder to you. Be honest with yourself—no one's watching!

I Am, Therefore I Am

Step 9: Own It!

Welcome to your life! I'm glad you finally decided to show up. It's very exciting from this point on! Oh, the successes you'll achieve and the experiences you'll have! Just make sure you're getting up every day and owning who you actually are.

Live your dreams, live with passion, and reach beyond—from the moment you wake up to the moment you close those starry eyes of yours! When people ask what you do, tell them. Let everyone know *who* you are and *what* drives you. In the process, you may even convince your old, negative self of what a positive person you have become!

What Do You Mean, It's Not All About Me?

Step 10: Give Back

This step challenges you to look past everything you've built for yourself and find ways, big or small, to give back. Mentor a child, donate to a charity, or volunteer your time. There are many ways to give, and with a source such as the Internet, you can find a way that suits your interests and needs. Remember, there is always a needy cause that could use your unique talents, services, or voice, so excuses don't fly here! Find something you care deeply about and figure out how to help. Some people think charity is only about *giving* of yourself or donating your money, but the rewards of working with others and helping to make a difference are priceless!

Congratulations! You have successfully climbed your own progressive 10-step ladder to personal victory. But when you get to the top, start climbing toward another goal and living beyond your initial dreams. Remember, there are always new mountains to climb and new frontiers to discover, so never limit yourself or live small. We are all amazing human beings who are capable of extraordinary feats, and selling yourself short is doing a disservice to humankind.

Dream big. Live big. Live passionately. And always ask yourself: "Where will my ladder take me next?"

Epilogue

~~~~~

IN CONCLUSION, the Watch Me! mind-set has to be applied to your innermost self. Take your frustration with not feeling complete in your current life and apply it to finding your true self and ultimate destiny through motivational and inspirational reading, journaling your goals and feelings, meditating for focus and conviction, and surrendering to your divine higher power.

You cannot just sit around and wait for miracles to happen. You must take an active role in defining your goals and refining your talents, so that when success comes knocking on your door, you're dressed and ready to go!

It may seem a little overwhelming to do all of this "self work," but it's a small sacrifice you should make now to save you from a troubling future that could potentially find you "lost in the midst of it all."

This step-by-step self-transformation starts with you willing to *let go* and understand the balance of control in your life. It continues with you focusing on your personal ladder toward self-exploration and goal setting, which will ultimately lead you to carrying out your destiny and higher purpose every day.

So take the time—you're worth it! And not only will you prove your destiny to the world, but more importantly, you'll also prove it to yourself!

Conclusion by Riana:
It's Never Really Over

I BELIEVE THE MOST IMPORTANT THING to understand is that your journey, like the concepts in this book, never really ends. Each day, each step we take, and each goal we set is in fluid motion—always evolving, changing, growing, and being reinvented and reevaluated.

We were born into this Earth school to learn many extremely important lessons that we will carry with us to the next stage of being. Yes, there is a lot to be done before that second stage! We have been granted a limited amount of time, and we need to do our best to reach our higher purpose dream before our time is done.

We were all meant for greatness, so I ask you: What will you do today to improve your journey in life? Start with your desire to change, and then incorporate the other four Ds (determination, dedication, devotion, and dare to dream) to get you going on your goals. Keep reading, learning, growing, and challenging yourself by creating and meeting your daily, weekly, monthly, and six-month goals for both personal/relationship and business/academic success. When you look back, you will see how your amazing life has unfolded, and you will be filled with a sense of pride and accomplishment.

In sharing the philosophy of the Watch Me! mind-set with you, I hope that you have stopped to rethink your direction, to revalue your time and relationships, and to decide that a spiritual sense of purpose is of the utmost importance in feeling a sense of accomplishment.

Always monitor the balance within your various life spheres for a calm, peaceful, and powerful personal approach to all your important relationships. Have the faith to know that our higher divine power did give us many blessings and talents that not only can bring us personal happiness and success, but also can ultimately allow us to serve and give back to our world.

I believe that we are *all* God's angels and are here to spread His light and goodness upon the world, one person at a time. If I have somehow touched your heart; taught you to set some worthwhile personal goals; fed your purpose with inspirational and motivational ideas; convinced you that your moods are entirely dependent upon your own self-thoughts, perceptions, and interpretations; and have taught you to actively choose love over fear with each decision, then I have indeed succeeded in some of my higher purpose goals.

Please share your love, light, sense of calm, ability to forgive, your spiritual belief, and your passion to give back to everyone you meet. Be a positive being to help those who are giving up on themselves, who feel stuck in their personal lives, or who are depressed because no one believes in them. Encourage them to seek the help of a spiritually-based and holistic counselor or coach to get refocused and make an unexpected change or a painful transition a positive growth period for them.

Buy them a copy of this book and encourage them to understand that all they need to do is to *start believing in themselves* and to start making the goals that will inspire their growth to reach their dreams. Share with them your personal knowledge, experience, and success in living the inspirational, spiritual, and motivational principles of the Watch Me! mind-set.

I thank you all for taking this journey with Alexi and me, and I truly pray that the words "Watch Me!" will burn forever within your hearts, minds, and souls as a glorious, bright shining light leading the way to your ultimate higher purpose to live beyond your dreams!

Since Our Last Conclusion: Update from Riana

I T'S BEEN AN AMAZING six years since our first book was written about the Watch Me! mind-set (Watch Me! *The Bold, New Motivational Attitude for Personal Success*), as there have been many successes, celebrations, and also challenges.

During challenges, is it said that pain is our greatest teacher, and I can't agree more. At such times, we must reinvent ourselves and do the soul searching needed to ask, "Why is this happening, and what am I supposed to learn from it?"

These trials in our life actually bring us back into our most spiritual center and presence, as we ask God to clarify an issue and help show us the way to heal. It is a time to seek and align ourselves with a new simplicity, a deeper spiritual devotion, and a conscious effort to live in the now so that we can experience every sign and message that presents itself and shows us what to do next.

It is a time to ask ourselves, "What do I want and need to do that I have put on hold for way too long?" So many of us get swept up in our to-do lists, daily grind, hectic schedules, and working just to survive. Our country has undergone a huge financial debt and mortgage crisis since 2008, in which so many have lost sight of their dreams as they lose their jobs and homes. I am finishing this book during Hurricane Sandy, the worst disaster to hit the east coast of NJ and many areas in and around New York City. Although the eye of the storm passed right by me in Egg Harbor Township, NJ, I was extremely lucky and only lost power for a few days. Many lost their homes in an instant, and many lost their lives.

Pure survival makes us forget our dreams and the purpose of our lives, and until we can meet our basic needs for food, water, sleep, shelter, safety and work/income. The next higher level of needs include friendship, family, love, sexual connection, and belonging which should be satisfied so you can focus your energy on your higher purpose goals and move on to advanced level achievements. If you are struggling with the level one, most basic needs category, get support from a counselor or coach, or your city's social services.

According to Abraham Maslow's hierarchy of needs, as described in his 1954 book *Motivation and Personality*, only after the most basic needs are mastered and met can you then build self-esteem, confidence, and achievement. The top tier in the hierarchy is self-actualization, which pertains to a person's full potential and the process of coming to realize that potential. Maslow describes this as "the desire to become more than what one is, and to become everything that one is capable of becoming." It is this highest level need that many struggle to reach and which this book addresses. Self-actualization is the process of being your highest and best self by serving others daily through the joy of our work. If your work is not meaningful or is not fulfilling your lifelong passion, reevaluate your life, get refocused, set up new goals, and fight the fear to make a change for the better. Risk new growth and face challenges using your goal-setting system to reenergize you, and dare to dream of being your best self and beyond.

Continued stress, anxiety, depression or a daily fight to live is telling you something: it is time for a change, time to take care of your mind, body, and soul. Get enough rest, eat healthy foods, read as much as possible about the issue you are facing, as well as motivational and inspirational books, and take the time to meditate and pray. Practice your spiritual faith to find the answers you seek. Please always believe in yourself, and never lose sight of your divine purpose.

Challenges can either break you or cause you to become your best self. Use the Watch Me! mind-set along with spiritual faith, and choose to make all of life's transitions a time for reflection, learning, and personal transformation. It may be helpful to see a certified coach or a therapist to help you process and prepare for these changes, and I would be honored to assist you along the way.

Over the years I have received so many blessings! I have watched my daughters grow into wonderful, giving, successful business-women who live with integrity and share their love and art with the world. I feel such bliss when sharing in both my daughters' joys and accomplishments. I have acquired a magnificent son-in-law, Charles (and his family), and have such incredible happiness that I am about to be a grandmother to Stephana and Charles's baby boy!

For thirteen years I have had the honor to be the coach and counselor for so many fabulous people, and in the past nine years, I have had the opportunity to work full-time in my private practice, Therapy by the Sea, in Atlantic County, NJ, helping hundreds of people of all ages. I received my certificates for relationship coaching (singles and couples), and my app, *My Relationship Coach*, is about to launch any day for smartphones and iPads. This will now give me the opportunity to help people from all over the world! I am also in the process of acquiring my Florida state license for mental health counseling; as I hope to retire there in the near future.

Many of my therapy and coaching clients have read about the Watch Me! mind-set and have felt so inspired by it that they have written heartwarming notes and testimonials about how it touched their lives. Many returned to buy more books for friends and family members who are going through challenging times. I feel so grateful that I could, in some way, do what I was born to do: help and inspire others through their deepest emotional pain and toughest transitions. As the book helps them, their payment benefits EPIC and my arts scholarship fund, so everyone wins!

As I do my daily work with married and committed couples who find their relationships in severe jeopardy, single people who are looking for love or who have experienced painful, traumatic breakups, or families with parent-child discord, I have seen many recurring issues emerging. I felt that I desperately needed to address these issues to ease the emotional agony of these clients.

This has led me to write my forthcoming book, *Love Beyond Your Dreams: Break Free from Toxic Relationships to Have the Love You Deserve*. I am also planning my third book in this series, *Relationships Beyond Your Dreams: Strategies to Stay Together during Today's Challenging Times*.

It is my goal to offer audiobooks, informative products, webinars, podcasts, and intensive weekend retreats for couples and singles in the near future. Information on upcoming events is available on my Web site, www.RianaMilne.com and on my app, *My Relationship Coach*.

Using the Watch Me! mind-set and staying keenly focused on my higher purpose, I pledge to continue my journey along with you to help us all reach our God-given potential, vision, and goals to live beyond our dreams!

May God bless you all!

The Day the Watch Me!
Mind-set Was Born

A Child of the World
By Riana Milne in 1974, age 16

Be strong, my child—
stand tall and heed,
know and understand
how confusing our world can be.
With the changing of times,
our secure society could erupt,
to leave a person with nothing
except himself
and his own mind.

Believe in what good
can be found in confusion.
You are you—you know
your needs and personal preferences.
Follow them through . . .

Not with the dream of how nice
things could be,
but with a goal to get what you deserve—
a happy life.

Beautiful things come from
your heart and soul.
Realize this and share
this God-given gift with others,
for He meant it to be that way.
And enjoy the gifts of others,
for they want to share their special gifts too!
Do let them . . .
and enjoy their qualities:
the good and the not so good,
for these traits keep life
interesting for all.

Breathe and take in the joys of life . . .
You are entitled to as much as any other!
It's all there waiting for the asking.
Don't be afraid . . .
Believe in your spirit and remember
how fate is determined
only for your best interest.

Bear others when you do not agree.
They are entitled to their own stories,
True or false
understand that people can be weak . . .
and hate to admit it.

Comfort them, and someday,
they too will comfort you.

But most important of all,
Find peace . . .
In yourself as well as in others.
Believe in your beliefs;
Don't change to the desires of others,
for your peace will soon desert you,
and you will have no mind . . .
if you allow others to govern it!

So stand up, my child!
Be proud of what You are . . .
For You are You!

Riana and her two daughters, Alexi and Stephana,
by the sea in Ventnor, NJ.

Haiku from Riana's Journal
(1973)

You were born to die
And there's a pause in between
Which is only Life

What will you do with yours?

How to Apply or Donate
to The Riana Milne Scholarship Fund
for the Arts

I PERSONALLY UNDERSTAND how critical the performing arts were to my life, my daughter's lives, and to the many students at Riana Model & Talent School in Erie, PA and New York City. Because creative people often choose careers and training outside of the typical college program, there is not much financial support to get the professional training they need to succeed.

This fund was established with the publication of our first book in 2006. With each book sold, I will donate two dollars to the general scholarship fund. However, for any school purchasing *Live Beyond Your Dreams: From Fear and Doubt to Personal Power, Purpose, and Success* as a textbook directly from By the Sea Books Publishing Company, the two dollars will go toward a scholarship award at *that particular school.* This book teaches profoundly important life skills needed for success. It is not just for those students who are interested in the arts, but for all adolescents who have a dream.

Applications for this scholarship opened January 1, 2007, and students may apply every January thereafter. Award winners will be chosen by May 1st of each year and a scholarship award will be presented at graduation. Seniors who are planning to graduate and who have a 3.5 GPA or better may apply. Since both my daughters graduated with a GPA over 3.5, I am setting the standard this high to reward those creative individuals who deserve a scholarship based on educational excellence—those who have a desire and dedication to develop their talent, regardless of race, gender, or financial need.

You may apply for a scholarship for the following professions: modeling, singing, acting (stage, film, or television), dancing, broadcasting (radio or TV), writing (music, poetry, other), or photography.

Please type an essay of 500 to 1000 words in 12-point Times New Roman font. Please discuss why you deserve a scholarship, and exactly what you would do with the funds awarded. Your essay should include the amount needed for the school, program, or services required to become a professional. These could include a model and talent school, a production studio for a music demo, a photographer for professional models' or actors' shots, a singing coach, or other professional services needed to launch your creative arts career. Training schools you hope to attend could include a *licensed* model, talent, acting, or dance school; a broadcast communications school, photography school, or a music production/singing school.

Along with your essay, send a professional talent resume, your most recent report card and proof of your GPA, and any support materials to prove your talent: photographs, writing samples, a demo CD of you singing or music you produced, or a DVD of your acting performance. Applications will be accepted yearly from January 1st through April 1st at midnight. Include your name, address, phone, and personal e-mail address, as well as your high school's name, address, and phone number, and a counselor/adviser's name.

Send your application package to this address:

Riana Milne
15300 Jog Rd, unit 109
Delray Beach, FL 33446 USA

For donations to the Scholarship Fund, please include your email address, and a receipt will be sent back to you by email for a tax deduction.

Send your questions to the following email:
BytheSeaBookPublishing@gmail.com,
Attention: Scholarship Fund.

Thank you, and good luck in your careers! Riana Milne

The EPIC Movement and Nonprofit Organization

EVERYDAY PEOPLE INITIATING CHANGE (EPIC) is a nonprofit organization committed to bringing safe, clean drinking water to a number of villages in the developing world.

Through the implementation of clean water wells, along with hygiene and sanitation education programs, EPIC provides a sustainable solution to the vast problems people in the developing world face today.

EPIC hopes to inspire *everyday people* to realize their potential to *initiate* positive *change* by recognizing that every single day is another opportunity to help put a stop the world's unnecessary injustices!

Every day provides you with the opportunity to be a part of something epic—*What did you do today?*

To **find** out more about how you can make a positive change, please **visit us and arrange your donation** at **www.epicthemovement.org.** Thank you so much for your contribution to this worthy cause.

With sincere thanks,
Alexi Panos and Tennille Amor
Cofounders of EPIC.

References and Recommended Reading

Assaraf, John, and Smith, Murray. *The Answer: Grow Any Business, Achieve Financial Freedom, and Live an Extraordinary Life.* NY: Simon & Schuster, 2008.

Ban Breathnach, Sarah. *Something More: Excavating Your Authentic Self* (audio recording). NY: Time Warner AudioBooks, 1998.

Browne, Sylvia. *Lessons for Life* and *Blessings from the Other Side.* www.SylviaBrowne.com.

Butler, Gillian, and Hope, Tony. *Managing Your Mind: The Mental Fitness Guide.* NY: Oxford University Press, 1995.

Byrne, Rhonda. *The Secret.* (DVD movie). TS Productions LLC, 2006.

Chopra, Deepak. *The Book of Secrets: Unlocking the Hidden Dimensions of Your Life.* NY: Random House, 2004.

Chopra, Deepak. *The Seven Spiritual Laws of Success: A Practical Guide to the Fulfillment of Your Dreams* (audio recording). San Rafael, CA: New World Library, 1994.

Chopra, Deepak. *Ageless Body, Timeless Mind: The Quantum Alternative to Growing Old.* NY: Harmony Books, 1993.

Coles, Robert. *The Moral Intelligence of Children: How to Raise a Moral Child* (audio recording). Los Angeles, CA: Audio Renaissance Tapes, 1997.

Covey, Stephen. *Beyond the 7 Habits* (audio recording). NY: Simon & Schuster, 2003.

Covey, Stephen. *Living the 7 Habits: Stories of Courage and Inspiration* (audio recording). NY: Simon & Schuster Audio, 1999.

Daniels, Dawn Marie, and Sandy, Candace. *Tears to Triumph: Women Learn to Live, Love and Thrive.* NY: Kensington Publishing, 2009.

Doman, Glen, *The Institutes for the Achievement of Human Potential*, www.laph.org.

Dooley, Mike. *Manifesting Change: It Couldn't Be Easier.* NY: Simon & Schuster, 2010.

Dyer, Dr. Wayne. *Inspiration: Your Ultimate Calling* (audio recording) Hay House Inc, 2006.

Dyer, Dr. Wayne. *Staying on the Path.* Carisbad, CA: Hay House Inc, 2004.

Edward, John. *One Last Time. A psychic medium talks to those we have loved and lost.* www.JohnEdward.net.

Erickson, Erik. Psychological Stages of Development Summary Chart. www.psychology.about.com/library/bl_psycholsocial_summary.htm.

Gafni, Marc. *Soul Prints: Your Path to Fulfillment* (audio recording). NY: Simon & Schuster Audio, 2001.

Hicks, Esther and Jerry. *The Astonishing Power of Emotions: Let Feelings Be Your Guide.* Carlsbad, CA: Hay House; 2007.

Hill, Napoleon. *Think and Grow Rich.* NY: Penguin Group, 2005.

Ilardi, Stephen. *The Depression Cure: The 6-Step Program to Beat Depression without Drugs.* Philadelphia, PA: Da Capo Press, 2009.

Lerner, Harriet. *On Mothers & Daughters: Breaking the Patterns that Keep You Stuck* (audio recording) Boulder, CO: Sounds True Audio, 1995.

Lieberman, David. *Instant Analysis: How You Can Understand and Change Self- Defeating Behaviors & Habits.* NY: Martin's Press, 1997.

Mackay, Harvey. *Pushing the Envelope: All the Way to the Top* (audio recording). NY: Random House Audio Books, 1999.

McNeilly, Robert. *Healing the Whole Person.* NY: John Wiley & Sons, 2000.

Miedaner, Talane. *The Secret Laws of Attraction: The Effortless Way to Get the Relationship You Want.* NY: McGraw Hill, 2008.

Miedaner, Talane. *Coach Yourself to Success: 101 Tips from a Personal Coach for Reaching your Goals at Work and in Life.* Chicago, IL: Contemporary Books, 2000.

Mims, Ana. *Keeping the Faith: How Applying Spiritual Purpose to Your Work Can Lead to Extraordinary Success.* NY: HarperCollins, 2007.

Moore, Thomas. *Care of the Soul; A Guide for Cultivating Depth and Sacredness in Everyday Life* (audio recording). NY: Harper Audio, 1992.

Orman, Suze. *Women & Money.* New York, NY. Random House, 2007.

Osteen, Joel. *Good, Better, Blessed: Living with Purpose, Power and Passion* (audio recording). New York, NY: Simon & Schuster, 2008.

Osteen, Joel. *Your Best Life Now: 7 Steps to Living at your Full Potential.* NY: Hachette Books Group, 2004.

Prochaska, James, Norcross, John, and Diclemente, Carlo. *Changing for Good: A Revolutionary Six-stage Program for Overcoming Bad Habits and Moving Your Life Positively Forward.* NY: Avon Books, 1994.

Robbins, Anthony, with Dr. John Gray. *Powertalk! On Creating Extraordinary Relationships* (audio recording). Los Angeles, CA: Audio Renaissance Tapes, 1996.

Roger, John, and Kaye, Paul. *Momentum—Letting Love Lead: Simple Practices for Spiritual Living.* Los Angeles, CA: Manderville Press, 2003.

Salzberg, Sharon. *Faith Trusting Your Own Deepest Experience.* London: Element Books, 2002.

Sha, Dr., and Master Zhi Gang. *Divine Transformation: The Divine Way to Self-clear Karma to Transform Your Health, Relationships, Finances and More.* NY: Simon & Schuster, 2010.

Shumsky, Susan. *Divine Revelation.* NY: Simon & Schuster, 1996.

St. James, Elaine. *Inner Simplicity: Regain Peace and Spirituality* (audio recording). NY: Bantum Doubleday Dell Audio Publishing, 1998.

Taylor, John Maxwell. *The Power of I Am: Creating a New World of Enlightened Personal Interaction.* Berkeley, CA: Frog Publishing, 2006.

Tolle, Eckhart. *A New Earth: Awaking to Your Life's Purpose.* NY: Penguin Group, 2005.

Tolle, Eckhart. *The Power of Now: A Guide to Spiritual Enlightenment.* Novato, CA: New World Library, 1999.

Urban, Hal. *Choices that Change Lives: 15 Ways to Find More Purpose, Meaning and Joy.* NY: Simon & Schuster, 2006.

Van Praagh, James. *Tuning into Healing/Forgiveness* (audio recording). NY: Penguin Audio Books, 1998.

Vitale, Dr. Joe. *Expect Miracles: The Missing Secret to Astounding Success* (audio recording). Gildan Media Corp, 2009.

www.Webmd.com. Web resource for herbal and holistic vitamins, remedies, and medicines.

Williamson, Marianne. *The Gift of Change: Spiritual Guidance for a Radically New Life* (audio recording). San Francisco, CA: Harper Audio, 2004.

Williamson, Marianne. *On Intimacy* (audio recording). www .marianne.com/books

Woods, Len. *Handbook of World Religions.* Uhrichsville, OH: Barbour Publishing, 2008.

Notes

Life & Relationship Coaching
provided by Riana Milne

For details, pricing information and to register for any coaching program, go to the web site www.RianaMilne.com or email: RianaMilne@gmail.com

Coaching services for those:
Single, Dating, Engaged, Married, in Painful Relationships, or Surviving the loss of a Loved one or relationship; Healing from affairs, Addictions, Abuse/Toxic relationships, Separation, Divorce, in Difficult transitions, Troubled teens, Parenting/family/sibling issues; Business/career coaching

- Individuals & Couples
- Dating Success Strategies for Singles
- Pre-Marital Relationship Coaching/Workshops
- Marriage/Couples Coaching/Retreats
- Gay/Lesbian Relationships
- Strategies to Stay Together
- Healthy Communication Skills
- Are you in an Abusive Relationship?
- How to Identify a Toxic Person
- Breaking Free from Toxic Relationships
- Surviving Divorce, Breakups & Toxic Relationships
- Are You Addicted to Love/a Person?
- After the Loss – Transition at any Age
- Re-Entering the Dating World
- Choosing a Healthy Life Partner

- Mid-Life Changes & Goals
- Finding Balance in Life/Relationships
- Life and Career Coaching
- Finding Motivation to Change
- Spirituality & Success—The Essential Connection
- Spiritual Healing & Wellness
- Be a Positive, Powerful Woman
- Mighty Men—The Evolved Male Partner
- De-Stress! Personal Time Management
- Sexuality & Intimacy Issues
- Stop Anxiety & Depression
- Raising Self Esteem
- Bereavement, Loss of a Loved One
- Overcoming Post Traumatic Stress, Grief
- Coaching for Parents/Difficult children and teens
- Teen & Children's Anxiety, Depression, Anger and other concerns
- Addictions in Relationships (Alcohol, Drugs, Gambling, Sexual Addiction, Eating Disorders)
- Are you Co-Dependent?
- Entertainment Industry Coach (Modeling/Acting/Singing)

Various Coaching packages are available world-wide.
For more information, or to apply for a Free Life & Love Coaching
Strategy session; go to www.RianaMilne.com

Virtual Training: **www.LifeandLoveTrainingAcademy.com**
App: **My Relationship Coach**
For Speaking Events: **http://rianamilne.com/riana-milne/**

Singles & Couples Group Coaching is available at:

www.LifeandLoveTrainingAcademy.com

Private Coaching with Riana can be arranged by applying for a complimentary Life & Love Strategy Session at www.RianaMilne.com; a $1000 value. Private Coaching Packages are available in Delray Beach, FL, USA or virtually through SKYPE at coachrianamilne.

Coaching packages available include:

1) VIP 1/2 Day

2) VIP Full Day

3) 6-month, VIP Diamond Coaching
(Bonus: includes the 90 Day Online Group Training Program)

Riana Milne
MA, LMHC, CCTP, CAP, SAC

Certified Expert Life, Dating & Relationship Coach

Visit Riana's website to get complimentary downloads of her two books, read educational articles, and see her most recent videos:

http://rianamilne.com/

Please keep in touch with us on our Social Media!

FB: **https://www.facebook.com/CoachRianaMilne**

Twitter: **https://twitter.com/rianamilne**

YouTube: **https://www.youtube.com/RianaMilne/videos**

LinkedIn: **https://www.linkedin.com/in/rianamilne/**

Instagram: **https://www.instagram.com/coachrianamilne/**

Pinterest: **https://www.pinterest.com/rianamilne/**

Google: **https://plus.google.com/u/0/+RianaMilne**

Riana's Speakers Page: **http://rianamilne.com/riana-milne/**

App: **My Relationship Coach**

Link for Apple phones and iPads: **https://itunes.apple.com/us/app/my-relationship-coach/id589020215?mt=8**

Link for Google play and Droid Smart phones:
https://play.google.com/store/apps/details?id=com.app_mycoach.layout&hl=en%C3%82%C2%A0%C3%82

Dating to Mating, Life & Love Transformation Program for Singles

Tired of doing all the right things and still attracting or settling for the wrong partner? Having a hard time breaking free of someone you know is Toxic and bad for you? Stop the dead-end relationships that leave you unfulfilled. If you simply can't find love, are newly divorced, or just experienced a hurtful break-up or loss of a long-time partner, learn the proven success strategies needed to gain dating confidence, reinvent yourself, and successfully find a loving partner. You'll know exactly what to do, who to avoid, and how to attract an emotionally healthy, loving mate for a life-long relationship!

Benefits:

- Break free once and for all from a toxic partner who is breaking your heart
- Stop attracting dysfunctional personality types that make you crazy
- Stop negative thoughts and behavior patterns that are sabotaging your relationships
- Heal emotionally from heart-ache by adapting a positive mind-set and confident attitude
- Reinvent yourself to become a successful, confident single before dating
- Improve all your life areas for more personal confidence and happiness
- Write an online profile that will get you the dates you desire
- Know the specific questions to ask while dating to discover any red flags
- Raise personal self-esteem and confidence while having fun dating
- Know the essential character traits mandatory in an emotionally healthy partner
- Be clear on your needs, requirements and desires for a life-long partner
- Use the "Law of Attraction" to call-in your perfect, life-long dream partner!

Sign up today at www.LifeandLoveTrainingAcademy.com

Relationship Rescue!
Life & Love Transformation Program for Couples
Taking Love from Toxic to Terrific!

Are you questioning whether to stay or leave your Relationship? Change for good the critical issues that destroy your troubled relationship and turn any toxic behaviors and unhealthy patterns into an emotionally healthy, loving, safe, evolved and sexually passionate Relationship that can be better than ever! Communicate your needs, requirements and desires to your partner in a comfortable and supportive way. Stop blaming behavior and listen with an open heart and positive mind, creating the emotional closeness necessary for a happier, more affectionate and loving relationship.

Benefits:

- Stop dysfunctional childhood coping patterns that sabotage and ruin your relationship

- Understand and heal any Adverse Childhood Trauma; for better trust & empathy

- Stop fighting, boredom, stress, resentment, anger and disappointments

- Stop any Unconscious Emotional Triggers & Negative, Repetitive Behavior Patterns

- Stop any toxic behaviors that hurt you, your partner and the relationship

- Use positive communication skills and choices to feel heard, safe, supported, loved and respected

- Learn how to get your needs, requirements and desires met by your partner

- Learn the Therapeutic break for peaceful, loving conversations and calm negotiations

- Life Coaching to become your best self, improve overall happiness, increase energy and life balance

- Increase your personal & relationship happiness levels with increased confidence & a positive mind-set

- Create romantic Date nights that are fun, and encourage sexual fantasy play

- Get back the affection, friendship and sexual passion you once had - while falling in love all over again!

Sign up today at www.LifeandLoveTrainingAcademy.com

Testimonials from Riana's Coaching Clients:

"Riana Milne came into my life and right away I knew she was meant to be there. Eighteen months ago, I was struggling, lost and helpless. Riana's supportive Coaching techniques led me to find myself and to make positive lifestyle changes after a difficult time in my life following a divorce. Because of her incredible insight into life issues and her ability to express direction in her books and coaching program, I gained the strength I needed to move forward and feel amazing! Today....I am stronger, happier and love myself more than I ever have. It has been an incredible journey of setting goals, focusing on the positive, reading and centering on positive and spiritual energy. The only books you ever need to read are LIVE Beyond Your Dreams and LOVE Beyond Your Dreams by Riana Milne. There is no other App you need to have on your computer or iPad other than Riana Milne's, My Relationship Coach! Sometimes people come into your life......I would highly recommend her Coaching program...I am now in a wonderful, emotionally healthy & evolved relationship - and knew EXACTLY what to do to attract this type of love into my life." **Lisa S.**

"I came across Riana online and was intrigued by her professional expertise and blog where she started her journey in helping people. I was really touched by what I read and decided to give her a try. I hadn't really felt a connection between a few other Coaches I have been to. Instantly, when I sat down and met with Riana, I knew that I had found my Coach! Coaching led me to gain my confidence back, getting to a point of happiness and self-worth again. Through my work with Riana, and the worksheets and her two books I read; it was an eye-opener and I was lucky to escape the biggest mistake of my life - that of a marriage to the wrong person. I am now in the most fantastic, healthiest relationship of my life! I cannot thank Riana enough for being such an amazing coach, person and mentor. She is sweet and caring, and provides great advice and asks questions that need to be asked and also guides you with answers you may not want to hear or be ready for. I have enjoyed opening up to her and becoming a better person for it and I am forever thankful. She's an amazing woman and an inspiration! I encourage anyone who is in need of help with themselves, or a relationship, to give her program a try - and you won't be sorry! Thank you so much Riana!" **Erin L.**

"I had never experienced a coaching program and since doing the Life & Love Transformation Coaching Program with Riana, I have totally turned my life around. I am now extremely focused and doing very well in both work and school, and have detached myself from toxic relationships because I know what signs to look for so that it doesn't happen again. Riana and this program has helped me see life and relationships for more than what they seem on the surface; making me now open to meeting new people and with the new-found confidence and self esteem I needed to be out dating and enjoy the process." **Christina S.**

"Riana came into my life by happenstance. I met through a close friend of mine, a producer that was doing a new reality series called "Radical Dating". "Radical Dating" is a show about dating in your 40's. After being cast on the show, I was introduced to my life/relationship coach. Enter Ms. Riana Milne. I wasn't sure what to expect as I have not been on a reality show before, let alone has any kind of coach. And truth be told, I didn't think I needed one, as I was doing just fine on my own. Well let me tell you how wrong I was. After three months of filming, I am a different person than I was when I started the show. I owe my positive changes to Riana. Small back story…I am a gay man in my 40's. I was in a relationship for over 6 years and then my partner passed away in an accident. That was 6 years ago. I have dated one person (3 months) in the last 6 years and that did not turn end very well. Suffice it to say, I had a few issues that I needed to deal with if I was ever going to be able to have a healthy long lasting relationship with anyone. I had a fear of abandonment (childhood issues), did not trust, made humor a mechanism of dealing with any issue, was a negative person, was not happy and the list goes on. I needed not only a personality adjustment but I needed a wakeup call. Through this "Radical Dating" program and with the help of Riana, I overcame all my obstacles. Riana is the most wonderful coach anyone could ever have in their life. She opened my eyes to a lot of things. She made me aware of issues I needed to overcome, brought more spirituality into my life and brought me to a place where I am truly happy with myself and my life. She provides a wealth of encouragement, motivation and strength. I will say this in conclusion…No one, and I mean NO ONE, can help you if you are not willing to help yourself. But if you are willing to help yourself and get over those obstacles, then Riana is exactly who you need to "be in your corner". She will pick you up, dust you off and help push you in the direction you need to go. I will say that if it was not for Riana, I would still just be going through the motions in this life of mine. She helped me realize I have a purpose and a strength that I did not even know I had. Thank you, Riana for everything you have done for me! I love and adore you and I am glad to know that you are always a phone call away!" **Scott T.**

"Almost six years ago, I felt my world spiraling out of control. I did not think highly of myself. In fact, I thought I was not good enough, not worth anything, and people/life would be better without me. Looking back, I can say I didn't know how to love myself. When I was 14, I lost my dad. Then, at 28, I lost my sister. At 35, I lost my mom. All the people I loved - "left" me. People would comment how strong I was and would praise me. In reality, it was a facade as I never really learned how to deal with all the loss. If that wasn't enough, I had a few not so good relationships. Everything in my life just kept whirling around in my head and then it would turn into anger and rage. After extensive research and reading many biographies, I came across Riana Milne's website. Something about her website intrigued me and I was impressed with her background, schooling, experience, and resume. I reached out to Riana through email, and within 24 hours, she responded. We spoke on the phone and a meeting was scheduled. My first meeting with Riana, I felt very comfortable and safe. She welcomed me in, and we started to discuss the list of my issues one by one. Riana asked questions, offered advice, and coached me how to open my eyes to view situations from a different aspect. Sure, there were many times I didn't necessarily like hearing the advice Riana had to offer, but I listened. After our coaching session(s) I would think about her advice, and the next session I would say, 'you were right.' But that's what good Coaches do. Through the last six years, working with Riana in our Coaching sessions, I have found her to be hard-working, honest, reliable, and respectful. Riana is unique from all other Life Coaches who I have seen. What makes Riana unique? She uses an approach to focus on purpose, desire, and goals. Riana also provides a wealth of encouragement and motivation. Life will always throw curve balls or obstacles in your path. To know I have my Life Coach, Riana Milne, in my corner is like having a security blanket. Riana was and is an essential part of helping me heal, accept, and love myself. Even though Riana is now in Florida, I know she is always there for me as she is a very caring person. I know all I need to do is call and she will find a time that works for both of us to have a coaching session. I highly recommend Riana for anyone who is struggling with any aspect of their life. Thank you, Riana." **Karen J.**

"I started to work with Riana in 2016. When I first met with her I was in a very low place in my life. I was coming out of a bad relationship, I was in a new relationship I wasn't happy with, I wasn't happy with my job and I was filled with anxiety and depression. I had met with therapists and psychiatrists to try to deal with the depression but nothing was working. I came out of my first meeting with Riana feeling great. She helped me take a natural approach to healing myself within, using her system. I started to meditate and take vitamins recommended by Riana and my anxiety and depression started to get better. She inspired me to believe in myself and gave me a lot of great career advice. Since meeting with Riana, I have started my own business, I know what to look for in a good partner and my entire outlook on life changed. I would have to credit Riana with turning my life around and helping me achieve my true potential!" **Dan**

"Hi Riana– I just wanted to share with you an update on my life and what has happened in my marriage since we spoke last December. My husband has finally moved out and I had to file a protective order for me and my son because things started to get violent, just as you said they would once things started resurfacing. I tried everything possible, the marriage counselor in our area saw everything and saw right through him, just like you. As you predicted, he only went twice and I have kept going and now I see the angle that she was trying to go about by focusing on me first, to get him to keep going to counseling. After the latest big incident, she told me – as you did, that I was dealing with an unstable, suicidal, irrational, and delusional person and that he would be my blood if I did not leave him. You both were so right! But regardless, when I started really looking at this whole relationship I had with this man for the past three years, I started looking at it from the outside in, and so many more things started being exposed. Every single thing on your Sociopathic checklist was him. As you suggested, I looked further – and found a secret life. I found other escort services that he had been looking into since I had found the one in Las Vegas, multiple women he was emailing, drugs, and much more—everything just came out... I feel like the word "fraud" that you used couldn't have been a better word, and I feel that I have been living with an imposter since the day we met. His real person that he is and always has been, is who he is now. I just wanted to send you a billion Thank You's for taking that time and speaking with me. Our conversation stuck with me especially during all of the difficult times when I was trying to decide what to do, and when

I started questioning if I was doing the right thing by leaving him. You are an angel sent from above! I can't explain the feeling of the biggest weight being lifted off my chest now that he is gone. I have already met with a paralegal to go over paperwork to file for the divorce. I just had to share, and say thank you once again. I really enjoy your Sunday Facebook Live and I will try to get on it this week and say hello :-) Take care and keep doing what you are doing! You have saved my life! Xoxo" **Alicia B.**

"Riana's Coaching Program has helped me recognize what an ACOA is (an Adult from Childhood Trauma – and it's affects it plays on one's self-esteem and in Partner choice.) She offered me plenty of information and questions to ask both myself – and my dates – to determine what level of growth someone from Childhood Trauma has achieved. I am so eager to further expand my knowledge in this area that has affected me so greatly in the past; then see what new experiences come my way! I now feel spiritually and consciously strong, and recognize that my self-care is so important. I have learned about my Requirements, Wants and Needs to focus on while dating, so I will now choose the right man for me. My mind-set is positive, strong and confident now!" **Christine B.**

"I was looking for answers I couldn't find, until I fell on Riana's profile. I tried a discovery session with her over Skype and since the first time I noticed how smart and interesting Riana is. I couldn't stop thinking about the things she said and decided like a strike of intuition to work with her. Before starting the work, she sends an amazing and practical workbook with 10 modules as well as 2 books she wrote. I believe the way the sessions were conducted are structured and scientific, it's not the usual coaching sessions like the ones I experienced before where I was talking randomly about any topic which used to get me stuck for months without any result. Riana helped me a lot in understanding some topics deeper, working on getting

over my past relationships and widening my horizons into new relationships and not fall into my usual toxic patterns again. Riana is at the same
time supportive and kind, and yet, directive, and firm from another side,
which is exactly what I needed. She is generous with her information and
cares about your progress. She is also spiritual and gives practical tools to
use and even recommends things you can do to improve your lifestyle
overall. She's always well dressed, creative, a great communicator, and
doing the right thing, supporting you as much as possible. She is surely
one of the best worldwide coaches I know of! I highly recommend
Riana for anyone looking for a Relationship coach or just a Self-
development / Life coach to help become the best version of you. This can
work anywhere in the world, I live in another continent and communication
was easy through Skype. I look forward to meeting Riana face to
face someday! :).

What I loved about You, Riana:
- your kind heart
- your professional approach
- I loved the ACOA concept; helped me to understand so many things!
- the workbook
- Your two books; LIVE & LOVE Beyond Your Dreams
- the smiley face in the box, amazing! (Coaching gift)
- the idea of the Individual & Group meditation on the beach,
  I wish I could be there
- how you are always perfectly dressed
- the fact that it's a program – and not just random coaching sessions!
- the modules of the Workbook
- Your Facebook Live videos (and the one's on You Tube)
- widening my horizons
- explaining clearly the pattern of relationships
- the extra support by email and text message – So Helpful!
- the good vibes
- the genuine smile

- the way you care sincerely when I am in a crisis mode
- Riana as a person! :D
- Everything I wrote in my testimonial, I really mean it!
-R. in Lebanon

At the start of this program I was a mess. I was doing badly in school, at work, in my love life, and it just felt as if nothing could go right for the longest time. I was depressed for months about myself. My confidence was at an all-time low and things just needed to change in my life. That's when I started this program. This program helped me in so many areas of my life. Riana helped me identify the things in my life that truly make me happy, and gave me exercises that helped me make those things a habit in my life. I have a speech impediment, so for the majority of my life I was extremely self-conscious about my stutter. But Riana was able to help get over the anxiety and self-doubt that my stutter gave me through this program and the exercises she had me doing. Riana has helped get my life in order and on track! I'm more focused in my goals and know how to achieve them. I'm more confident in myself and don't worry about what other people think regarding to my stutter. This program truly is a life changing experience; I even met the girl of my dreams! Thank you, Riana!" **Daniel S.**

"I'm currently 17 years old, and I have struggled for about half my life with depression, anxiety, suicidal thoughts, and family issues. It wasn't until about a year ago, I started on a positive path, thanks to my therapist Riana Milne. My conditions suddenly worsened about a year ago and I knew it was finally time for me to see someone. After appropriate research to find a good therapist, I went with Riana. From the moment I met with her, she made me feel extremely comfortable and made me feel as though I wasn't in this alone. On my first visit, I shared my story with her, something I had never done with anyone. Simply because it was extremely hard to talk about and I didn't want people to think I was crazy. With the aid of

Riana and another doctor she referred me to, I have been on a slow but successful road to recovery. Riana gave me ways to reduce my stress, in addition to advice to deal with friends and family. Not only has she helped with my mental conditions, but with everyday life. It has also been a hectic year trying to apply for college and scholarships while maintaining my grades and obtaining a job. She gave me great tips and was able to lead me every step of the way. She also continues to impress me with all she has accomplished in her life, while battling struggles of her own. I would recommend Riana Milne to anyone seeking any type of assistance to get through whatever your difficulty might be." **Ally M.**

"Riana is amazing! She has helped our family through turbulent waters on many occasions. Riana has a gift at connecting and making you feel comfortable by opening you up to really identfy the problem and then offers practical ways to work through the issues. I trust Riana with my most cherished treasure- my family, and highly recommend her to anyone!" **Glen M.**

"I found Riana by the grace of God. She saved our marriage. We now have a better marriage than we thought we could have. Riana has taught both my husband and I how to really love each other and communicate our feelings. She also helped us with other issues that were destroying our marriage and got through to my husband which I never thought would happen. Riana saw me many times alone and really helped me to understand myself. We are still in therapy, but not as often as we were. My husband actually looks forward to going to our sessions! We know if we slip, we can come see her and we come out of her office feeling renewed and re-motivated!" **Laura A.**

"I had a lot to work on and correct as I came to Riana as an ACOA with abandonment concerns, and was choosing partners who were no good for me. Riana helped me change my mindset and overall self-worth. Daily meditations reduce my stress levels and I am now able to stay positive even on the rough days. She taught me to value myself and know my worth, my requirements and non-negotiables when choosing an emotionally healthy partner. I have already had positive experiences in my career goals, personal life and relationships. I am ready for an evolved partnership and I'm now dating someone exclusively for over 3 months, who also wants marriage and a family! I have learned to follow my dreams, take risks, and not be afraid anymore to be alone. My biggest strengths have become to stay positive, and I feel attractive and amazing about myself!" **Jamie C.**

"I have had two separate coaching experiences with Riana, the first was focused just on me following an extended period of time with a "significant other" that had been on a long, frustrating and disappointing decline. The second, which followed along after this initial work, was with my partner who had also been separately working in advance with Riana. The work Riana and I did together was extremely helpful. I suppose it is natural to question yourself when a long-term relationship begins to dissolve, and I was no different. I had almost become convinced that I was a core reason for many of the problems in my relationship - and that this was somehow the result of personal failings. The self-assessment work we did together enabled me to re-establish that I wasn't suddenly "unworthy", but instead I was still fully able to be an extremely strong partner - with the right person. That allowed the question to become one of compatibility, obviously less difficult than thinking there might be a need for major personality "adjustments". Feelings of personal inadequacy dissipated. My long-term partner and I then engaged in couples coaching with Riana. We completed an assessment of ourselves, views of the relationship and our partner. This was useful; it showed that there was a great deal of caring, attraction and trust between us & allowed us to narrow the issues to a few, spending our time on these points. Further, we feel comfortable that neither of us is "the problem", which allows us to remain friends and "love from a distance". I strongly endorse using Riana as a Coach." **Bill W.**

"I'm so thankful to Riana for helping me land my new job! I was working in a lower level management position and was feeling ready for the next step and a new challenge in my career. As a collage graduate with management experience, you would think interviews would be a breeze for me, but I felt anxious and unsure of myself moving up. Riana took all my best qualities and helped me present them in a way that made me look like a shining star that would be an asset to my company. We went over my resume, and career development plan. Most importantly, Riana gave me the self-esteem & confidence to walk into the interview and get that job! I will always remember Riana asking, "Why not you?" I took that with me into the interview, and I will always remember it with each step I take in my life - Why not me?!" **Erin S.**

"Riana was an essential part of helping me to heal myself and to rebound after a very difficult divorce. After 5 years of trying to do this for myself, it wasn't until I hired a Life Coach, Riana Milne – to really speed up the process. I'm so glad I chose to do the Coaching, vs Counseling – which helped my entire family. My son had failed to launch, getting lost while he tried to help his mother move on, and now he is totally on the right track, back in school and working hard earning a great income. My daughter was angry and didn't want me to move on, and had a difficult time accepting any woman I chose to date. I admit, I was choosing the wrong type of woman, spinning my wheels and ending up depressed and just immersed in my work. Today, my life is totally different, and it's wonderful to see my kids so happy and successful! I have an amazing woman in my life that I will be asking to marry soon. If you are thinking of hiring Riana, don't hesitate! It is well worth the investment to finally feel so fantastic and confident about life." **Johnny B**

"Riana has a true passion for helping others navigate through life's roadblocks and helping one get to their ultimate goals - be it in relationships, career, weight issues or self-esteem. I always remember someone telling me; "What makes you think doing the same thing over and over is going to produce a different result?" This was true for me before coaching. Riana gives you valuable tools each week to get to your goals in a positive and constructive way. After ending a 5-yr relationship, she helped me pick up the pieces and move forward in my life. In her LOVE Beyond Your Dreams book it says to "Be who you want to attract." If you want the best, you have to BE the best in all areas of your life; that includes your health, appearance, finances and your home. I also realized in our meetings that it was important to have a strong spiritual and faith based part of my life, and look for a partner that has this as well. I have found it gives one a good moral compass which helps in dealing with all parts of your life; be it in business, friendships or in one's sacred relationship. One of my favorite sessions with Riana was on the beach learning meditation and doing the Gratitude Prayer. It starts off with deep breathing, acknowledging the things you are grateful for; then visualizing what you want and would like in your life and finishes up with asking God; "What would you like me to know?" I am grateful for all the positive and constructive advice and knowledge Riana has shared with me. I hope if you are at a crossroads in your life and need guidance that you will do yourself a great favor and hire Riana." **Betsy A.**

"Riana has been amazing in helping me understand how and why an individual is toxic from relationship to relationship. Her book, Love Beyond Your Dreams, is a MUST read. I'm stronger because of her coaching and I know she was the coach for me. An online search led me to her. I called a few offices, but kept searching when it just didn't feel right. When I called Riana, she took the time to listen and get to the heart of the matter on our very first call. At the time, that helped like you wouldn't believe. Everyone needs support at some time. Her compassion came right through. Her methods of coaching work!" **Krystal B.**

"We did the couples intensive with Riana, and I can honestly say it has completely changed our lives and our marriage. We went from the verge of separation and divorce to wanting to restore our love and get on a new and healthy path to improve our marriage and be happy again. We've spent three years in traditional therapy and felt stagnant. Finding Riana was a God-send and we are so grateful to her for all her amazing and knowledgeable guidance. Thank you!!" **Iola & Chris K.**

"Words cannot even begin to describe how this program has completely changed my life; mentally, physically, and emotionally. I was in one of the worst places in my life when Felix and I broke up, I didn't see any way out of the heartbreak and certainly couldn't see the light at the end of the tunnel. I thought my relationship was so perfect and was moving in the right direction since we had just gotten back from a romantic trip to Paris and he was moving down to Florida and supposed to be living with me. It was only after we broke up that I realized I had completely lost myself in the 9 months we were dating. I couldn't even recognize myself! I went from being so strong, independent, confident, and ready to take on the world in anything that was thrown at me. I became completely dependent on my BF which was hard when he lived all the way in New York. I thought it was ideal living so far apart since we could still have our own lives, but when we did see each other it was completely focused on us. Over time, I now realize how much it mentally affected me and changed my behavior. I was seeking attention from other guys since he was never around, I was relying on him to make it better when I had a bad day, when I was mad or upset at something that had nothing to do with him I somehow managed to make it his fault; I had become completely co-dependent. I couldn't sleep, eat, or concentrate at work. I knew I needed help to get back on track and found literally my saving angel Riana. I wasn't looking for just therapy, I needed more than to just talk about my problems and feelings; I needed some sort of direction. That's why this coaching program sounded fantastic. I have in all aspects of my life adapted the "Watch Me" attitude from the Live Beyond Your Dreams book. In my life, I had always had people telling me I was never going to be anything and my self confidence was taking a hit. Now I apply the "Watch Me" mindset to everything again! I wasn't sure of my criteria or what I needed or wanted in someone I was dating. Riana's amazing book, Love Beyond Your Dreams will now forever be my go to guide whenever I'm looking to meet someone, or even when I'm in a relationship and am seeing some warning signs. It will forever be on my night stand for me to review. I will also always have my Life & Love Transformation Workbook, which I think is where I learned the most about myself. There is only so much information that sticks when just reading, so actually applying the knowledge and reflecting on how it applies to me really helped me a lot. This program may have only been 90 days, but I have gained a true friend and mentor that I look up to and I know this knowledge will last me a lifetime! Thanks for everything Riana." **Korine S.**

"I had just come to the end of a 3-year relationship and I was overcome with feelings of misery and loss. I reached out to Riana for help, coaching, and counseling. By closely following the "Watch Me" program, I began to realize that I had allowed myself to remain in a toxic relationship for far too long. My ex had slowly eroded my self-confidence and clouded my ability to see my value as a partner, and as a person. By setting goals and taking meaningful steps to achieve those goals each day, week, and month, and I was able to build my self-esteem and distance myself from the painful breakup. I learned to count my blessings and to get in touch with my spiritual side. As I took steps to improve my appearance, my finances, and my work and family relationships, my eyes were opened to the new possibilities that awaited me. I did find new love with a woman who is beautiful, charming, witty, and kind. My life has taken a 180-degree turn in just a few short months. I would recommend Riana's Coaching program for anyone who feels that their life needs a tune-up, but you must have an appetite for self-improvement and a willingness to do the work. It changes your life! I promise you won't be disappointed with the results!" **Mark L.**

"Dear Riana - There's a spirit of helpfulness that shines through everything you do, and even though the warmest of thanks would never be enough to repay you, please know how appreciated you are and what a true blessing you've been. Thank you for ALL your help and wisdom over the years; it really helped me to get through some very difficult times! Your suggestions have really helped change an almost impossible situation! God Bless you, Riana, on your journey!" **Doreen V**

"Riana is a truly genuine soul who has taught me to see life in a new light. Through coaching, listening, sharing and reading I have learned a new appreciation for not only what I have, but also the wonderful possibilities that lie ahead! Riana has many gifts, but her passion of helping people has touched me personally and changed my life forever." **Tiffany C.**

"After a 35-year marriage came almost to a crashing end, I needed to talk to someone outside of my family and friends. I was lucky enough to have been referred to Riana at Therapy by the Sea. Riana's Relationship Coaching got my wife & I through one of the most difficult times in our life and help me understand and deal with the feelings of guilt I had as I learned to stop all destructive, toxic behaviors that ruined our marriage. We are happier and better than ever; and look forward to our future together! I cannot thank Riana enough for saving our marriage, transforming my life in every way; and encouraging my wife to give US another chance. I would recommend anyone with relationship issues to contact Riana!" **Tony M.**

"Riana has helped many people, myself included, discover who they are and find their inner strength. She has a natural gift for helping people become more self-aware and better equipped to deal with life's naturally occurring obstacles. I would recommend Riana to anyone looking for guidance in their everyday lives." **Jerry G.**

ORDERING INFORMATION
Love Beyond Your Dreams: *Break Free of Toxic Relationships to Have the Love You Deserve*

Please see Riana's Web site, http://www.rianamilne.com/ for other products available, and get information on other books, how to receive Relationship or Life Coaching, set therapy appointments, attend speaking events, seminars, and to join her mailing list.

Get Riana's free app, **My Relationship Coach,** *for your smart phone.*

Link for Apple phones and iPads: https://itunes.apple.com/us/app/my-relationship-coach/id589020215?mt=8

Link for Google play and Droid Smart phones: https://play.google.com/store/apps/details?id=com.app_mycoach.layout&hl=en%C3%82%C2%A0%C3%82

E-mail orders: BytheSeaBookPublishingCompany@gmail.com

Phone orders: 201-281-7887 (please have credit card ready)

Postal orders: By the Sea Books Publishing Company
c/o Riana Milne, 15300 Jog Rd., Suite 109,
Delray Beach, FL 33446

Name _____

Address _____

City _____ State/Province ____ Zip/Postal Code _____

Telephone _____ E-mail _____

Per book cost: $16.95 US; $20.95 CAN and other countries
$4.00 US shipping, $6.00 outside of USA
Volume discounts available – please call for information

Payment: ☐ Check   ☐ Credit Card: ☐ Visa   ☐ MasterCard

Card Number _____ Expiration _____

Exact name on card _____ Billing Zip Code _____

_____ **check here if you would like to order – Live Beyond Your Dreams –** *from Fear and Doubt to Personal Power, Purpose and Success;* Riana's first book in the series. The same ordering and price information applies.

Please state here – *Book Dedication to* – Riana will be glad to sign your book!

_____

eBook versions available at www.amazon.com, www.barnesandnoble.com, and on many other platforms.

Thank you for your order! Satisfaction guaranteed.

Success is a journey not a destination –
half the fun is getting there.
- Gita Bellin

— Notes —

Notes

Notes